Gun (

Gun Curious

*A Liberal Professor's
Surprising Journey Inside
America's Gun Culture*

Davᴵᴅ Yamane

Exposit
Jefferson, North Carolina

ISBN (print) 978-1-4766-9587-7
ISBN (ebook) 978-1-4766-5355-6

LIBRARY OF CONGRESS AND BRITISH LIBRARY
CATALOGUING DATA ARE AVAILABLE

Library of Congress Control Number 2024003153

Front cover image by Les Cunliffe/STILLFX

Printed in the United States of America

Exposit is an imprint of McFarland & Company, Inc., Publishers

Exposit

*Box 611, Jefferson, North Carolina 28640
www.expositbooks.com*

For Sandy, my lifeline,
who encouraged me to believe that
knowledge can build a bridge

Table of Contents

Acknowledgments

I am an old scholar, but when I began this study in 2012, I was new to guns. I had spent my entire career as a sociologist of religion before this academic midlife crisis. Entering a new field was invigorating, like becoming a graduate student again. I knew little about guns, much less the academic study of them, so like my kids on the opening day of pool season, I dove with abandon into the scholarly "literature" (the accumulated body of knowledge) on the topic. At first, I was drowning even in the shallow end of the pool. I managed to stay afloat thanks to the support of others. Today I feel more comfortable swimming around in the deep end, which I hope this book reflects.

A lot has happened since I began studying American gun culture. My kids—Paul, Hannah, and Mark—all graduated from high school and college. I got divorced and remarried. I moved three times. I gained a stepdaughter and two grandchildren, Emily, Zoey, and Ollie. I lost my father, Raymond, and my writing accountability cat, Mango. I have laughed countless times while shooting and shed tears of anger and pain too many times following shootings. I have traveled the country learning about guns and explored the depths of my conscience about gun violence. It has truly been a surprising journey and one never traveled alone. Over the course of more than a decade working on this project, I have accumulated a huge collection of IOUs.

Wake Forest University has supported this work, not only by paying my regular salary, but through research funding and teaching leaves. The academic freedom provided by being a tenured faculty member has allowed me to pursue this often controversial topic and to teach a Sociology of Guns seminar every year without interference.

When I first began my fieldwork, people in gun culture were rightfully skeptical about having a liberal professor poking around. Early on, I would introduce myself at gatherings by saying, "I'm a sociology

professor, but please don't hold that against me." After I took his flagship MAG-40 course in 2012, I asked Massad Ayoob if he would provide a letter of introduction I could use when approaching others. He
generously agreed, and that letter allowed me to establish myself in the
field well enough that very soon no introduction was needed. By the time
I observed the Suarez International Pistol Gunfighting School in 2017,
Gabe Suarez startled me by declaring, "The warriors fight and the histo-
rians write. David is our Thucydides." Although I want to resist the char-
acterization, there is a kernel of truth in his exaggeration. Many in gun
culture have entrusted me to tell their story fairly and factually. I feel the
burden of that trust and I hope this book repays it in part.

Many of my gun culture debts can be seen in this book's text and
notes. Some have influenced me so fundamentally that they are in the
DNA of the work itself. Michael Bane, John Correia, Kevin Creighton,
Craig Douglas, Tom Givens, Ashley Hlebinsky, John Johnston, Tam Keel,
Danny Michael, Randy Miyan, Rob Pincus, Karl Rehn, John Richardson, and Sean Sorrentino deserve special recognition. Not many other
sociologists were working on gun culture when I began my study. Fortunately, early on my friend Black Hawk told me to look at the UC-Berkeley
Sociology Department's website for a graduate student named Jennifer
Carlson. Three books and a MacArthur genius fellowship later, Jenny is
still my guiding light in the field.

As I discuss in the introduction, my lunchtime presentation at the
National Firearms Law Seminar was a pivotal moment for me as I sought
my voice on this issue. Thanks to Sarah Gervase for that invitation. I have
developed, tested, elaborated, and refined my thinking about guns in a
number of other settings. I'm grateful in particular for opportunities provided by: The Copeland Colloquium on "The Symbolic and Material Construction of Guns" at Amherst College (2017); a Gun Studies Symposium at
the University of Arizona (2017); the Wake Forest University Law School's
"Race and Guns in America" webinar (2021); the Outdoor Writers Association of America Annual Conference (2021); an author's workshop at the
University of Connecticut for a special issue of the ANNALS of the American Academy of Political and Social Sciences on gun violence (2022); a
Deseret News Elevate Panel on "Gun Violence in America—Moving
Beyond Partisanship" (2022); a workshop at Saint Anselm College on "The
Ethics, Law, and Social Science of Firearms and Self-Defense" (2022); a discussion of gun culture and gun violence at the Lutheran Ethicists' Network
annual meeting (2023); the Duke Center for Firearms Law and University of Wyoming Firearms Research Center annual works-in-progress

workshop (2023); and the Vail Symposium's "Conversations on Controversial Issues moderate by Clay Jenkinson: Gun Violence in America" (2023).

At an academic workshop recently, one of the participants expressed hope that his recently published book would sell well because he needed to recoup some of the $15,000 of his own money he had spent researching the book. I was taken aback by this at first, until I realized I have spent at least that much of my own money in my dozen years researching and writing this book. To help pay for this work, I set up a "Buy Me a Coffee" account to crowdfund support. There are too many contributors to name them all and I do not want to name the biggest contributors without permission. But you all know who you are, and I hope you consider this book an installment payment on the balance due.

Many friends, old and new, read and commented on drafts of this work. Crucially, some are deeply involved in gun culture and others are totally outside of it. They tried to help me get the tone of this book right so it would appeal to diverse audiences including gun enthusiasts, gun skeptics, and the gun curious. Any shortcomings are my own. Thank you for your time and energy B.J. Campbell, Chris Cheng, Kevin Creighton, Chris Cypert, Jess Dawson, Michael Helms, Ashley Hlebinsky, Anne Hoppe, Tam Keel, Tom Klitus, Joel Mier, Randy Miyan, John Richardson, Khal Spencer, and Nick Unger. My part time writing coach Brendan O'Meara of the Creative Nonfiction Podcast helped me at some key points in my writing journey.

A few people in my life help me with my work but, more importantly, enrich my life with their friendship. My longest-standing friend in the academy, Black Hawk Hancock, has gone from taking my writing critiques for years to dishing them out abundantly in this project. My writing accountability partner, Lynn Neal, never wavered in her confidence that I could do this, even when my resolve faltered time and again. Communications professional and dear friend Robin Lindner gets a couple of credits in this book, but she has accumulated many more off the books for her years of love and support.

Getting this book into your hands has not been easy. I have been told by more publishers than I care to count (thirty-three, for the record) that there is no market for this book on American gun culture. For some, there is no market for books on guns generally; for others, no market for my low-heat, balanced take on guns. And an indeterminate number simply do not want to publish a book that is not fundamentally critical of guns and gun culture. As one reviewer of the proposal for *Gun Curious* wrote, "The views put forth here are repressible."

To his credit, my agent Don Fehr got the idea of this book immediately when I queried him. He took me on, helped me to develop a strong proposal, and for nearly a year searched for a gun curious publisher. In the end, not even his considerable reputation in the industry was enough. Just as I was contemplating self-publishing or starting the project again from scratch—something I had already done once six years earlier—I received a LinkedIn message from Lisa Camp. In addition to being a fellow Wake Forest University parent, she also graduated from Wake Forest with a bachelor's degree in sociology (and psychology, but no one's perfect). More importantly, she is the executive editor at McFarland & Company, an independent publisher of academic nonfiction books located in Jefferson, North Carolina, just eighty miles from my home in Mocksville. We scheduled a lunch meeting and, like Don eighteen months earlier, Lisa got the project right away. I am grateful for her support and that of the entire McFarland team, especially Dré Person , Adam Phillips, and Karl-Heinz Roseman. This is truly a home-grown North Carolina book.

Gun Curious is dedicated to my life partner Sandy, the only other person who has read every word of this book, without whom none of this would be possible or meaningful.

Glossary of Gun Terminology

These definitions were initially sourced, gathered, and/or written by Ashley Hlebinsky and Daniel Michael for use in the Cody Firearms Museum, Buffalo Bill Center of the West, Cody, Wyoming, USA. They are used and adapted here with permission of the authors. Note that these are practical rather than legal definitions.

Action: The way a gun operates.

Assault Rifle: A machine gun that is single-user portable and selective fire (has semi-automatic, automatic, and/or burst modes), with a detachable magazine that chambers an intermediate cartridge.

Assault Weapon: A catch-all term that typically centers around features of certain semi-automatic firearms, including but not limited to detachable magazines, pistol grips, bayonet lugs, and folding/telescoping stocks. The precise definition, however, can change depending on individual state and/or federal proposed legislation.

Automatic: A firearm that fires continuously when a trigger is pressed and stops when the trigger is released, the firearm is out of ammunition, or it malfunctions.

Barrel: The component of a firearm through which projectiles travel.

Bolt Action: A firearm with a breech that is opened by turning and sliding a bolt.

Bore: The hollow portion inside a gun barrel.

Break Action: A type of firearm in which the action opens at the breech to load ammunition into the chamber.

Breech: The rear end of the barrel.

Bullet: Projectile.

Caliber: The internal diameter or bore of a gun barrel.

Carbine: A shorter rifle, usually with a 20-inch or less barrel.

Cartridge: A type of ammunition that contains a bullet or shot, propellant, and a primer within a case.

Case: The housing of cartridge components (metallic, paper, plastic).

Chamber: The part of the barrel in which a cartridge is inserted before being fired.

Cylinder: The rotating portion of a revolver, consisting of multiple chambers.

Firearm: A portable gun.

Flintlock: A firearm that uses a piece of flint to strike a steel plate to spark and fire the gun.

Forearm: A wooden or synthetic stock, forward of the breech, where a shooter can rest their hand to support the firearm. The forearm is there to protect the shooter's hand from the heat of the barrel.

Frame: Also known as the receiver; the part of the firearm that holds together the barrel, hammer, and trigger.

Gauge: A term of measurement to describe the internal diameter of a shotgun barrel. It is determined by how many lead balls of that diameter make one pound; the smaller the bore, the higher the gauge number because smaller bores take more round balls to make up a pound.

Gun: A device incorporating a tube from which bullets, shells, or other projectiles are propelled by explosive or expanding gases.

Handgun: A short-barreled firearm meant to be fired by holding it in one or both hands, rather than resting the stock against the user's shoulder. The term pistol is often used interchangeably.

Lever Action: A firearm that uses a lever to chamber a cartridge and, typically, eject a spent case.

Magazine: A container, detachable or fixed, where ammunition is stored while feeding a repeating firearm.

Matchlock: The first ignition system, utilizing a slow-burning match to fire the gun.

Metallic Cartridge: Contains all components of a cartridge (bullet or shot, propellant, and a primer) within a metal case.

Musket: A military long gun, typically smoothbore, meant to be fired from the shoulder or off a rest.

Muzzle: Open end of the barrel from which projectiles emerge when fired.

Percussion Cap: The cap used to create the spark of a percussion ignition firearm. It contains a fulminate, typically mercury.

Receiver: Also known as the frame; the part of the firearm that holds together the barrel, hammer, and trigger.

Revolver: A type of firearm, usually a handgun, that has a revolving cylinder.

Rifle: A firearm with *rifling*, designed to be fired from the shoulder.

101 PARTS OF A GUN

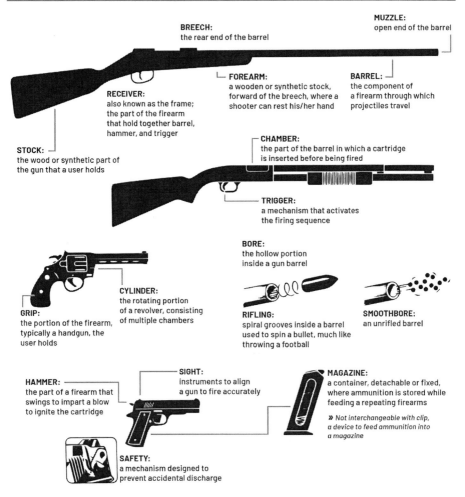

MUZZLE:
open end of the barrel

BREECH:
the rear end of the barrel

FOREARM:
a wooden or synthetic stock,
forward of the breech, where a
shooter can rest his/her hand

BARREL:
the component of
a firearm through which
projectiles travel

RECEIVER:
also known as the frame;
the part of the firearm
that hold together barrel,
hammer, and trigger

CHAMBER:
the part of the barrel in which a cartridge
is inserted before being fired

STOCK:
the wood or synthetic part of
the gun that a user holds

TRIGGER:
a mechanism that activates
the firing sequence

BORE:
the hollow portion
inside a gun barrel

CYLINDER:
the rotating portion
of a revolver, consisting
of multiple chambers

GRIP:
the portion of the firearm,
typically a handgun, the
user holds

RIFLING:
spiral grooves inside a barrel
used to spin a bullet, much like
throwing a football

SMOOTHBORE:
an unrifled barrel

HAMMER:
the part of a firearm that
swings to impart a blow
to ignite the cartridge

SIGHT:
instruments to align
a gun to fire accurately

MAGAZINE:
a container, detachable or fixed,
where ammunition is stored while
feeding a repeating firearms

» Not interchangeable with clip,
a device to feed ammunition into
a magazine

SAFETY:
a mechanism designed to
prevent accidental discharge

Courtesy the Cody Firearms Museum.

Rifling: Spiral grooves inside a barrel used to spin a bullet, much like throwing a football.

Safety: A mechanism designed to prevent accidental discharge.

Semi-Automatic *(self-loading)*: A firearm in which one round is fired each time the trigger is pressed. The firearm fires one round and chambers another to be ready when the user presses the trigger again.

Shot: Collective term for a group of bullets or pellets.

Shotgun: A smoothbore gun (*no rifling*) that typically fires shot.

Shotgun Shell: A form of ammunition loaded with shot or slugs, designed to be fired from a shotgun.

Sight: Instrument to align a gun to fire accurately.

Silencer: A sound suppression device that also hides muzzle flash and causes recoil reduction. Often called a suppressor, or sometimes in non–U.S. settings, a moderator.

Single Action: A type of firearm in which the trigger essentially does one action. A person must cock a hammer before pressing the trigger to fire the gun.

Slide Action *(pump action):* A firearm that has a moveable forearm to chamber a round to be ready to fire and eject a spent case after a round is fired.

Smoothbore: An unrifled barrel.

Stock: The wood or synthetic part of the gun that a user holds.

Trigger: A mechanism that activates the firing sequence.

Wheel-lock: An ignition system that utilizes a serrated disc that spins slightly to spark a piece of pyrite and fire the gun.

Preface

Because guns do not have a teleology, people use them for a range of purposes, from good to evil. Gun owners are human, so we see the full range of human triumphs and tragedies among them. Gun culture is part of American culture, so America's flaws also stain gun culture. This recalls Immanuel Kant's observation, "Out of the crooked timber of humanity, no straight thing was ever made." But media and scholarly attention are disproportionately drawn to the evil, tragic, flawed, and crooked.

Reflecting my liberal "tragic optimism," my approach to guns has a different point of departure.[1] Rather than focusing on crime, injury, and death with firearms, my work is based on the proposition that guns are normal and normal people use guns. This is not an article of faith or a belief statement for me; rather, it is based on my empirical observations of guns and gun owners over the past 13 years. When I say guns are normal and normal people use guns, I mean it in two senses. First, guns and gun ownership are common, widespread, and typical. Second, guns and gun ownership are not inherently associated with deviance or abnormalities.

In today's binary world, this observation codes me as "pro-gun," and not just in the view of their cultured despisers. One of the students in a pistol course I was observing at Gunsite Academy in Arizona said to me, "It is nice to have someone working on this from the pro-gun side." I was taken aback by this comment because I have never seen my work as "pro-gun." What I write about guns is based on my search for truth, not a political position. I am pro-understanding.

Understanding is the heart of this book. It is the foundation of critical thinking, empathy, and learning. It contributes to effective communication, decision-making, innovation, and problem-solving. The human desire to understand is intimately connected with curiosity, defined by the great pragmatist philosopher William James as "the impulse toward better cognition."[2]

In fact, my curiosity-driven search for understanding is how my journey into the world of guns began over a decade ago. I was gun curious, both personally and professionally.

Curiosity is the sociological enterprise's driving force. In his classic 1963 book, *Invitation to Sociology,* Peter Berger declared, "It can be said that the first wisdom of sociology is this: things are not what they seem." Social reality is complex and difficult to apprehend at first glance, and with each new discovery about some aspect of the social world, new complexities are revealed. Consequently, sociologists must constantly question what we see, not accept seemingly obvious answers, and pursue the truth even though it is ultimately elusive. Berger warned those considering his invitation, "People who feel no temptation before closed doors, who have no curiosity about human beings, who are content to admire scenery without wondering about the people who live in those houses on the other side of that river, should probably also stay away from sociology. They will find it unpleasant or, at any rate, unrewarding."[3] I accepted the invitation to sociology long ago; the curiosity in *Gun Curious* reflects this.

My understanding of American gun culture now includes 13 years of personal experience as a gun owner and 12 years of sociological research. It incorporates hundreds of hours of fieldwork, innumerable conversations with gun owners, immersion in various old and new gun media, and extensive engagement with scholarly analyses and cultural criticisms of guns. *Gun Curious* tells the story of this surprising journey inside American gun culture.

When I embarked on my personal and professional exploration of guns, I thought back to the great German-American sociologist Reinhard Bendix, whom I had the good fortune to meet at UC-Berkeley not long before he died in 1991. Though I was a mere undergraduate and he a distinguished faculty member, Bendix graciously spoke with me about the sociological enterprise I was just joining. He referred me to a passage from the philosopher Baruch Spinoza's *Tractatus Politicus* that I have attempted to embody in my work in the ensuing three decades and that I hope is the animating spirit of *Gun Curious*:

> *I have sedulously endeavored not to laugh at human actions, not to lament them, nor to detest them, but to understand them.*

* * *

In his influential book *Gun Fight,* a history of the conflict over the right to keep and bear arms in America, UCLA law professor Adam Winkler observes the polarization of our contemporary public discourse about guns.[4] Each side warns of threats from the other. Gun owners are reduced to being "gun nuts" and gun control advocates are "gun grabbers" at heart. My journey, by contrast, has taught me that there is a broad and deep middle of the American population between the most conspicuous advocates at the two extremes. These less visible individuals, neither enthusiasts nor critics, are often simply curious about guns.

I can relate. I am a "card-carrying liberal" Asian American sociology professor from the San Francisco Bay Area who, for the first forty-two years of my life, never saw, touched, or fired a real gun. In 2011, I transitioned from gun curious to gun owner. Social scientists and the media too often portray gun owners as bigoted zealots and ignore people like me who represent the normality of gun culture in America. This story weaves together my personal experiences and sociological observations of becoming a gun owner to take readers on a journey through gun culture in a way no book yet has. In doing so, I explain America's unique relationship to firearms for readers motivated by sympathy or antipathy or just plain curiosity about guns in the United States.

Gun enthusiasts are, of course, a natural audience for *Gun Curious* because it tells our story fairly and factually. I hope firearms skeptics will also read this book to better understand why gun ownership makes sense to tens of millions of Americans. Interested outsiders, including the gun curious, should appreciate how this book richly describes an unfamiliar but intriguing social world. Recalling Peter Berger's admonition, people who are content to believe what they have always believed about guns, gun owners, and gun culture should probably not read this book. But I invite those whose minds and hearts are open to learning something new to join me on this journey.

* * *

Open minds and hearts are as important now as ever. Despite my liberal optimism, I cannot help but share the common feeling that cultural and political divisions are engulfing the United States. Guns and gun violence are a common flashpoint.

Case in point: Like many Americans, I reluctantly watched events unfolding at the George R. Brown Convention Center in Houston in May 2022. The National Rifle Association held its annual meeting and exhibits just days after the slaughter of children at an elementary school in Uvalde, Texas, and not two weeks following the massacre at a grocery store in Buffalo, New York. The two sides in our polarized gun debates were on full display. Inside the convention center, Ted Cruz, Donald

Trump, and others planted the flag for gun rights. Outside on Discovery Green, David Hogg, Beto O'Rouke, and others rallied the crowd for gun control.

Neither side could hear the other, being literally divided by Avenida de las Americas and the convention center walls. But a figurative divide was even more significant: neither cared to hear the other. Both sides took the multifaceted reality of guns in American society and simplified it to fit into their one-dimensional containers.

While this culture war over guns rages among cultural and political elites, many everyday Americans want answers that go beyond slogans like "from my cold dead hands!" and "protect children not guns!"

As a liberal professor who became a gun owner in my forties, I have a foot in each of two worlds that see guns so very differently. Being "betwixt and between" statuses helps me to see the issue from both sides and positions me to act as a translator from one side to the other. *Gun Curious* shows why guns make sense to those of us who own them, how I understand the risk of negative outcomes associated with firearms, and what responsible gun ownership can look like in the twenty-first century.

This book takes the normality of guns and gun owners as a starting point, but also has implications for how we approach the wicked problem of gun violence. Addressing gun violence in the United States systematically and comprehensively requires Americans with diverse values and beliefs to have empathetic conversations across our differences about guns. We cannot repair this American divide until we begin to talk to each other with the goal of mutual understanding.

To be clear, *Gun Curious* does not provide immediate policy solutions to the problem of gun violence in the United States, much less its most idiosyncratic form seen in Uvalde and Buffalo. It does, however, speak across the divide evident in Houston that inhibits the conversations we desperately need to have right now.

Introduction:
How a Liberal Professor
Became a Gun Owner

Like many preteen boys, even in the deep blue liberal cultural bubble of the San Francisco Bay Area, I passed time with my friends in the late 1970s shooting BB guns. We would drink cans of Shasta soda as we walked to a pond up the hill behind the high school. When they were empty, we used the cans as targets. We also shot at whatever else caught our eyes—rocks, trees, the water. At one point, I can't remember exactly when or why, I saw a bird sitting on a tree branch across the pond. It seemed too far away to hit, but showing off for my older friends, I took aim and pulled the trigger anyway. The bird did not react at all. It just fell from its perch, like a stone. Although my friends were impressed, I felt queasy.

I didn't touch a gun again for 30 years.

* * *

This aversion was never seriously tested because my social environment and personal interests insulated me from guns for decades. Gun violence was a non-issue in my childhood home of Half Moon Bay, a small coastal town thirty miles south of San Francisco. Through high school, I played sports, revered Dr. Martin Luther King, Jr., and protested apartheid in South Africa. As I began college in 1986, my concerns were Ronald Reagan, the threat of global nuclear annihilation, and the sale of missiles to Iran to fund the right-wing Contra rebels in Nicaragua. I served as President of the College Democrats at American University in Washington, D.C., and was profoundly troubled by the homelessness and racial inequality I saw all around me in the nation's capital.

When I fled the profane world of Washington politics for the sanctity of the Ivory Tower, the liberal ideals of my youth followed me and grew

5

stronger. Through my undergraduate degree in sociology from the University of California at Berkeley, guns were not a part of my everyday reality and my intellectual concerns were bigger than the small arms of American gun culture. When I went to graduate school in Wisconsin, an area of the country more flush with firearms, I lived in Madison—"the Berkeley of the Midwest"—and never encountered a gun in person or conversation. Moving to Indiana for my first faculty job at the University of Notre Dame, my personal and professional bubbles continued to protect me from gun culture. This was for the best given my youthful act of aviancide.

Even after George H.W. Bush used it as a slur in his 1988 presidential campaign against Michael Dukakis, I have never shied away from the "card-carrying liberal" label. Far from fearing the "L-word" as a scarlet letter, I prided myself on being liberal. I still do. I believe we should feed the hungry, clothe the naked, care for the sick, empathize with prisoners, and welcome strangers, and that local, state, and federal governments play an important role in this. I also believe our government should safeguard civil rights and that the courts should ensure those rights when it fails to do so. My first book was on *Student Movements for Multiculturalism* and, as a fourth-generation Japanese-American with working-class roots, I believe that diversity is an important value for higher education.

Nothing in my background as I entered my fifth decade of life in 2008 would lead anyone, myself included, to think I would be asked to give a keynote address at the 2019 National Firearms Law Seminar (NFLS). Held immediately before the National Rifle Association's annual meetings and exhibits, the day-long event gathers several hundred attorneys and others for a variety of sessions on different aspects of guns and law like "Marketing Practices Liability in the Firearms Industry" and "How U.S. Export Controls Regulate Firearms and Ammunition." During the seminar,

Polaroid picture of the author wearing an "Abolish Apartheid: Divest Now" t-shirt and pin just prior to graduating from high school in 1986 (photograph courtesy Sandra Stroud Yamane).

an invited guest makes a special presentation to edify attendees as they eat lunch. In 2019, I was that guest.

My stomach turned as I surveyed the Regency Ballroom at the Indianapolis Hyatt from the podium. I saw table after table of conferees hungrier for their catered lunch than another lecture. I felt nervous even though I was thoroughly prepared for the moment. I had already imagined myself giving the lecture, saw myself standing at the front of the room, felt the audience looking at me, and heard the sound of my voice speaking. Yet I was still anxious about how my ideas would be received. The speech itself was a blur. My wife Sandy told me it went well. People laughed and expressed appreciation at the right moments as I told the story of "How a Liberal Professor Became an Armed American."[1]

* * *

Shortly after I entered my forties, in the spring of 2010, a dramatic life change led me to rediscover guns. I separated from my first wife, moving out of my suburban home in Winston-Salem, North Carolina, and into an apartment. I had not been a renter since I was in college some twenty years earlier. Fortunately, I could afford to live in one of the better complexes in town. It was home to many older long-term residents, younger or relocating professionals, and some families. Management did its best to keep college students out, which I appreciated because I did not want to live near anyone I might have in one of my sociology classes at Wake Forest University.

But even in a nice apartment complex you have vacancies and turnover, and this transiency means you don't always get to know your neighbors as well as you could, or should. In the three years I lived there, at least four tenants occupied the unit above mine. I never had a conversation with any of them—or anyone else at the complex—beyond everyday courtesies. The sole exception was a woman in her mid-forties who lived alone in a unit upstairs on the back side of my building. We must have kept a similar schedule because I would see her in the parking lot more often than other residents. Over a few months, we progressed from simple greetings to slightly longer chats, about work or the weather. We talked enough to feel apartment neighborly, but not well enough that I knew her name.

During this time, my kids would spend every other weekend with me. I was just getting home with my daughter Hannah and younger son Mark one Saturday afternoon in October 2010 when I noticed my neighbor distressed and arguing with a man I did not recognize. Her bony arms connected to narrow shoulders that topped her slight frame; she could not have weighed more than one hundred pounds. Still, she stood in the open driver's side door of her car, blocking the much larger man from getting in as she pleaded with him not to take it.

Adrenaline raced into my bloodstream, tightening my focus on the unfolding conflict. Before considering the consequences, I stepped toward them and asked, "Is everything OK?"

The man looked at me menacingly and said, "I'm her boyfriend," adding with emphasis, "*Just mind your own damn business.*"

"I have my kids with me. I don't want any trouble," I told him, then asked her again, "Is everything all right?"

He backed away from her and she said, "Yes."

They went to her apartment and we went to ours.

Hannah and Mark did not ask me about what had just happened and I said nothing to them about it. But the acid that soured my stomach scolded me. I was supposed to protect them but endangered them instead. For what? To help someone I hardly knew?

The next day, a frantic knocking on our apartment door startled us. I looked through the peephole and saw my neighbor. Her face was taut and her eyes were as wide and blue as swimming pools. Although it was after noon, she looked like she had just woken up. Different sections of her blonde hair crossed each other and her clothes hung at odd angles.

Adrenaline again filled my body as I looked at the trouble outside my door. She clearly needed help, but questions sped through my mind: Where was her boyfriend? Was he right behind her? If I opened the door, would he force her and himself inside? Would he kill her then me for helping her?

These questions gave way to a mandate: Protect Hannah and Mark first. I hurried them into one of the bedrooms and shut the door. I didn't tell them why and they didn't ask. The extraordinary knocking and my concerned expression told them all they needed to know. As they hid in the bedroom closet, I let my neighbor in. She told me through tears that the guy she was with the day before had threatened her with a knife and stolen her cell phone and car.

I felt torn between helping the broken person in my apartment and the potential consequences of doing so. If he is in the parking lot, he knows where I live. He knows I have kids. I am vulnerable. *We* are vulnerable.

Thinking again of Hannah and Mark, I urged my neighbor back outside where she used my phone first to call her father and then the police. At least half an hour later the police arrived to take a report for the crime of "unauthorized use of conveyance." The incident report I later found online noted that drug/alcohol use was involved, the offender and victim were related to each other as boyfriend/girlfriend, and the case was closed due to the victim's refusal to cooperate.

* * *

This episode was just the latest in a series of incidents involving my neighbor that led the apartment management to evict her. Initially and temporarily reassured, this experience forced me to face the fact that no one is immune to the possibility of violence. I also confronted the reality that my impulse to be a Good Samaritan to my neighbor endangered both me and, more significantly, my kids. Not just in those moments but going forward as well. I realized I had no means of protecting us if my neighbor's boyfriend/dealer decided to seek retaliation for my intervening in their dispute and involvement in reporting him to the police.

He knows where I live. He knows I have kids. And when seconds count, as the cliché suggests, police are just minutes away.

Recalling this encounter even many years later can still make me feel light-headed and sick to my stomach. A major difference between then and now is that I write these lines with a handgun within arm's reach. I am sure some friends and colleagues will be shocked to read this. My 12-year-old bird-killing self would certainly be surprised.

To be clear, I did not immediately drive from the harrowing experience with my neighbor to the local Gander Mountain Firearms Superstore to buy a gun. Doing so was not yet within the realm of possibility for me. BB guns aside, I had never even seen, much less handled or fired, a real gun. However, the feeling of insecurity and desire to protect my family played a major role in my conversion from being an orthodox liberal who knew nothing about firearms into an average American gun owner.

* * *

As a sociologist, I know I did not make my decision to buy a gun in a vacuum. It was facilitated by living in a particular historical and social context. "Men make their own history," Karl Marx famously wrote, "but they do not make it as they please; they do not make it under self-selected circumstances, but under circumstances existing already, given and transmitted from the past."[2] Had I been living in my childhood hometown of Half Moon Bay, California, instead of Winston-Salem, North Carolina, it is unlikely that I would have sought an armed solution to my problem of insecurity, at least not as quickly as I did. The same would be true had I been living in Winston-Salem early in the twentieth century instead of the twenty-first. Unbeknownst to me, even before deciding to buy a gun, I was already getting caught up in the vast and complex net of American gun culture.

A few months before the hostile encounter at my apartment complex I made an important discovery lying on a bed at the Country Inn and Suites in Columbus, Georgia. I was there with my oldest son, Paul, for a tennis tournament and passing time during a rain delay by channel surfing on the TV. By dumb luck, I landed on a History Channel marathon showing back-to-back-to-back-to-back-to-back episodes of the inaugural season of *Top Shot*. With no cable television subscription at home, I had no idea that a mainstream channel would air a program that combined the basic premise of the reality TV show *Survivor* with a shooting gallery on steroids captured by high-speed videography. What I saw was a revelation to me. To this day, I remember the trick shot showdown in episode seven of that first season. Tara Poremba hit all of her targets using a Winchester Model 1873 rifle Annie Oakley style—backward over her shoulder using a mirror to aim—and Chris Cerino drove two of three nails by hitting them on the head with bullets fired from a Smith & Wesson M&P double action revolver. I did not realize it then,

Sig Sauer P226 semi-automatic 9 mm pistol similar to the one used by the author to take his first shots (photograph courtesy Tamara Keel).

but the excitement of watching these feats of marksmanship planted in me a seed of interest in firearms.

Flash forward six months from the *Top Shot* marathon to a conversation with my friend (and now wife) Sandy over peppermint lattes at a local Starbucks. Neither of us recalls how we got onto the topic of guns, but we both distinctly remember the point at which Sandy told me she carried a Beretta M9 service pistol in the United States Coast Guard.

I asked incredulously, "You carried a gun?"

"Yes," she replied. "I even received an expert medal for pistol and sharpshooter distinction on the M16."

My personal distance from guns was related, in part, to my distance from military service. Although my father served in the U.S. Army, it was nothing he ever talked about with us kids and he never owned a gun while we lived in California.[3] I knew Sandy served in the Coast Guard, but it never occurred to me that she would have carried a sidearm as part of her daily responsibilities. Now gun curious because of *Top Shot* and sensitized to their possibility by my disturbing apartment encounter, Sandy's story came at just the right moment. It inspired me to overcome my longstanding fear of guns by learning how to shoot.

Sandy paved the way for this by calling her Davie County High School classmate Jimmy Staley, a gun trainer for the North Carolina Highway Patrol. Jimmy invited us to his nearby farm for a shooting lesson. Jimmy loaded a magazine with 9 mm cartridges that we had picked up at the local Walmart on the way there, inserted it into his Sig Sauer P226 semi-automatic pistol, and handed the gun to me. A full-size duty weapon used by many law enforcement agencies and the Navy SEALs, the grip filled my hand. Fully loaded with 15 rounds of ammunition it felt heavier than the two-and-a-half pounds it weighed. Jimmy showed me the proper way to grip the Sig and said, "Go ahead."

In January 2011, as a 42-year-old, I shot a real gun for the first time.

* * *

Nothing I had seen on TV or in the movies prepared me for the shock of an explosion literally an arm's length from my face. My eyes instinctively closed and my ears rang from the gun's 160 decibels, more than twice as loud as a jet engine taking off. Guns also observe Newton's Third Law of Motion—for every action, there is an equal and opposite reaction—so the combustion that forced the projectile down the barrel and out of the muzzle at 1,250 feet per second also drove the gun back toward me. Although I was able to absorb some of the impact of this recoil with my arms and body, the muzzle still flew upwards by at least 45 degrees giving me the sense that it was going to fly out of my hands.

Anxiety prevented me from storing more memories of that precise moment, but I know I missed the target entirely. As I shot my way through the first magazine, Jimmy would suggest small adjustments to my grip or stance or sight alignment or trigger press. With his coaching, I walked each consecutive shot closer to the bullseye.

At the end of our session, Jimmy said, "You did all right."

Expecting to be frightened, I instead had fun and felt challenged. The experience was not unlike golfing. You can have fun golfing even if you are not a good golfer. And getting better at golf, or even just making a couple of good shots during an entire round, is enough to bring you back. Getting into guns was most assuredly not my intention that day, but I was hooked after shooting fewer than fifty rounds.

* * *

With my gun curiosity piqued, I didn't have to look hard to find firearms all around me. I realized the annex to our local sports arena holds gun shows several times a year. I noticed ground signs advertising concealed carry classes on many heavily trafficked street corners. I saw billboards on area highways displaying advertisements for local gun stores. I also discovered, with astonishment, that many of the highly educated professionals I played tennis with owned guns. One had several long guns that were passed down from his grandfather. Another had two semi-automatic pistols in his basement that he used to shoot regularly. Several women in our tennis community also owned handguns, mostly for self-defense.

Realizing how common and normal guns were to so many people around me, I felt like I was the only person in North Carolina who *didn't* own a gun.

I fed my growing interest in firearms by lurking in online forums, watching television programs, listening to podcasts, and reading blogs, magazines, and books about guns. I was amazed to see just how much content about guns was available on every media platform. I joined the Carolina Shooters Club online forum, but there were scores more in which I could have participated. From *Top Shot* on the History Channel, I graduated to some of the many gun-related programs available on the Outdoor Channel and Sportsman's Channel like *Shooting Gallery* and *Shooting USA*. Of the many podcasts available, I settled early on Bob Mayne's *Handgun World Podcast* and Tom Gresham's *Gun Talk Radio*, both of which are pitched to a broad audience and so did not overwhelm me with technical minutiae and insider talk as narrowcasting often does. Through blogs, I came to know a wide variety of gun people, indirectly and directly, far and near. Today I count as friends John Richardson, who writes his *No Lawyers Only Guns and Money* blog in the Blue Ridge Mountains a couple of hours to the west of me, and Sean Sorrentino, who used to write *An NC Gun Blog* in the Research Triangle a couple hours to the east. Given my advanced age, I also consumed "dead tree media," passing hours at my local Borders bookstore thumbing through books and magazines about every conceivable aspect of firearms.

As I became increasingly interested in guns, the sociologist in me saw that I was becoming increasingly enmeshed in American society's longstanding culture of firearms.

* * *

In 1970, two-time Pulitzer Prize-winning historian Richard Hofstadter published an influential essay called "America as a Gun Culture."[4] In it, Hofstadter lamented the uniqueness of the United States "as the only modern industrial urban nation that persists in maintaining a gun culture." He accurately observed that America's gun culture is rooted in the widespread, lawful possession of firearms by a large segment of the population going back to before the nation's founding. As the country developed, so too did our gun culture.

"What began as a necessity of agriculture and the frontier," Hofstadter observed, "took hold as a sport and as an ingredient in the American imagination." Hunting became not only a source of food but a dominant form of recreation for many, and casual target shooting competitions were commonplace on the frontier in the nineteenth century. At mid-century, fraternal shooting clubs called *Schützenbünde* flourished in many cities with sizable German populations including New York, Cincinnati, Milwaukee, and San Francisco. The National Rifle Association (NRA) played a significant role in promoting America's gun culture from its founding in 1871 to promote better marksmanship through long-range rifle competitions.

Into the twentieth century, hunting continued to be an important part of U.S. gun culture, particularly in rural areas, but also among urbanites looking for a temporary escape from city life. The gun industry also increasingly promoted guns as objects of (typically masculine) desire using mass advertising techniques developed in the early twentieth century to fuel consumer capitalism. Especially as part of socialization into hunting, receiving a "real" rifle became a rite of passage from boyhood into manhood for many. For the older and wealthier, gun collecting as an avocation and business arose in conjunction with this evolution away from a purely utilitarian view of guns.[5]

People still own guns for many different reasons today. Hunting, recreational and competitive shooting, and collecting continue to be important aspects of U.S. gun culture. As I built my personal arsenal, my initial focus was on small caliber handguns and rifles that would be inexpensive and easy to plink with at the range. I also bought a double-barreled shotgun so Sandy and I could participate in shooting sports like wobble trap and sporting clays. My experience shows that fun remains an important point of entry into gun culture and a major reason for remaining in it.[6]

Nevertheless, American gun culture's center of gravity has shifted over the past half-century. Most gun owners in twenty-first-century America—especially new gun owners like me—point to self-defense as the primary reason for owning a gun. In a 1999 ABC News/Washington Post poll, twenty-six percent of respondents cited protection as the primary reason for owning a gun; by 2013, that proportion had grown to forty-eight percent. Hunting, sport shooting, and gun collecting declined by a roughly equal amount. More recently, a national survey of gun owners in 2019 found nearly sixty percent of respondents indicated "to protect my family, to protect my community, for my own protection" as their primary reason for owning a firearm.[7]

Not long after my trip to Jimmy Staley's home range in January 2011, I came across Michael Bane's *Down Range Radio* podcast. Bane is a leading figure in the gun media today. In an episode covering new trends for the coming year, Bane distinguished between "Gun Culture 1.0" and "Gun Culture 2.0." Gun Culture 1.0, according to Bane, is the historic gun culture that Hofstadter described, and Gun Culture 2.0 is the contemporary culture centered on armed self-defense. This distinction provided the conceptual language I needed to describe the broader social and cultural movement I was just entering. What I thought was my unique personal experience of getting into guns was actually a more common process of becoming part of Gun Culture 2.0.[8]

* * *

My approach in describing this process is not prescriptive—do *this*, not *that*—but descriptive. I leverage my personal and sociological curiosity as I journey inside American gun culture. I begin by establishing both the cultural and anthropological normality of guns and gun ownership.

From there, I explore why gun ownership makes sense to an increasingly diverse cross-section of the U.S. population. Along the way, I answer various questions I faced as my gun-owning career developed. Why guns? Which guns? How many and for what purposes? Do I need an AR-15? How do I get a concealed carry permit? What about the risks associated with gun ownership? What kind of training do I need?

Public and policy debates about guns are dominated by those most committed to gun rights or gun control. But the loudest voices are not the most representative. We can only hear a broader range of quieter voices by getting closer to the ground. We need to listen for the ideas expressed around a fire pit, bourbon in hand, and no recording devices present. Or at a fun shoot on a makeshift range on the back-forty of a farm. Or while reloading magazines in between sessions at a gun training course. *Gun Curious* elevates these more muted voices, especially my own, and in doing so tries to model a more civil discourse about guns in America than our current shouting match.

1

Guns Are Normal
and Normal People Use Guns

My involvement in gun culture has profoundly shifted my perspective on guns and gun owners. Several years into my transition to gun owner and gun studies scholar, I was a guest on my fellow North Carolinian Sean Sorrentino's *GunBlog VarietyCast*. Sean and I discussed my background, project, and problems with academics' dominant approaches to studying guns. When he asked me at the end for my big takeaway, I said something that turned out to be more significant than I expected. "The thing that has surprised me most about getting into gun culture these past six or seven years," I said, "is that *gun owners are people, too*. If you just read the scholarly literature on guns, you would not know that."

In the years since that podcast appearance, I have refined this perspective into a motto: *Guns are normal and normal people use guns.*

When I say guns are normal and normal people use guns, I mean it in two senses. First, guns and gun ownership are common, widespread, and typical. Second, guns and gun ownership are not inherently associated with deviance or abnormalities.

The problem with this approach is normality is not newsworthy. It is not of concern to social scientists. It doesn't mobilize the interest of advocacy groups. It can even be hard for me to tell interesting stories about something that is, in many ways, so unremarkable. And yet it is my dominant experience of guns and gun owners.

When my wife Sandy and I first started dating, she worked as the plant nurse at the Ingersoll-Rand factory in Mocksville. She treated injuries and promoted wellness for the hundreds of workers building Ingersoll's industrial air compressors. An unexpected benefit of her job was getting to know many people for whom guns are a normal part of life. In the fall of 2012, one of them invited Sandy to attend a group fun shoot on his family farm just outside the city limits. All the host told her about the "Invitational Shoot" was "show up at 10:00 a.m. sharp for the safety briefing and bring your guns and ammo." I was her plus-one.

Sandy and I left her parents' house in Mocksville and headed out on County Home Road, past the Davie County Detention Center, into the countryside. Turning onto a barely marked dirt road, my imagination ran to a disorganized bunch of people shooting aimlessly at tree stumps and into the woods. Having to open a steel frame cattle gate and drive through an actual cow pasture to get to the site reinforced this prejudice. But when we arrived at the parking area, I saw a cleanly mowed field and u-channel fence posts draped with yellow police tape demarcating the range. Paper, steel, and plastic bottle targets were neatly arrayed one hundred yards down range. Wooden picnic tables established the firing line and served as shooting benches. A separate range for handgun shooting was off to the side at a ninety-degree angle to the rifle range. There were also several more picnic tables alongside a canopy with a grill and coolers filled with non-alcoholic drinks. I was impressed.

Our first stop was a sign-in area where we were required to complete a long liability release form, as you would at any gun range. When enough people arrived, we grouped up for a safety briefing by a National Rifle Association certified Range Safety Officer (RSO). During the briefing, my mind drifted to the potential danger of shooting alongside people I had just met. One mistake by one person could be fatal. As it turned out, there was always an RSO present while the range was "hot," and other shooters informally reinforced safety standards on the firing line. During one break for hot dogs and sweet tea, we heard stories of people in previous years being asked to leave for not safely handling their firearms.

In addition to being safe, firearm owners in general are very generous with their guns and ammo. This is especially true of firearms collectors who, like collectors of any material thing, are passionate about their guns. As a result, that morning Sandy and I had the opportunity to try a World War II-era carbine, a $3,500 modern semi-automatic rifle, and a .22-caliber AR-style plinkster. The highlight of the event for many people, however, was shooting the .50-caliber rifle.

My fellow shooters and I had a hard time walking past the fifty-cal without stopping and staring. A .50-caliber bullet and the rifle that fires it are both extremely large in comparison to the rifles people typically shoot. The .50-caliber round is more than twice as wide and long as a typical AR-15 bullet and weighs nearly ten times as much. The rifle itself is five feet long and weighs more than thirty pounds. Too long to fit on the picnic benches and too heavy to shoulder, the fifty-cal was set up to shoot on the ground.

During the Invitational Shoot, anyone who wanted to try the fifty-cal—not a Barrett M82A1 with its $10,000-plus price tag, but a $2,500 ArmaLite AR-50—could do so by paying three dollars for a single round of ammunition. Sandy and I did not give away our shots, not knowing if or when the opportunity would come again.

After an RSO's brief overview of the AR-50's bolt action, I got in a prone position behind the rifle and aimed at a water-filled milk jug 100 yards down range. This would be an easy shot on a weapon whose effective range is 1,800 yards, but for some reason I laid down on the wrong side of the rifle, shooting it right-handed rather than from my dominant left-hand side. I could not get my cheek placed correctly on the stock nor my eyes fixed on the scope well enough to get a steady aim on the target. I readjusted so many times that I lost track of the target altogether. Feeling everyone's eyes on me, I just pulled the trigger when I thought I was close. A big cloud of dust short and left of the target showed everyone how badly I missed. It wasn't until we walked down range later that we saw how badly I really missed. I actually nicked one of the u-channel stakes at the edge of the range.

Sandy laughed. To this day, she never misses an opportunity to remind me that I took out the fence while she drilled a 20-ounce Aquafina bottle on her first attempt. Although I felt embarrassed, no one else appeared to care much. We were just a group of recreational shooters having a good time.

It is impossible to know how much of this unproblematic shooting takes place in the U.S. out of the public eye. Some 30 to 40 people gathered on a private range on someone's farm for a safe and fun day of shooting, eating, and socializing. To remix one of rapper Ice Cube's famous lyrics, "Even though I didn't get to shoot an AK, it was still a good day."

* * *

No one knows what proportion of the U.S. population owns guns. As with religion, the federal government does not keep official records or collect statistics on gun ownership. So, we depend on surveys conducted by organizations like Gallup, the Pew Research Center, the National Opinion Research Center, and others. These surveys not only produce different estimates, but they also underestimate gun ownership rates.

My educated guess is that forty percent of adults, more than ninety million civilians, personally own the four hundred million guns (plus or minus) in the U.S. Millions more who do not personally own guns live in gun-owning households.[1]

On any given day, an overwhelming majority of America's tens of millions of gun owners will not experience or cause any adverse outcomes with their hundreds of millions of guns. According to the National Center for Health Statistics, in 2019 there were 14,861 homicides using firearms. Even using the faulty assumption that a different person committed every homicide using a different gun, a mere 0.019 percent of gun owners and 0.0037 percent of guns are involved in firearm homicides annually. Looked at the other way around, at least 99.98 percent of gun owners and 99.996 percent of guns are not involved in homicide in any given year. Even if we add suicides (23,941 in 2019), accidental deaths (485 in 2019), and non-fatal firearms injuries (84,776 in 2017), only 0.16 percent of gun owners and 0.03 percent of guns at most are "responsible." That means 99.84 percent of gun owners and 99.97 percent of guns are not associated with any of these negative outcomes.[2]

Considering these numbers calls to mind sociologist Charles Kurzman's book, *The Missing Martyrs*. In it, Kurzman takes the question of Islamic terrorism and turns it on its head, asking, "Why are there so few Muslim terrorists?" This is an important but unasked question. After all, there are over a billion Muslims in the world and revolutionary Islamists who seek to convert them to terrorist violence. "As easy as terrorism is to commit," the book's description reads, "few Muslims turn to violence."[3] With slight editing, this could be rewritten to raise an equally important but unasked question: "As dangerous as guns are, why are there so few negative outcomes with them?"

Questions like this are not new to me. Taking up the academic study of guns more than a decade ago, I was struck by how hard it was to find scholarship on the normal use of firearms by normal gun owners. Despite the longstanding presence of a robust, legal gun culture in the U.S., the social scientific study of guns is dominated by criminological and epidemiological studies of gun violence.[4] In this respect, the field has not progressed much since sociologists James Wright and Linda Marston observed in 1975 that "the vast, overwhelming majority of the 90,000,000 or so privately owned weapons are not involved in accidental shootings or intentional deaths. Most gun owners studied in this paper are probably responsible persons who use their weapons for legitimate recreational activities. In this respect, the data presented here may contribute more to the sociology of leisure than to that of social problems." Three years later, James O'Connor and Alan Lizotte concluded similarly: "Hunting, gun collecting, and sport shooting are activities which involve large numbers of people for whom guns occupy a central but routine and legitimate place. These activities have been generally ignored by researchers interested in gun ownership and violence; but involvement in these activities surely accounts for most gun ownership in the country." The core of gun culture has shifted from leisure to self-defense since these early assessments, but the "routine and legitimate place" of guns in many Americans' lives has not.[5]

Given the fraught nature of gun violence today, I must pause to say unequivocally that I am not attempting to minimize the importance of understanding and reducing firearm injury and death, including accidents and self-harm. To suggest that one cannot simultaneously recognize the normality of gun ownership and seek to reduce negative outcomes with firearms is a pernicious false dichotomy. There is no question that firearms homicide, suicide, and injury rates in the U.S. are higher than many other economic peer countries that afford their citizens less freedom and responsibility regarding gun ownership. But like many health disparities, certain people with guns disproportionately kill or injure themselves or others. I explore the unequal risks of negative outcomes with firearms at length in Chapter 7.

My point is that the complex social realities that produce these health disparities are harder to think about and study than a myopic focus on guns themselves. At its worst, this myopia leads to an inappropriate conflation of gun culture with the deviant and criminal use of guns.

* * *

In July 2017, the gun violence reporting organization *The Trace* ran a story about the work of photographer Garret O. Hansen.[6] Hansen was introduced to American gun culture when he took a job as an assistant professor of photography at the University of Kentucky in Lexington. Once there he was surprised to find that "it was not uncommon for friends and colleagues, including those of a liberal tilt, to fire off a few rounds after work before grabbing a beer." As I did a few years earlier, Hansen found that target shooting at the range is normal for a large swath of the American population. Hansen himself tried shooting and subsequently thought to combine the shooting he had discovered (with guns) and the shooting he did professionally (with cameras).

Among his series of works, which have been displayed in galleries and museums across the country, is "Silhouette." For the pieces in this collection, Hansen gathered cardboard backings that are used to hold paper targets at gun ranges. In a darkroom, he made prints of the cardboard which he then turned into one-to-one replicas in mirrored Plexiglas. Hansen describes the experience of viewing the works when they are displayed: "As viewers approach the piece, they see their own reflections hollowed out by the countless bullets." For the final work in this series, "Memorial," Hansen used twelve panels to depict the actual monthly gun homicides in Kentucky in 2016. In his view, "This work acknowledges and lays bare the heavy price of having a heavily armed civilian population."[7]

Although Hansen's work is visually stunning, his analysis and *The Trace*'s coverage of it follow a very common narrative structure that moves from normal people engaging in the normal activity of having fun target shooting at a gun range to homicidal violence involving guns. But this narrative movement from gun culture to gun violence assumes a connection that needs to be documented empirically. After all, "a vast majority of legal gun owners never experience the illegal use of guns firsthand."[8] In this way, gun owners on balance are just like the large majority of us who exercise the rights to free speech, assembly, and religious practice responsibly.

My initial thought in reading *The Trace* story about Garret Hansen's work was that he should actually be more concerned about his colleagues' grabbing a beer after going to the range than about the target shooting itself. In terms of public health, gun ownership compares favorably to alcohol consumption.

* * *

Like guns, alcohol has been part and parcel of the everyday lives of people on this continent, at least since British colonist George Thorpe distilled alcohol from Indian corn mash in the Berkeley settlement near Jamestown, Virginia, around 1620. The many personal and social ills associated with alcohol abuse led to the historic and failed "noble experiment" banning alcohol with the ratification of the Eighteenth Amendment to the U.S. Constitution in 1920 until the repeal of Prohibition with the ratification of the Twenty-First Amendment in 1933.[9]

Since then, public health scholars have continued to document the toll that alcohol takes on individual lives and our society as a whole. These include immediate risks such as accidental injury, risky sexual behaviors, miscarriage, stillbirth, and fetal alcohol spectrum disorders.

Long-term health risks of alcohol use include high blood pressure, heart disease, stroke, liver disease, digestive problems; cancer of the breast, mouth, throat, esophagus, liver, and colon; diminished learning and memory; depression and anxiety; and social problems such as lost productivity, family dysfunction, and unemployment.[10]

Despite this alcohol-use epidemic in America, any person over twenty-one years of age can walk into most supermarkets, liquor stores, wine stores, beer stores, bars, or restaurants and buy alcohol. There are no laws specifying "prohibited persons," no permits required, no criminal background checks, no mental health assessments, no registration, no additional fees beyond the cost of the product and sales tax. Alcohol is widely advertised on old and new media platforms, especially on its biggest stages, like the Super Bowl and World Cup. Two years ago, I bought a quarter of a barrel of Kentucky straight bourbon whiskey—sixty 750 ml bottles—in a single day.

San Francisco forced its last gun store, High Bridge Arms, out of business in 2015. In 2023, I asked Google's artificial intelligence (AI) experiment Bard, "How many liquor stores are there in San Francisco?" The AI chatbot responded: "According to the San Francisco Department of Public Health, there are 867 liquor stores in San Francisco. This number has steadily increased in recent years, with an average of 10 new liquor stores opening each year." Given the daily toll taken on individuals and our society as a whole, why are more people not up in arms about how easy it is for people to access such a destructive product?

In fairness, some are as up in arms about the scourge of alcohol as guns, like journalist Ted Alcorn, who has criticized both. Alcorn highlights alcohol's particularly devastating relationship to violence and violent death. His work is supported by a report on alcohol misuse issued in 2023 by the Consortium for Risk-Based Firearm Policy and the Center for Gun Violence Solutions at the Johns Hopkins Bloomberg School of Public Health. The report reveals that alcohol kills approximately three times as many people annually as guns. Alcohol is also one of the largest risk factors for homicide and suicide and is a major contributing factor to gun violence.[11]

Given these facts, it is interesting that no one holds me—a lawful alcohol owner and user—responsible for the misuse of alcohol by (many, many thousands of) others. No one looks to me to "be part of the solution rather than part of the problem." No one requires me to have a 0.00 blood alcohol content before driving because so many others drink and drive. No one asks me how many more people have to die before drinkers, "for the good of their fellow citizens," give up alcohol.[12] No one asserts that I value alcohol more than children because I drink. No one suggests we should institute more common sense laws because if we can prevent *even one more death* due to alcohol, we must do so.

Despite the many negative outcomes associated with its consumption, alcohol is less criticized by scholars and activists than guns, except when they focus on alcohol use by gun owners. Certainly, the death and destruction caused by alcohol usually happen more slowly and less dramatically than gun injury and death. But I also think that these critics recognize that responsible alcohol use is possible, despite the fact, reported by Alcorn, that "the science is increasingly clear that alcohol use confers no health benefits and any level of consumption poses risks."[13] I am thinking here of the social scientists who analyze guns as risk factors for injury and still enjoy hoppy IPAs, the moms who demand action on guns and consume California Chardonnays, and the *New York Times* staff who editorialize against guns by day and drink craft cocktails in Brooklyn at night. What allows them to see that alcohol is normal and normal people consume alcohol but not view firearms the same way? Perhaps the idea of alcohol control hits too close to home.

I can hear critics objecting that this argument is an instance of "whataboutism," an attempt to distract readers from the problem at hand by drawing attention to a different problem. In my defense, I am trying to draw an analogy between guns and another risk factor for negative outcomes that most people who condemn and seek to control guns do not similarly criticize, even though it is even more harmful and less regulated. If guns and alcohol, or gun owners and alcohol users, or the gun violence epidemic and alcohol epidemic, were similarly stigmatized, this analogy would be irrelevant.

* * *

Through my research and publications, I have developed a reputation for analyzing the inner workings of American gun culture and understanding gun owners on their own terms. Early in 2017, the nonpartisan Pew Research Center asked to consult with me on a survey of gun owners they were preparing. I spoke with members of their research team for an hour or so, emphasizing the importance for anyone studying guns in America to recognize that guns are unproblematic for a large part of the U.S. population.

When the survey results were released in June 2017, I was impressed, and not just because they used several questions I suggested. One particularly ingenious question that had not even occurred to me was, "Regardless of whether or not you own a gun, have you ever fired a gun?" A remarkable seven out of ten American adults (72%) answered yes. That is nearly 180 million people. Viewed the other way around: A minority of American adults (28%) had never shot a gun. If that is not a normal behavior in our society, I do not know what is.[14]

Pew also reported that a majority of the population currently lives with a gun in their home or has in the past. In terms of personal gun ownership, instead of simply asking respondents whether or not they currently own a gun, Pew wisely had currently gunless respondents indicate whether they could see themselves owning a gun in the future. Over one-third (36%) said they could. These are the gun curious.

Only a minority of American adults (33%) told Pew they both do not currently own and cannot ever see themselves owning guns. Let's call them *No/Nevers*. If I had been asked this question any time before 2010, I would have been a *No/Never*. I quite quickly and unexpectedly became gun curious and then a gun owner. An untold number of others would find themselves in my shoes during the Great Gun Buying Spree of 2020+, when many of the gun curious got off the fence about guns and even some *No/Nevers* had a change of heart.

On Friday, 13 March 2020, President Donald Trump declared a national emergency concerning the novel coronavirus disease (Covid-19) outbreak in the United States. The following Monday, gun sales peaked at approximately 176,000 for the day, according to an analysis of data from the National Instant Criminal Background Check System (NICS). Gun sales were so robust in the first month of the Covid-19 pandemic that total sales for March 2020 (6.95 per 1,000 people in the U.S.) exceeded the previous record month, set in December 2012 following the Sandy Hook Elementary School massacre. Sandy Hook amplified existing concerns that the recently re-elected President Barack Obama would seek strong gun control laws, including an "assault weapons" ban. With gun sales in April and May 2020 also exceeding the previous year's figures, it was clear that Covid-19 had supplanted President Obama as the "greatest gun salesman in U.S. history." As it turns out, this was just the beginning of a gun-buying spree that spiked again in the summer.[15]

As the reality of the coronavirus pandemic was settling in, nation-wide protests were breaking out following the May 25 death of George Floyd at the hands of Minneapolis police officers. Some of these protests had violent elements, including looting and property destruction. At the same time, calls to "defund the police" spread. Although not as high as March's record, gun sales in June again exceeded two million. Fueled by the ongoing pandemic, protests for racial justice, and a contentious presidential election campaign, gun sales remained high through the end of the year. According to the National Shooting Sports Foundation (NSSF), the primary firearms industry trade group in the U.S., background checks for firearms sales in 2020 were sixty percent higher than in 2019.[16]

As the social challenges of 2020 extended into 2021, so too did the gun buying. Six of the top ten days with the most gun sales ever recorded were in March 2021. It is easy to imagine that these were just gun super-owners adding more and more firearms to their existing arsenals. There is surely some truth to this. But we also know from a survey conducted by scholars at Northeastern and Harvard Universities that nearly one-quarter of gun buyers in 2020 were new gun owners, and that these new gun owners were especially likely to come from non-traditional demographic backgrounds: women, Black and Latinx people, and people of diverse sexual identities.[17]

Many find these exceptional sales figures shocking and appalling. But as someone who has spent more than a decade immersed in American gun culture, I find them remarkable for how clearly they reflect the centrality of defensive gun ownership today. Faced with social uncertainty and unrest, many people find peace of mind in dogs, camera and alarm systems, gated communities, wasp spray, and other security technologies. It is also perfectly normal that a broad swath of Americans look to guns for safety and security.

* * *

My lunchtime address to the 2019 National Firearms Law Seminar about becoming a gun owner (described in the Introduction) was a coming-out moment of sorts for me. My friend and YouTube gun celebrity John Correia recorded the presentation and the positive reception I received encouraged me to post the video on my own (much more modest) YouTube channel. Another friend Robin Lindner, a communications professional, edited the raw footage into a coherent 36-minute video that we uploaded in May of 2019. Although it falls well short of the millions of views that Correia's Active Self Protection videos get, the 11,000+ views of "How a Card Carrying Liberal Professor Became a Card Carrying Liberal Armed American" to date are respectable for a 40-minute-long lunchtime lecture by a sociologist to a bunch of lawyers.

Knowing that many scholars and activists stigmatize guns and gun owners, I made the video public with some trepidation. Although I never actively hid my gun ownership, I did not actively promote it. If people wanted to infer that my hanging out in gun culture was strictly arms-length research, I did not disabuse them of that notion. But something unexpected happened with the release of my video: people started coming out to me as gun owners—or at least as gun curious. This included several fellow Wake Forest University faculty members.

Guns are very normal in certain parts of the United States. In other social circles, such as among my tribe of professors, they are much rarer. As much as some of us prize diversity, the reality is that our social networks tend to be quite homogenous. Sociologists call this propensity for birds of a feather to flock together *homophily*, meaning "love of the same."[18] We see it in those with whom we study, work, and play, who we date and marry, and especially who we connect with on social media. Homophily also affects our exposure to firearms. People who do not own guns tend to know other people who do not own guns. This becomes a problem for those of us who do.

As political scientist Mark Joslyn has argued, it is not simply that firearms are uncommon in gun-poor social networks. Guns and their owners are disdained. Joslyn documented this using a "thermometer" to gauge the feelings of gun nonowners toward owners. Respondents were asked to rate their feelings toward various groups on a scale of 0 to 100. Scores above 50 reflect "warmer" (more favorable) feelings and scores below 50 reflect "colder" (less favorable) feelings. The average feeling thermometer score for nonowners toward gun owners was 49 "degrees," with the most common score a frosty 0 out of 100. Joslyn summarized these results by observing that a "significant percentage of nonowners felt very negatively or cold toward gun owners" and nonowners held "clearly unfavorable" feelings overall. Nonowners felt colder toward gun owners than they did toward two other groups known to be stigmatized in American society: atheists (= 50 degrees) and Muslims (=53 degrees). Only one group fared worse than gun owners: members of the National Rifle Association (=42 degrees).[19]

To be fair, criminologists study crime and public health scholars study pathology. Sociologists study what's wrong with society, not what's right. We teach courses on "Social Problems" and "Deviant Behavior"; the unproblematic or nondeviant are unmarked. To study what is normal about guns falls outside sociology's analytic wheelhouse. That said, some biases go beyond mere disciplinary preferences.

Take Jonathan Metzl, for example. Metzl is Frederick B. Rentschler

II Professor of Sociology and Medicine, Health, and Society at Vanderbilt University and a leading sociologist studying guns. The Social Science Research Council tapped him to lead an initiative on "social science research pathways into understanding American gun violence, gun culture, and its discontents." He served as editor of a special issue of *Palgrave Communication* on "What Guns Mean: The Symbolic Lives of Firearms" (to which I contributed an article); wrote a book about how the politics of racial resentment has fatal consequences for white Americans, including gun suicides; and most recently published *What We've Become: Living and Dying in a Country of Arms.*[20]

As is often the case, it was in the less formal setting of a professional meeting that Metzl's fundamental view was laid bare. At the annual meeting of the American Sociological Association in 2018, Metzl organized and presided over a panel on "Guns and Violence in Trump's America." In his opening statement, he reviewed various negative outcomes associated with guns and then, as if grasping for words, concluded with exasperation, "*Guns are bad.*" I tweeted from the session that he had just summarized the dominant social scientific approach to guns.

Of course, this does not mean Metzl is a bad person or scholar. I consider him a colleague and benefit from his work in the field of gun studies. But my view that guns and gun ownership are normal contrasts sharply with most of my fellow social scientists. When I tell my colleagues I am studying "gun culture," they frequently hear me saying "gun violence," since they primarily associate guns with negative outcomes. Or they will respond, "Good, more people need to be studying gun control," betraying their political views on the issue of guns. It falls too far outside their experience with guns to think of them in any way other than negatively. Although sociologists are my people professionally, their understanding of guns and gun culture is profoundly disconnected from my own experiences these past 13 years. But I do understand this stance toward guns; for the first 20 years of my academic career, I shared it.

No individual scholar is responsible for covering the entirety of any object of study. The problem is when the collective effort of scholars working on a particular topic focuses so relentlessly on only one part of it. I am reminded of the parable of the blind men and the elephant. In the story, each man learns about an elephant by touching a single part. Consequently, they have limited and different understandings of the animal. In the case of gun culture, however, the blind men do not even examine different parts of the elephant. They only explore its anus.

* * *

Coming from outside gun culture, I had no idea just how common guns are in many parts of our social world. In 2005, I moved to Wake Forest University in Winston-Salem, North Carolina, and the liberal academic bubble insulating me from guns began to break down. Much of the credit for this is due to my native North Carolinian wife. Sandy grew up in the next county over from Winston-Salem, in the most redneck city in the state of North Carolina: Mocksville.

This title is not just my opinion. It is based on an analysis by Road-Snacks, an infotainment website that analyzes various types of data to offer humorous but telling insights into different communities. Among the many redneck criteria used by RoadSnacks, Mocksville ranked number one in three key categories: tobacco stores, fishing shops, and gun stores per capita.[21] So, guns were as normal a part of life for Sandy growing up in Mocksville in the 1970s and '80s as they were abnormal for me in the San Francisco Bay Area. Hunter safety education was taught as a mandatory part of her physical education class with Ms. Steelman at Davie County High School, where rifles were routinely stored on gun racks in the back windows of trucks in the school parking lot during hunting season.

This difference in our social backgrounds persisted into adulthood. Riding with Sandy on State Highway 421 in a rural area outside of

Deer stand the author mistook for a children's fort in a Yadkin County, North Carolina, farm field (photograph courtesy Sandra Stroud Yamane).

Winston-Salem one afternoon, I looked out at an open cornfield and saw a wooden structure that seemed very out of place. It looked like a free-standing tree house, an elevated square enclosure with a ladder and window openings.

I mused, "Sandy, isn't that a weird spot for kids to build a fort?"

Sandy looked at me as if I were from another planet, which I sort of was, and said, "That's a deer stand."

She also had to explain to me what deer stands are used for.

Despite this abnormality, she married me anyway.

2

Top Shot and the Human-Weapon Relationship

The television show *Top Shot* profoundly affected my understanding of the normality of guns and helped create the conditions for me to become a gun owner. But for a long time, I viewed it simply as an entertainment sopapilla with a light dusting of firearms education and a drizzle of history. I could not see the deeper connection between a *Survivor*-inspired competition with guns and the kind of survival impulse I felt when confronted by my mortality in the parking lot of my apartment complex back in 2010. Enter Randy Miyan, Executive Director of the Liberal Gun Owners, who helped me see the deep evolutionary roots of the human-weapon relationship, an ongoing relationship in which we *Homo sapiens* participate as a species.

To tell the whole story of this breakthrough, I have to go back to the year 2000. I had just finished my second year as an assistant professor when the first episode of the first season of the reality competition show *Survivor* aired in May. With the guillotine of tenure hanging over my neck and three kids under six years old, watching a relatively new genre of television was not on my to-do list. That year proved millions of my fellow Americans had different priorities. *Survivor: Borneo* was the highest-rated show of the year, averaging nearly thirty million viewers weekly—exceeding the audience of *ER, Friends,* the World Series, and the NCAA basketball finals—and capped by over fifty million viewers for the season finale. The show became a cultural phenomenon, so ubiquitous that even though I never watched a single episode, I knew all about the villainous Richard Hatch, who nakedly embodied the show's motto, "Outwit, Outplay, Outlast," all the way to the $1 million prize and the title of Sole Survivor.

I did not intend to watch Season 2 of *Survivor,* scheduled to premiere following Super Bowl XXXV in January 2001. But the Baltimore Ravens'

34–7 win over the New York Giants was so boring that I fell asleep on the sofa trying to watch the game. When I woke up as the game was ending, my drowsiness kept me on the sofa and the TV on CBS. I was not alone. Forty-five million people reportedly watched the *Survivor* Season 2 premiere.[1]

Having been seduced by the *Survivor: Australian Outback* premier, I eagerly tuned in week after week to see the latest installment of a novel, unscripted soap opera. Although personal nurse Tina Wesson won the competition, the hero and star was a 27-year-old auto-customizing Texan named Colby Donaldson. He not only played the game masterfully but was telegenic and a good talker to boot. After the show, he appeared in commercials for Schick razors and played himself in an episode of *Curb Your Enthusiasm* in which Donaldson and another "survivor" debate who had the worst experience. (In absurdist Larry David fashion, Donaldson competes against a Holocaust survivor.)

The significance of all of this for my story of becoming a gun owner is that when I was hotel cable channel surfing between my son's tennis matches in Georgia, I paused on The History Channel's reality competition show *Top Shot*. Not because I was interested in guns, but because Colby Donaldson was the host. Given the formative influence of *Top Shot* on my views of the normality of guns, I often find myself reflecting on the chain of events that led me to that point. I woke up from the Super Bowl just in time to see the premier of *Survivor: The Australian Outback* and got hooked on the show and its de facto star. We happened to be on a rain delay at my son's tennis tournament and had access to cable TV the very moment when The History Channel was airing a *Top Shot* marathon. I recognized Colby Donaldson as the host and decided to watch the show. In my more *Celestine Prophecy* moments, I think it had to be more than a coincidence.

* * *

Top Shot was a marksmanship competition show that ran for five seasons on The History Channel. It shared Colby Donaldson and the fundamental elements of the reality competition format in common with *Survivor*. Amateur and professional shooters were divided into two teams that competed against each other, with the losing team voting to send two teammates to an elimination challenge. The loser of the head-to-head challenge leaves the show with Colby's solemn pronouncement, "You've fired your last shot." Eventually, the two teams merge, more challenges and eliminations follow, and by the end, a single player wins the competition and a $100,000 cash prize. In Season 1, former

British Army Captain Iain Harrison beat gun trainer Chris Cerino and competition shooter J.J. Racaza for the title "Top Shot."

I became obsessed with *Top Shot*. Season 2 premiered in February 2011, the week after I bought my first gun. I would live tweet on my Blackberry during each episode and later in response to appearances by contestants on Tom Gresham's syndicated radio show *Gun Talk,* another gun-themed program I was fanatical about at the time. I got drawn into the weekly *Top Shot* episodes even though I knew the producers heavily edited the show to create dramatic storylines filled with tension between heroes and villains. The *Survivor* formula works.

Despite the show's drama, *Top Shot* still featured iconic weapons and interesting marksmanship challenges. Episodes started with a canned introduction in which Donaldson says of the competitors, "Each shows the timeless skills of a true marksman, not just with one weapon, with *any* weapon." I mentioned the Season 1 trick shot challenge in this book's introduction. In that same season, contestants shot a Beretta 92F pistol while riding on a zipline, severed a rope with a Winchester Model 1873 rifle, and played poker by shooting cards with a Colt Peacemaker revolver. During Season 2, cast members faced a novel challenge involving "primitive" weapons: a tomahawk and a blowgun. History repeated itself in Season 3. Donaldson introduced a team challenge by reminding the contestants, "A true marksman is not determined by guns alone." Flashing his familiar wry smile and achromatic teeth, he declared, "We are about to go primitive." Donaldson introduced a weapon that surprised even a *Top Shot* superfan like me. "We are going old school here, gentleman. For the first time on *Top Shot,* we're featuring mankind's first measure of marksmanship." A dramatic pause was followed by laughter when he unveiled a box of *rocks.*

Donaldson followed this big reveal with an equally revelatory comment: "Success with this weapon was critical to early man's survival." This statement about the profound role of rocks in human history raised the possibility that beyond the show's *Survivor*-esque manufactured drama lay something deeply significant about weapons and marksmanship. I could never quite put my finger on it until I met Randy Miyan, who helped me see the connection between primitive weapons and the history of human beings, our evolutionary development, and our contemporary social reality.

* * *

When Randy Miyan visited my Sociology of Guns seminar at Wake Forest University in the spring of 2019, my students did not quite know what to make of him. He wore jeans, an untucked blue Oxford shirt with a gray t-shirt peeking out below the hem, and adidas running shoes—a stark contrast to my standard suit and bow tie. Miyan stood out physically, reaching six feet four inches in height even without his ball cap. The well-worn trucker's hat teamed with a ponytail to keep his hair somewhat under control. Miyan also created some cognitive dissonance in my students by discussing his background in Buddhism and Taoism, his practice of meditation, and his exploration of the depths of nonviolence prior to his involvement with the Liberal Gun Owners (LGO).

LGO is an organization for "gun enthusiasts who identify as liberal, centrist, free-thinking, or independent." Unlike its membership-based cousin, the Liberal Gun Club, you cannot join LGO. You can, however, participate with nearly five thousand others in its heavily vetted and moderated private Facebook group. The formation of a social media community for liberals who enjoy guns is the first and original prong of the LGO mission, as conceived in 2007 by then-21-year-old college student, Adam Sorum.[2]

With its incorporation as a 501(c)(4) nonprofit in 2017, LGO elevated Miyan from Facebook group administrator to full-time, paid Executive Director. It also added a second prong to its core mission: interfacing with the public as a liberal voice within gun culture. LGO's distinctive perspective centers on "simultaneous proponency." According to Miyan, this means "equal support of both firearms ownership rights and the reduction of firearms-related violence." In the LGO lexicon, this equal embrace of firearms ownership (FO) and public safety (PS) is "The FOPS Nexus."

Four years into his tenure as LGO Executive Director, Miyan took the FOPS Nexus public in the form of a white paper called *The Liberal Gun Owners Lens* (hereafter *LGO Lens*). In February 2021, I opened this 165-page document he emailed me. Like my students two years earlier, I did not know what to make of Miyan and his work. To construct this analysis of the human-weapon relationship, he could not rely on his 15 years of experience as an Earth-valued carpenter, most recently specializing in yurts, nor his Ohio University bachelor's degree in business administration, for which he never did research beyond a "passable strong–B paper." Miyan had to take a two-year-long deep dive into the ocean of transdisciplinary scholarship on human origins, including work in archaeology, paleoanthropology, and evolutionary biology. In Jacques Cousteau fashion, he returned to the surface teeming with information that lays a solid foundation for my own orienting claim that guns are normal and normal people use guns.[3]

When I spoke to him about the *LGO Lens'* backstory, Miyan described it as "a Russian nesting doll discovery process." The idea of the FOPS Nexus was present early on, with the public safety side focused on school shootings. But he soon realized that LGO would also have to address church shootings and mass shootings and suicide and violence in communities of color, and with this came a recognition that "basically, everything, anything that touches guns I needed to know about." Around this time, I asked Miyan to guest lecture in my class. I did not remember this part of the story, but in his telling, when I was describing to him my approach to teaching the Sociology of Guns, I did a sort of Jerry Seinfeld impression. "*Hey, guns. What's up with that?*" Although we laugh about it now, the consequences for Miyan were quite serious. "That's all that was in my head for months," he reflected. "Hey, guns. What's up with that?"

Pulling apart the Russian nesting dolls, Miyan realized the foundation of the LGO position would have to answer this question. He eventually came around to his answer: "The first answer is *Homo sapiens.* Humans. That's what's up with that. That's really the first answer. We do guns because we do projectiles. So, if we're going to do this and understand it, we have to go all the way back to where we start from." From this realization, Miyan figured out the four-pillar framework that now guides his work in just two days. "But getting to that couple of days took almost two years," he recalls. And it would take him another two years to research and write just Pillar 1 on *The Human-Weapon Relationship: Anthropology, Evolution, and Human Innateness.*

* * *

The first pillar of the *LGO Lens* holds that widespread contemporary civilian ownership of firearms is a continuation of an unbroken 300,000-year history of involvement with "the advancing projectile weapon." In other words, the human-weapon relationship is behaviorally normal for *Homo sapiens* as a species.

"The Human-Weapon Relationship is not merely some superficial, cultural construct," Miyan writes in the *LGO Lens.* "It is also not some minor, anthropologic side story. It is not a vestige. It certainly cannot be understood by encapsulating it as something which belongs to one geographical region, which is merely the result of frenzied commercial interest, or which is inherently criminal or deviant." Instead, as paleo-anthropologist John Shea observes, "Projectile weaponry is uniquely human and culturally universal. We are the only species that uses

projectile weaponry, and no human society has ever abandoned its use."
To understand this, we need to "stretch our consideration backward
through the evolutionary line of general, hominin development," Miyan
insists, "back millions of years into the past."⁴

At the outset of the Pleistocene Epoch (2.5 million to 12,500 years
ago), there were three hominin groups (bipedal primates, including
humans) in Africa: *Australopithecus, Paranthropus,* and *Homo*. Toward
the end of the epoch, only the *Homo* genus survived. Subsequently, at
least three *Homo* species spread around the Earth: *Homo neanderthalen-
sis* (Neanderthals) in Europe, *Homo floresiensis* in Indonesia, and *Homo
sapiens* in Africa. By the end of the epoch, according to Shea, *Homo sapiens* were "the sole remaining contestant of *Survivor: Pleistocene*."⁵ How
and why *H. sapiens*—that is to say, *we*—won the evolutionary title of
Sole Survivor is an open question that continues to captivate students of
human origins.

Although complex, multi-causal, and only partially understood,
some paleoanthropologists have begun taking a closer look at a comparatively neglected piece of the puzzle: projectile weapons. Biologist
Paul Bingham developed a novel theory that places the ability to deliver
"death from a distance" at the core of what scholars of human origins
call the "human uniqueness problem." How did *Homo sapiens*, and only
Homo sapiens, develop traits such as advanced cognition (especially
language but also technology), prosociality, and a capacity for social
learning that allow us to dominate the planet? Bingham puts prosociality center stage, arguing that "unique human attributes all derive from
social cooperation with members of the same species (conspecifics) inde-
pendently of genetic kinship." Other animals generally cooperate only
with close kin and "compete aggressively with non-kin conspecifics."
Early Pleistocene proto-humans did not come upon the adaptive advantage of cooperation out of an altruistic spark within but through an
evolved ability to collectively punish group members who are "socially
parasitic." In Bingham's simpler term, those who are "cheaters."⁶

Of particular interest for our purposes here is that Bingham roots
the adaptive advantage of coercively enforced kinship-independent
social cooperation in a prior evolutionary development: a "novel physical
virtuosity at ... accurate, high-momentum throwing." Bingham and his
collaborator Joanne Souza observe that "humans throw the way a chee-
tah runs or a dolphin swims—with elite skill." We are, they say, "born to
throw." This anatomical advantage would later be parlayed into evolutionary success in our ancestors' "capacity to kill or injure ... *remotely,*

from many body diameters away." The offensive and defensive benefits of this for hunting and conflict with other hominins are obvious. For Bingham, however, this ability to deliver death from a distance is more important for the central role it plays in the coalitional enforcement of social cooperation by reducing the personal risk of those who would impose punishment on socially parasitic behavior. This point is central to the *LGO Lens*, especially the suggestion that our ancestral behavior remains central to human societies. Today we simply "prefer newer projectile weapons when we can get them."[7]

Although *Homo sapiens'* excellence in throwing was not always in evidence on *Top Shot*, the rock-throwing challenge in Season 3 is not so gimmicky from the perspective of human evolutionary survival and development. Later advancements in weaponry also took advantage of our anatomical gift for throwing, even as subsequent technologies overcame the limits of human power.

* * *

Paleolithic culture began with the working of stones into tools by hominins over 3 million years ago. The first Stone Age tools were those used to hammer, chop, cut, or puncture. From cutting implements used to butcher scavenged animals it was a short step (in evolutionary time) to figuring out a way to use sharpened stones to hunt game or defend against competing hominin groups. Miyan's prehistory of the human-weapon relationship in the *LGO Lens* gives an "honorable mention" to pointed stones discovered at the Kathu Pan 1 archaeological site in South Africa. These 500,000-year-old stone points bore evidence of both impact and "hafting"—a technological process that allows projectile points to be attached to a staff—making them the earliest evidence we have for a multicomponent thrusting spear.[8]

Even my contemporary, domesticated mind can recognize that having to be at spear's-length to injure a two- or four-legged Stone Age predator is suboptimal in the real-life game of survivor. Fast forward 100,000 years and the *LGO Lens* points us to evidence from an archaeological site in Schöningen, Germany, for spears whose shaft taper suggests that they were engineered for throwing. Hand-thrown spears as projectile weapons are certainly an advancement over hand-held spears as contact weapons.[9]

The next developmental step was to amplify human anatomical power through mechanization with technologies like the atlatl. Akin to tennis ball throwers commonly seen at dog parks, the atlatl is a lever used to propel a spear at a higher velocity than could be achieved with the throwing arm alone. I first learned of the atlatl not from the *LGO Lens*, but in the sixth episode of Season 4 of *Top Shot*. When the red team lost a bullseye competition to the blue team, they had to send two of their members to compete in the elimination challenge. In discussing who to nominate, Google employee and amateur shooter Chris Cheng upset his teammate, big game hunting guide Tim Trefren, by going around the room and assessing the strengths and weaknesses of each member's performance. Lips taut and foot tapping rapidly, Trefren finally jumped in to say, "Chris, don't take this personally. I'm sitting listening to you find everybody's fault in the room but your own, and that pisses me off. I want you in elimination with me." In an on-camera interview spliced in with the real-time footage, Trefren explained, "Back home if we were all sitting in a bar and that conversation comes up, it wouldn't have been, I'm challenging you at the elimination. That's ass-kicking words."

When Cheng and Trefren arrived for the elimination challenge practice session, host Colby Donaldson reminded them that "only one of you will survive the competition, and survival is a primitive instinct." Cut to a wide shot of Donaldson holding a nearly six-foot-long dart in his left hand and a much smaller stick in his right. "The atlatl," he declared, to surprised laughter from the two competitors. To teach the contestants how to use the device, primitive weapons expert Jack Dagger reprised his appearance from Season 3's rock-throwing episode. Dagger explained that energy created by swinging the atlatl is transferred to the dart and delivered toward the target at upwards of one hundred miles per hour. "One of the beauties about atlatl throwing is you don't have to be a big, strong man to perform well." This quickly became apparent in the practice session. In the same way that Joe Montana throws a football better than Arnold Schwarzenegger, Cheng took to the atlatl more easily than Trefren. Although the Wyoming hunter got out to an early lead in the ten-throw competition, the Silicon Valley project manager made a bullseye on the furthest target in the eighth round to generate an insurmountable lead in the "Atlatl Battle." Cheng would go on to win Season 4 of *Top Shot* and the two main prizes: $100,000 cash and a contract to represent Bass Pro Shops as a professional shooter. He left his job at Google, wrote a book about succeeding in shooting and life, came out as a gay man, and has since been an advocate for gun rights and diversity within gun culture.

In his voice-over explanation of the atlatl, Donaldson explained, "This projectile throwing device is considered one of the first true

The author (left) with History Channel's *Top Shot* Season 4 champion Chris Cheng in Santa Cruz, California, 2021 (photograph courtesy Top Shot Chris Cheng).

weapons systems." Combining a separate projectile and delivery device, the atlatl builds on and amplifies the evolved human capacity for throwing that Bingham and Souza see as vital for *Homo sapiens'* survival and dominance. As Randy Miyan observes in the *LGO Lens*, only modern humans possessed advancing projectile weapons, and they likely played a key role in our success over competing *Homo* species like Neanderthals. More importantly for this work, the atlatl creates a model for later, even more powerful weapon systems like the bow and arrow and, eventually, the firearm.

* * *

Today's widely owned semi-automatic rifles and pistols are part of the unbroken thread of the human-weapon relationship stretching back to rocks in the uniquely evolved hands of our prehistoric ancestors. The ability to deliver a lethal blow from a distance was significantly advanced by the discovery and harnessing of the power of gunpowder, and its eventual application to handheld firearms. Cannons were the first product of the application of the "Gunpowder Revolution" to weaponry. Using the explosive power of chemicals (a compound of charcoal, potassium nitrate, and sulfur) rather than human or mechanical power to launch projectiles dramatically increased the weapon's destructive force. The difference between using a cannon and a human arm, sling, or catapult to launch a rock or ball is clear. If you say "hand cannon" today, the typical gun owner will likely think of an extremely large handgun like the Desert Eagle or .500 Smith & Wesson Magnum, guns that make "Dirty Harry" Callahan's .44 Magnum revolver seem modest by comparison. But the term hand cannon has deep roots in firearms history, dating back to the fourteenth century when people literally held small cannons in their hands.

From the first cannons to today's small arms, the basic operation of firearms has been remarkably consistent over time. A projectile is propelled down a barrel by expanding gases produced by a rapidly burning ("exploding") propellant. The early hand cannons took at least two people to operate, one to hold the weapon and one to ignite the powder. Efforts to design an ignition system that could be operated by one person set in motion the evolution of personal firearms from the fifteenth century to today, beginning with the matchlock and culminating in the closed cartridge. The early history of firearms—as told in the museum at the Springfield Armory National Historic Site in Massachusetts, for example—is often organized not by size, length, or caliber, but by the firing mechanism.

The invention of the matchlock allowed a single individual to operate a firearm more easily. Pulling the trigger lowers a slow-burning cord (the "match") onto a pan of priming powder which ignites the gunpowder in the barrel causing an explosion that launches a projectile out the open (muzzle) end of the barrel. Limitations of this ignition system—susceptibility to weather and the tactical disadvantage of having a burning match—motivated the invention of the wheel-lock replaced the match with a rotating steel wheel and pyrite to generate the spark necessary to ignite the powder. It was a short step from the wheel-lock to the snaplock, snaphance, and eventually the more widely recognized flintlock.

The match, wheel, and flintlock systems all depended on igniting the priming powder in a pan, limiting the weapon's speed and portability. A revolutionary development, therefore, was the percussion cap, which encloses a priming compound that detonates when struck by a hammer released by a pull of the trigger. This cap-and-ball system was far more reliable and facilitated the development of very small handguns like the Philadelphia derringer, as well as repeating arms like the rotating barrel "pepperbox" pistol of the 1830s and the early Colt revolving cylinder "wheel gun" introduced in 1836.

Although the percussion cap system advanced repeating firearms, it still kept the primer, propellant, and projectile separate. After the handheld cannon itself, a second revolutionary invention was the closed metallic cartridge, a technology that allowed for the development of modern repeating firearms. The self-contained cartridge encased the three key elements in a single unit and allowed guns to be breech (rather than muzzle-end) loaded. Firearms that could be shot more than once without reloading existed for centuries, as early as the late 1400s when a matchlock with a 10-shot revolving cylinder was invented.[10] But breech-loading cartridges made the modern repeating firearm with a single barrel possible. Arguably, from this point forward, all subsequent developments in rifles and handguns have been incremental and cosmetic.

What is not merely cosmetic is the human-weapon relationship itself. The *LGO Lens* characterizes the human-weapon relationship as "a biosocial tattoo on human innateness which was inked-in during a substantial time-frame of exceptional survival pressures." Although he gives short shrift to rocks as projectiles, Miyan follows Paul Bingham in emphasizing the anthropologic continuity of projectile weapons, from the spear to the atlatl to the bow and arrow to the firearm.[11]

For Miyan, we cannot simply ignore these historical facts about the uniqueness of human individuals and communities. "The modern firearm did not just fall out of the sky to spite the efforts of those who seek to create peace on Earth," he writes. "It certainly is not merely the result of some aberration of human behavior. Firearms are simply the most recent iteration of The Human-Weapon Relationship."[12]

* * *

Homo sapiens won the real-life, evolutionary game of *Survivor* by learning to create and maintain "alliances" through cooperation with non-kin conspecifics. But that cooperation is underwritten, then as now, by weapons-based "pro-human suppression of inhumane behavior." Today, this is anchored in the United States not just by state-sponsored military and police forces, but also by widespread civilian ownership of firearms, especially modern semi-automatic pistols and rifles.[13]

Human history profoundly overlaps with—indeed, is driven by—"the history of developing more and more lethal projectiles, which could be hurled further and further," according to neurologist William F. Brown. Taken to its logical conclusion, "The analogy to modern missiles is exact, even if the projectiles now have intercontinental ranges, and rocket fuel has replaced the bow or arm as the force needed for sending those modern projectiles on their way." According to Bingham and Souza, the expanding range of projectile weaponry allows us to scale our kinship-independent social cooperation, at least to the level of the modern nation-state, even if the "global village" remains a dream imagined by the World Council of Churches. Less grandiosely, we can observe with Paul Bingham, "No one will ever find any human society anywhere that exists without coercive weaponry in the hands of some or all of its members. These weapons might be bows, atlatls, guns, throwing stones, or something that we have not yet thought of, but they will always be there, no exceptions."[14]

In human societies today, the state claims—consensually or not—a monopoly on legitimate violence. This does not mean that only the state's violence is legitimate; it means the state gets to decide whose violence is legitimate. This often means restricting civilian ownership of coercive projectile weaponry. The U.S. is an outlier in allowing its citizens to own firearms—and the violence they embody—independent of the state. This right of citizens to keep and bear private arms is enshrined in many state constitutions and has been supported recently by the United States Supreme Court in its *Heller* (2008), *McDonald* (2010), and *Bruen* (2022) decisions.[15]

Widespread civilian ownership of firearms in America is a fact regardless of one's view of recent Second Amendment jurisprudence. In early American history, guns were commonly owned by those who could legally do so. One reliable estimate found guns in 50 to 73 percent of male estates and 6 to 38 percent of female estates. These rates compare favorably to other common items listed in male estates like swords or edged weapons (14% of inventories), Bibles (25%), or cash (30%).[16] Even as the nation has settled, industrialized, and urbanized, levels of firearms ownership remain exceptionally high. As discussed in the previous chapter, I estimate that forty percent of all American adults personally own at least one of some 400 million privately owned firearms in the U.S.

The anthropological normality of projectile weapons among *Homo sapiens* historically sets the stage for the cultural normality of firearms in the United States today.

3

Becoming a Gun Super-Owner

Gun inequality: US study charts rise of hardcore super owners.
—The Guardian

Meet America's gun super-owners—With an Average of 17 Firearms Each.
—The Trace

In 2016, the results of a National Firearms Survey conducted by scholars at the Harvard School of Public Health and Northeastern University the previous year were released exclusively to *The Guardian* newspaper and the gun violence reporting organization *The Trace*. Both outlets published stories by Lois Beckett emphasizing that just three percent of American adults own half of the guns in the United States. *Mother Jones* called this "the Craziest Stat About Gun Ownership in America."[1]

Because many people outside gun culture cannot understand why a person would own a single gun, owning 8 or 140 guns is that much more inconceivable. This misconception about gun ownership levels was highlighted when I first presented my research on guns at the 2014 annual meeting of the Society for the Scientific Study of Religion. My study was the first in nearly twenty years to explore how different aspects of an individual's religiosity influenced their likelihood of owning firearms.[2] Consequently, my paper did not fit neatly into any of the meeting's dozens of panels. I presented in a session called "Studies in Identity and Humility," alongside papers on dispositional humility, democracy in Sub-Saharan Africa, and gender attitudes across religious groups.

This kind of session is what meeting organizers call "Research Potpourri." It's like the leftovers category on the game show *Jeopardy*, though the literal translation from French often applies: putrid pot. Our late afternoon Saturday time slot did nothing to bolster attendance,

43

either. I presented "Clinging to Guns and Religion? Exploring the Connection Between Firearms and Faith in America" (hat tip to President Barack Obama) to an intimate gathering of friends and associates of the panelists.

Knowing my audience would not know much about guns, I began by laying out what I took to be some mundane background information. Unique among the industrial democracies of the modern West, I said, the United States is awash both in a sea of faith and of firearms. At the time, the Small Arms Survey estimated 270 million civilian-owned firearms in the U.S. The private ownership rate of 88.8 guns per 100 people in the U.S. is the highest in the world, well ahead of runner-up Serbia's rate of 58.2 per 100 and third place Yemen's 54.8. I saw the audience's attention growing as I recited these statistics.

Although this amounts to nearly one firearm for every person in the country, I continued, these weapons are not evenly distributed throughout the population. A majority of the adult population does not personally own any guns, so the minority of Americans who do own guns frequently own more than one. The 2004 National Firearms Survey fielded by researchers at the Harvard School of Public Health found that forty-eight percent of individual gun owners owned four or more firearms, and three percent owned more than twenty-five firearms. The average gun owner, I noted, owned 6.6 firearms.[3] This number drew an audible gasp from the audience. Having been involved with guns and gun culture for almost four years at that point, this response startled me. It reminded me of how uncommon firearms are for some people and my own initial surprise at learning how common they are for others.

This interaction with fellow scholars reminded me of some basic social processes that influence how people experience and understand firearms. The concept of homophily captures the idea that people tend to form connections with people like themselves (discussed also in Chapter 1). In lay terms, birds of a feather flock together. In his study of the "gun gap" in American life, political scientist Mark Joslyn explored people's perceptions of how common guns are in their friendship networks. Drawing on data from the Pew Research Center, Joslyn found that only one percent of gun owners said none of their friends own guns. Among gun nonowners, twenty-one percent said none of their friends own guns.[4] People whose social networks are gun-free zones have a hard time understanding the prevalence of guns among those whose networks are gun-rich.

The 2004 National Firearms Survey I drew upon in my presentation was replicated in 2019. The same group of researchers found that gun owners' personal arsenals had shrunk slightly from 6.6 on average in 2004 to 5.02 in 2019. However, these simple means remind us that averages can conceal as much as they reveal about who owns how many guns. For example, my real estate agent friend owns one gun, a small .380-caliber pistol that she keeps in her purse while showing houses. A fiftyish African American man I met at a local range keeps his only gun, a 9 mm semi-automatic handgun, in his house because "all the kids running around strapped" in his neighborhood. Sandy and I own twenty guns between us, seven hers and thirteen mine. Taken together, the four of us own twenty-two guns in total. This averages out to 5.5 guns each, only slightly higher than the mean number of guns in the 2019 National Firearms Survey. But the underlying distribution of guns among us varies considerably. Only I am a gun super-owner. Gun super-ownership is far from an exclusive club, boasting some eight million members. My experience shows that accumulating a super-owner level arsenal is actually quite easy, and sensible.[5]

* * *

As much as I enjoyed my first experience shooting with Sandy and Jimmy Staley, I did not rush straight from Jimmy's home range to the gun store. My first post-shooting trip was to my local Borders bookstore to learn more about firearms. In my free time during the final days of the winter recess in January 2011, I would grab a couple of their many books about guns and sit at the Borders Café for hours, soaking up as much information as possible. (The fact that I used Borders essentially as a free library and it is now out of business is not lost on me.) I supplemented this reading by listening to podcasts, surfing the web, and browsing magazines like *Guns & Ammo.*

Although I was in over my head wading into the shallow end of this deep pool of accumulated firearms knowledge, my curiosity was piqued.

Part of the disbelief at the arsenals amassed by gun super-owners results from a lack of familiarity with firearms themselves. I get this, both as someone who was unacquainted with guns for most of my life and as someone who tries to understand Sandy as a shoe super-owner. From the outside, a gun is a gun is a gun is a gun, just as a shoe is a shoe is a shoe is a shoe. But even a basic understanding of firearms highlights the many differences, large and small, that taken together create the vast diversity of guns that are owned for a variety of different purposes.

Single-user portable firearms are divided into two broad categories: handguns and long guns. Long guns are further subdivided into shotguns and rifles. Handguns, as the name suggests, generally have twelve-inch or shorter barrels and are designed to be fired while being held only in the hand. Long guns have longer barrels (typically at least sixteen inches for rifles and eighteen inches for shotguns) and also include stocks (butt and fore-end) that allow the weapon to be braced against the shoulder (shouldered) and fired with two hands. The inside of the barrel (bore) of a shotgun is smooth, as was the case with muskets like the British Brown Bess and the French Charleville. A rifle is also designed to be shouldered, but its bore has spiral grooves (called rifling) that impart spin to the projectile as it leaves the barrel, like Joe Montana throwing a football with a perfect spiral.

Firearms are further distinguished by their action—the parts of the gun that determine how rounds are loaded (chambered), fired, ejected, and re-chambered. For handguns, the major action types are break-action single shots, revolvers, magazine-fed semi-automatics (each trigger pull creates one firing cycle), and automatics (the gun cycles as long as the trigger is pressed and there is ammunition available). Shotgun actions include break-action, slide (pump) action, lever-action, and semi-automatic. Rifles can also be break-action single shots, semi-automatics, and automatics, to which we add rifle-specific actions such as bolt (seen on sniper rifles and in biathlon competitions) and lever (the famous Winchester Model 1873 seen in many movie Westerns).

Gun cranks will note that the distinctions here are too simple. There are, for example, bolt-action shotguns and handguns. Furthermore, early firearms like muzzle-loading long guns did not technically have an action. Rather, they entailed an extensive process to load and fire, twenty-eight steps for the matchlock musket according to Jacob de Gheyn's 1607 *Exercise of Armes for Calivres, Muskettes, and Pikes*.[6] Different action types developed once firearms were loaded from the breech rather than the barrel.

Such technical hair-splitting reinforces my point: classifying small arms by type and action yields at least twelve categories. And we have yet to consider the subject of gauges and calibers.

Although they share with rifles a longer barrel and stock, shotguns are identifiable because their ammunition is shotshells—a plastic tube (hull) loaded with a primer that ignites the propellent powder when struck by the gun's firing pin, a wad that collects the explosive energy, and metallic projectiles. The projectiles are traditionally lead pellets (shot), though other metals are used out of environmental concern. There are also shotshells loaded with single solid projectiles called slugs. The gauge of a shotgun is determined by the number of bore-sized balls that can be made from one pound of lead, the most common being 12-gauge and 20-gauge.

Matters do not become any easier when we switch from gauges to calibers. Colloquially, caliber refers to the diameter of the projectile fired from a handgun or rifle. More accurately, it refers to the diameter of the bore of the barrel as measured from the top of the lands (the narrowest part of the bore, as opposed to the grooves that constitute the rifling). To add to the confusion, calibers are measured in hundredths of an inch in the United States, thousandths of an inch in the United Kingdom, and millimeters in Europe and beyond. Common handgun calibers are 9 mm, .40, .45, .38, and .380. The most popular rifle calibers include .223, 5.56 mm, .30, and 7.62 mm. Akin to shotshells, handgun and rifle ammunition comes in cartridges composed of a metal case, primer, propellant powder, and projectile. Although often used interchangeably, only the projectile in a round of ammunition is a "bullet."

If all this were not enough, the small arms universe is made even more complex by constant innovation driven by profit-motivated entrepreneurialism, a desire to subvert government regulation, or the basic human creative impulse to do things just because we can. There are pistol caliber carbines: rifles that shoot handgun rounds like the 9 mm, contemporary semi-automatic equivalents of the Thompson submachine gun. There are AR pistols: AR-15-pattern rifles with the buttstock removed to allow firing without being shouldered and avoid minimum barrel length requirements established by the government. AR pistols are often outfitted with pistol braces that attach where the stock would ordinarily be and stabilize the gun on the forearm rather than the shoulder. The capacity of gun enthusiasts and gun manufacturers to innovate routinely exceeds the government's ability to regulate.

If these paragraphs describing gun types, actions, and calibers have your head swimming, then you are exactly where I was sitting at Borders trying to piece together the complex puzzle of firearms. At some point I realized that I did not need to understand everything about guns; I just needed to know what gun to buy first. My initial research led me to focus on .22-caliber semi-automatic pistols.

* * *

The .22 LR (Long Rifle) is a very small round, the bullet measuring less than a quarter-inch in diameter and weighing thirty to forty grains (less than three grams). By comparison, 9 mm Luger bullets range from 115 grains to 185 grains and .45 ACP bullets are typically 230 grains. The

.22-caliber bullet's modest weight means it does not require as much propellant to get it moving through the barrel and toward the target. For the
shooter, this means it has a lower "report" than larger caliber guns—that
is, it does not make a very loud bang, has minimal muzzle flash, and does
not send the gun back toward the shooter as forcefully.

Moreover, .22-caliber rounds are relatively inexpensive. Prior to the
post–Sandy Hook ammo shortage in 2013, I could buy boxes of 500 for
around $20 (compared to $25 for 100 rounds of 9 mm). The .22 LR cartridge can also be shot in widely available pistols, revolvers, and rifles.
These properties have made .22-caliber firearms a popular choice for
established shooters, children, and newbies like me for some time.

When I decided to buy a .22 caliber pistol, I still had dozens of different models to choose from. Sandy's fondness for Berettas from her
days in the Coast Guard led me to look hard at the U22 Neos from the
500-year-old Italian gun maker. Its design angles gave it the appearance
of something out of *Star Wars*. I also knew of the German manufacturer
Walther Arms from James Bond's use of its PPK pistol. The Walther P22
pistol's ambidextrous safety lever and magazine release attracted me as a
left-handed shooter.

Pouring over reviews led me to a well-known and respected gun I
had never heard of nor seen before: the Ruger Mark III. As the name suggests, the Mark III is the third iteration of the Ruger Standard Model
semi-automatic pistol, the first gun manufactured by Sturm, Ruger & Co.
in 1949. Although designer Bill Ruger based the Standard Model on the
Japanese Nambu, it evoked memories of the historic German Luger P08
for many. By its fiftieth anniversary in 1999, Ruger had sold over 2 million Mark-series pistols. More than twenty years later, it remains in production as the Mark IV.

There are no public gun ranges in the City of Winston-Salem, so
I spent my earliest days as a shooter at Pro Shots Range, in a strip mall
north of the city, and at Sportsman's Lodge, across the river in the next
county to the west. Both indoor gun ranges offered many popular guns
for rent, including the Ruger Mark III. The target model's blued steel,
black grips, and traditional lines make it aesthetically bland, at least
compared to the Beretta Neos, but it was by far the easiest to shoot, most
accurate and reliable of the .22 LR pistols I tried. The gun store operating
inside Sportsman's Lodge, Morris Firearms, had the Mark III in stock, so
on 28 January 2011, I put a $100 non-refundable deposit down on the $335
gun and made my way to the Forsyth County Sheriff's Office to apply for
a pistol purchase permit.

Until the spring of 2023, North Carolina was one of a handful of states that required residents to receive permission from the local sheriff to purchase a handgun. North Carolina's pistol purchase permit law was reminiscent of New York's 1911 Sullivan Act, which required applicants to show evidence of "good moral character" and "proper cause" to possess a handgun. Under the 1919 North Carolina law, the "good moral character of the applicant" and the need to possess the weapon "for protection of the home" had to be established before a permit could be issued. Clerks of the Superior Court were originally empowered to issue pistol purchase permits, but responsibility was shifted to county sheriffs in 1959. Although the good cause language in the statute was broadened to include "(i) the protection of the home, business, person, family or property, (ii) target shooting, (iii) collecting, or (iv) hunting," the good moral character language remained, with the following caveat: "the sheriff shall only consider an applicant's conduct and criminal history for the five-year period immediately preceding the date of the application." The recent elimination of the pistol purchase permitting system in North Carolina parallels the liberalization of concealed carry laws in the U.S. that has been underway for decades (a trend I cover in Chapter 5).[7]

When I made my way downtown to the Forsyth County Sheriff's Office, I brought with me a form that basically stated I was not prohibited from owning a firearm under federal law and gave my reason for requesting a permit. I also had to submit a list of my residential addresses for the previous 20 years and a "release of court orders concerning mental health or capacity." By applying, I was also submitting to a criminal background check.

Waiting in the bland lobby of the dated office building, I felt self-conscious about announcing to the others there that I was going to buy a gun. Despite my recent experiences, I was still a liberal professor at heart, more aware of negative outcomes associated with guns than positive ones. I also still harbored enough negative stereotypes about gun owners as uneducated, toxically masculine, political retrogrades that the idea of being a gun owner was not entirely comfortable for me.

When my number was called, I tried not to make eye contact with anyone else as I approached the glass partition separating me from the Sheriff's Office staff. Along with various messages taped to the window, like "Do Not Tap on Glass," a burgundy hardcover Gideons Bible caught my attention. Applications for handgun purchase permits in North Carolina were taken under oath on the Christian Bible. Violations of that oath, as indicated by another message on the window, were punishable as

perjury, a Class II felony. No mention was made of the fate of the applicant's eternal soul. Safe in the knowledge that my application was completely truthful, I submitted my paperwork, swore the oath, and slid
twenty-five dollars cash under the glass, five dollars each for five handgun purchase permits.

My permits were available within days, so I went directly from
the Sheriff's Office to Morris Firearms in early February to pick up my
first gun. Chuck Morris collected my purchase permit and balance due,
and minutes later I was shooting on one of Sportsman's Lodge's eight
indoor lanes. More than a decade later, the Ruger Mark III continues to
be a great starter pistol. I always use it to introduce novices to shooting,
including students in my Sociology of Guns seminar at Wake Forest who
take their first shots with it during our class field trip to the gun range. It
is also still fun for me to shoot after all these years.

* * *

For many, buying guns is like eating potato chips, you can't stop
at just one. The Ruger Mark III was perfect for me to learn the fundamentals of marksmanship, but it was also comparatively heavy at over
two-and-a-half pounds. This feature, which made the gun pleasant to

**Student shooting the author's Ruger Mark III .22-caliber pistol (photograph
courtesy Robin Lindner/RLI Media).**

shoot because it reduces recoil, also made it potentially difficult for my then sixteen, fourteen, and eleven-year-old kids to use. Its semi-automatic action also meant that the gun would continue to fire with each press of the trigger until the magazine was empty—ten rounds in the case of the Mark III. My research suggested a lighter single-action gun would be easier and safer for my kids.

Although a single-action revolver can hold multiple rounds in its cylinder, firing it requires manually cocking the hammer and pulling the trigger. The gun will not fire again until the user repeats that cycle. The Ruger Single-Six is a popular variant, introduced in the 1950s and based on iconic nineteenth-century revolvers Hollywood was re-popularizing at the time. After inspecting the Single-Six at two gun stores in neighboring cities and balking at the $400 price tag, I found my way to a local pawn shop in Winston-Salem. They didn't have the Single-Six, but I saw a used Ruger Bearcat .22 LR single-action revolver in the glass case. Also released in the 1950s and resembling a shrunken version of the famous Remington 1875 Single Action Army, its more compact and lightweight size made it a better starter revolver for my kids. The $250 cash price won me over. I used another of my pistol purchase permits and doubled the size of my arsenal.

After buying these two guns, it was just a matter of time and money before I reached hardcore super-owner status. Before the end of the year, I bought not one, not two, but *three* .22-caliber rifles. Wanting a scoped rifle to work on precision rifle shooting, I sought out a classic and affordable bolt action from the Czech firearms manufacturer Česká Zbrojovka (CZ). One of my students at Wake Forest told me his uncle owned a hardware store that sold guns an hour up the mountain in North Wilkesboro. A day trip there yielded a CZ American 452, my first rifle. Although a more accurate gun than I was a shooter, the CZ 452 also revealed my impatience, as sitting at a shooting bench working the bolt for each shot was far from the most exhilarating experience I have had behind a gun. It was time for a semi-automatic .22 caliber rifle.

Nearly synonymous with this category is the Ruger 10/22. With millions sold since the 1960s, the 10/22 is affordable and widely available. I had no trouble finding one with a black synthetic stock at Davie Outfitters in Sandy's hometown of Mocksville. On a roll, a few hours later that same day, I was at the Gander Mountain big box store thirty-five miles away in Mooresville buying a Rossi single-shot .22-caliber rifle for the kids. This is how I became the owner of five guns in a single caliber, each a different gun with a different purpose.

* * *

The different uses to which people put their guns are more fundamental than the technical differences between guns I described earlier.
A pistol, rifle, or shotgun can be used for self-defense. Handguns can be
used for hunting, along with shotguns (for winged animals) and rifles
(for land animals and varmints). All three types of firearms are used in
various sporting competitions, such as those contested in the Olympic
Games: skeet and trap with shotguns, and precision target shooting with
rifles and handguns. Today there are also several different action shooting sports. Many of these, such as those sponsored by the United States
Practical Shooting Association (USPSA) and International Defensive
Pistol Association (IDPA), are centered on handguns, though there are
also "3-Gun" competitions that require competitors to shoot handguns,
shotguns, and rifles in the same course of fire.

I wanted to get into shotgun sports like trap and sporting clays,
so I purchased a CZ Redhead 12-gauge over/under shotgun (gun #6). I
wanted a shotgun for home defense, so I picked up a Mossberg 590-A1
12-gauge tactical shotgun (gun #7).

As I became more familiar with firearms, I entertained the possibility of carrying a concealed handgun. Having just a little knowledge
of firearms made me susceptible to my own unconscious incompetence.
I did not know what I did not know. It never occurred to me that working at a gun shop does not make someone an expert on firearms nor does
it require them to put the customer's best interest first. As a result, the
first pistol I bought for concealed carry was a special edition Sig Sauer
P238 .380-caliber semi-automatic with a corrosion-resistant Nitron finish, rosewood grip panels, and tritium night sights. It was a very attractive but terrible gun for me, not least because the external safety on
the single-action-only P238 is designed for a right-handed shooter. I
am left-handed. To be fair, the gun store owner never told me I *should*
buy the P238. But he also did not advise against it even when he saw me
improvising a way to sweep the safety off by bringing my left thumb over
the slide. When the external safety on the gun worked its way off over the
course of a day riding cocked-and-locked in my left-handed concealed
carry holster, I quickly became conscious of my incompetence. I knew
what I didn't know.

I subsequently traded the Sig P238 for a striker-fired 9 mm Beretta Nano (gun #8) in 2012, to which I added a smaller Kahr Arms P380
(gun #9) in 2013, which I supplemented with a 9 mm Glock 43 subcom-
pact pistol (gun #10) in 2017, which I upgraded just before the Covid-19

pandemic in 2020 to a compact 9 mm Glock 48 (gun #11). Although today I only regularly carry the Glock 48, I have heeded the gun culture advice that "two is one, one is none" and kept the others as backups.

One Christmas Sandy gave me a full-size 9 mm pistol, the FNX-9 (gun #12) manufactured by the American division of the venerable Belgian company, Fabrique Nationale Herstal (FNH). Being left-handed presents some challenges in shooting shotguns, rifles, and handguns. The typical shotgun stock is cast-off (bent slightly to accommodate the right-handed shooter), and almost all semi-automatic shotguns eject empty shells to the right—across the line of sight of the left-handed shooter. Most bolt-action and semi-automatic rifles are also designed for the right-handed shooter. A handgun's slide stop lever, magazine release, and safety are typically on the left side of the gun, to be operated by the thumb of the dominant right hand. The FNX-9, by contrast, was fully ambidextrous. In its design, it was perfect for me. On the range, it was a struggle. I could not shoot the FNX-9 as accurately as other 9 mm pistols I tried.

Reading reviews online, I saw some chatter about issues with the FNX-9's sights—the parts of the gun attached to the top front and rear of the slide to facilitate aiming. I wondered if my gun shipped from the factory with bad sights. This idea was reinforced when I took a course with the famed trainer and shooter Massad Ayoob (read more in Chapter 8). Ayoob tests a lot of guns and mentioned during our class that he was once sent a gun from a major manufacturer that was shooting some six inches off at twenty-five feet because the manufacturer put the wrong sights on the gun at the factory. My theory was confirmed! The FNX-9 sights were certainly bad. All I needed was to have Ayoob shoot the gun to verify this. I imagined myself on the phone with FNH USA customer service telling the skeptical agent, "I *know* the sights are bad because I had *Massad* freakin' *Ayoob* test the freakin' thing, OK?!"

Ayoob was kind enough to return to the range with me at the end of his course to shoot the FNX-9 and see if the sights were faulty. About ten yards down range, we put up a plain brown cardboard target with no visible points of aim on it. I loaded the gun's magazine to capacity with seventeen rounds and had a second full magazine available for the test firing. Bracing himself against a post, Ayoob aimed the FNX-9 and put the first shot in the center of the target. He paused momentarily to look at the hole. He aimed again and put a second round *through the same hole*. Massad Ayoob set the gun down on the shooting bench and stated earnestly, in a deep baritone that anyone who has heard him speak can never forget, "The sights are fine."

In that moment I had to confront the harsh reality of my own limited ability as a shooter. This, of course, did not stop me from trying to find a "better" gun. Although what journalist Paul Barrett called "America's gun" was always an option, for months I resisted getting a Glock.[8] Synonymous today with polymer frame semi-automatic pistols, the Glock's ubiquity and plainness left me cold. Sandy's best friend Ina, a gun enthusiast and former Coast Guard trainer, calls them "an ugly ass bullet-throwing box." But on a trip to Sportsman's Lodge, I shot my friend's .45-caliber Glock 21. And I shot it well. Not Ayoob-level well, but better than the FNX-9. The Glock's shootability exceeded its utter lack of character and not long after I bought a fourth generation 9 mm Glock 17 (gun #13) at a gun show in Hickory, North Carolina.

* * *

In addition to protection against people (63%), hunting (40%), collecting (34%), sporting use (28%), and protection against animals (20%), the 2015 National Firearms Survey found that 40 percent of respondents said they owned guns for "some other reason."[9] Although I often feel pressure to justify owning guns, a common reason for owning particular guns is "just because." This is the reason I own a .223 caliber semi-automatic rifle, as I explain in Chapter 4. For the present accounting, I simply note that in 2014 I had the opportunity to take advantage of "Friends and Family" pricing through a friend who worked for Remington Arms Company. I used it to buy a Bushmaster XM-15 (gun #14), which is modeled on the Colt M4 Carbine used by the U.S. armed forces.

Subtracting the FNX-9 that I sold to a friend who wanted something to keep in his RV while camping, my current arsenal numbers thirteen firearms. Although this is fewer than the gun super-owner average of seventeen, it does not include Sandy's seven guns, which are part of our household arsenal of twenty. Or, as some gun culture friends would call it, "a good start."

* * *

The author of the hardcore super-owner stories in *The Guardian* and *The Trace*, Lois Beckett, was the best journalists covering the U.S. gun beat at the time, so if one reads beyond the headlines a more complex story emerges. Beckett observed among gun super-owners "serious hunters, firearms instructors, gunsmiths, people who love tinkering with and customizing their firearms, and Americans worried about feeding or defending their families in the wake of a disaster scenario." And, although many may think of themselves as "just an accumulator," to quote Phil Schreier of the NRA National Firearms Museum, some are indeed serious firearms collectors.[10]

Rather than recoiling from it, gun people I know proudly embraced the label gun super-owner. Liberally employing wink emojis, my social media contacts questioned the commitment of people owning *only* 140 guns. One gun store acquaintance of mine laughingly questioned a mere eight guns as the threshold for hardcore super-ownership. Another friend highlighted the regular auctions held—often due to divorce or death—involving hundreds of guns at a time from a single collection. Others joked about gun hoarders and made comparisons to the number of Hummel figurines and comic books and Squishmallows and model trains and tea sets some people own.

Forbes magazine Senior Contributor Elizabeth MacBride spent more than a year writing about the business of guns. Among her conclusions was, "Some people say guns are tools—but nobody buys 10 chain saws in varying colors and speeds."[11] It is truly hard to fathom that Mac-Bride spent so long reporting on guns and learned so little. Although most people do not buy ten chain saws, I own more than ten tools for yard work. I have a (1) lawn mower, (2) trimmer, (3) blower, (4) shears, (5) lopper, (6) hoe, (7a) stiff rake, (7b) leaf rake, (8a) shovel, (8b) spade, (9) mattock, (10) tiller, and more. I own dozens of writing tools—including pencils, roller balls, ballpoints, highlighters, sharpies, and more than 10 fountain pens. None are exactly the same. All do different things for me.

Although I lovingly give Sandy a hard time about owning so many pairs of shoes—her shoe armory overflows into a home office closet, after all—I get why she has so many. I personally have different tennis shoes for hard courts and clay, different running shoes for trails and treadmills, different boots for hiking and working in the yard, different dress shoes for real business attire and business casual, and four pairs of Birkenstocks.

Being a yard tool super-owner, pen super-owner, or shoe super-owner is like being a gun super-owner in many but not all ways. My yard tools, pens, and shoes are unlikely to injure or kill me, though I sometimes feel that way when I am raking leaves, writing, or exercising. Being safe and responsible is more important when it comes to firearms. I have also done yard work, written with pens, and worn shoes most of my life. They have always been familiar to me. I had to travel a much greater distance, socially and psychologically, to go from owning zero guns to owning one. Becoming a gun owner at all was harder than going from one gun to being an average American gun owner with five guns. And without it being a conscious goal, ascending to the rank of hardcore super-owner was quite easy.

* * *

"So, do *you* own a gun?"

People often ask this question when they find out I study gun culture and am not completely appalled by it.

Do I own a gun?

How should I answer this question when I know for many the real question is one which a colleague once asked me, "You're not a gun nut, are you?"

I could certainly play a semantic game and answer, No, I do not own *a* gun. But what would the response be if I told the truth?

Yes, I own guns.

Yes, I own several.

Yes, I own 13.

Hello, my name is David, and I am a gun super-owner.

4

Living with AR-15s

Why do civilians own AR-15s? This is one of the questions I hear most frequently when people learn I study American gun culture. Sometimes genuine curiosity motivates the question, but more often it is a statement masquerading as a question: Civilians should not be able to own AR-15s. Or, as assault weapons ban advocates from Barack Obama to Hilary Clinton to Joe Biden have put it, "Weapons of war have no place on our streets."[1]

The passage of an assault weapons ban thirty years ago makes clear that this is not a new issue. But each civilian mass public murder committed with an AR-15 reopens a wound that never has enough time to heal. Words cannot adequately express my overwhelming feeling of anguish and anger at the image, just last week as I type this, of someone walking into a bowling alley with a rifle and intentionally killing people. Heartbreaking. Sickening. Incomprehensible. Awful.

Understandably, mass public shootings in places like Lewiston and Uvalde and El Paso and Las Vegas and Sutherland Springs and Sandy Hook—places where people rightfully expect to feel safe—evoke powerful emotions. These events naturally fuel questions, especially about civilian ownership of "military-style assault rifles," that are often put to me as an expert in American gun culture by journalists, acquaintances, friends, and family members. Unfortunately, I find it ever more challenging to put forward my honest answers to these sincere questions without fear of accusations that I care more about guns than children, have blood on my hands, am on the wrong side of history, or worse. Talking respectfully across differences on AR-15s feels impossible.

The situation is made worse as these emotions around the AR-15 are channeled into partisan political activism. Although there is no inherent conflict between opposing gun violence and supporting gun rights, to embrace both is to be politically homeless today. The massacre at Sandy

57

Hook in 2012 was a turning point. As *Wall Street Journal* reporters Cam-
eron McWhirter and Zusha Elison observe in *American Gun: The True
Story of the AR-15,* "Half a century after Eugene Stoner invented the rifle,
[the AR-15] had arrived as the fulcrum of America's great gun divide."
Invoking a perfect image, McWhirter and Elinson characterize the
AR-15 as "just a cultural chew toy for angry partisans."[2]

A common discussion of AR-15s today goes something like this:

"There's no reason for civilians to own military-style assault rifles."

"I reject the term 'military-style assault rifle.' These are widely
owned semi-automatic rifles."

"Same difference. Your fetish is built on the backs of the grade
school children who continually forfeit their lives."

"Here are several reasons civilians have for owning them."

"Come on. You're too smart to buy what you are peddling here."[3]

The issue is so fraught and polarizing that several times I seriously
considered dropping this chapter on AR-15s entirely. I saw nothing productive coming from explaining why owning them makes sense to many
Americans.

In truth, I sit uneasily between "Come and Take It" and "Ban Assault
Weapons." I wish I didn't. AR-15s would be much easier to discuss, and this
chapter far easier to write, if I wasn't trying to avoid being driven to one
side or the other by partisans on this political wedge issue. As I describe
below, I bought an AR-15 in 2014. It is not part of my identity, a totem or
tribal emblem, a central part of my family security plan, or even something I use very often. I know I will scandalize some strong Second Amendment advocates in saying this, but I personally do not stand to lose much
from an "assault weapon ban." At the same time, I know I will scandalize some strong gun violence prevention activists in saying I do not think a
ban on AR-15s will make an appreciable difference in reducing gun injury
and death overall, much less the mass public shootings that most concern
people.[4]

I know this position will not satisfy passionate believers who tip to
one or the other side of the fulcrum. I don't love AR-15s. I don't hate
AR-15s. As I have become more familiar with them over the years—their
development and relationship to military weapons, functionality, flexibility, and diverse uses—I have learned to live with them.

* * *

For some Americans, there is a true fascination with guns—their
history, their mechanical operation, what they can do, and what they

stand for. These people are not unlike collectors or aficionados or obsessives in other areas of life like automobiles, trains, boats, or bicycles.[5] Several were in attendance at the informal farm shoot Sandy and I attended in Davie County back in 2012, including one who encouraged us to shoot a World War II-era rifle he brought from his collection.

I knew little about historic firearms at the time, but a few attributes of the rifle stood out immediately. It was a carbine. That is, a rifle with a shorter barrel and lighter weight. Carbines are often compact versions of a full-length rifle, like the British No. 5 Mk I "Jungle carbine" to the Lee-Enfield service rifle. The solid wood and metal construction of our new friend's carbine made it quite heavy compared to the modern rifles I had held. And then there was the steel butt plate. The butt plate is designed to protect the wooden stock, but it is also the part of the rifle that contacts the shooter's body when shouldering the gun. When properly mounted, the butt of a rifle fits into the shoulder pocket, the fleshy area below the collarbone and inside the shoulder. When shooting my small .22-caliber rifles, I did not experience any ill effects of not getting the gun mounted correctly. As Sandy and I would soon find out, the same is not true when shooting a more powerful rifle.

It turns out that we were shooting a Mosin-Nagant M44, a variant of the Mosin-Nagant 91/30 rifle developed in Russia in 1891 and in use through World War II. The M44 carbine fires the same 7.62x54 mm round as the full-size 91/30. A 7.62 mm bullet is the same diameter as the .308 Winchester that is popular for hunting game like deer and elk. When fired through the comparatively short and light M44 rifle, substantial recoil must be absorbed by the shooter. It's just physics. Rifles today typically have shock absorbing rubber recoil pads designed to protect the rifleman's shoulder rather than butt plates to protect the rifle itself. With the Mosin-Nagant, whatever skin, fat, and muscle you have in your shoulder pocket is the recoil pad.

As usual, Sandy eagerly jumped in to shoot first. Sitting on the bench she rested her elbow on the top of the table and pulled the stock into her shoulder. Aiming at a paper target one hundred yards away, she settled into the sights and pulled the trigger. The recoil drove her back nearly half a foot.

"Holy crap!"

Sandy's hearty laugh was met by the owner's knowing chuckle. "Did that wake you up?"

"Sandy," I said, motioning to the table, "there's four more rounds for you to shoot."

She grabbed her shoulder and declined but added with a big smile, "That thing's awesome. Wow!"

The owner responded with evident pride, "It kicks like a Russian mule, don't it?"

The Soviet military developed the M44 carbine in 1943 in response to the rise of urban street fighting during the Second World War. But to my untrained eye, it looked like a classic hunting rifle with its traditional wooden stock and bolt-action. This is no mere coincidence. There has never been a clear line of demarcation between "military" rifles and "civilian" rifles. Sometimes rifle designs are used for both civilian and military purposes concurrently, sometimes civilian designs are descended from military weapons, and sometimes military designs are influenced by civilian firearms.

The American long rifle—commonly known as the Pennsylvania or Kentucky rifle—played a role in our successful revolution against the British crown. But this weapon of war was also commonly used at the time to harvest game and to shoot at targets for competition and diversion. What many today would consider an innocuous-looking traditional hunting rifle is actually a weapon based on military designs like the nineteenth-century German Mauser Model 98, cousin to the Mosin-Nagant 91/30. The American long rifle itself was a modified version of European hunting rifles, suggesting that superior technologies can be found in civilian hands before they are adapted to military purposes (see also the discussion of the .223 Remington cartridge for the AR-15 below).[6]

Rifles actually used in war also diffuse into the civilian marketplace. After the Civil War, Union soldiers were allowed to keep their military-issued firearms. The M1903 Springfields of World War I and M1 Garands of World War II poured into civilian markets thanks, in no small part, to the Civilian Marksmanship Program. But this story should not just be understood from the supply side of the equation. There has long been consumer demand for military service firearms or variants of them like sporterized Springfields, M1s, and Mausers. This is especially true among military veterans. The AR-15 has been the standard service rifle since the 1970s so it is not surprising to see demand for civilian variants. As my friend and gun writer Kevin Creighton pointed out to me, today's reviled AR-15 is a modern variant of medium-caliber, semi-automatic, magazine-fed rifles like the Remington Model 8 and Winchester Model 1910 that are more than one hundred years old now.[7]

There is nothing inherent in any of these widely owned rifles that makes them "weapons of war." A rifle in the hands of a civilian harvesting game is a hunting rifle. The same weapon in a competitive shooter's hands is a sporting rifle. The same rifle in the hands of a civilian defending herself is a defensive firearm. In the hands of a mass shooter, it is a murder weapon. And in the hands of a soldier in battle, it is a weapon of war. Of course, for those people who primarily associate AR-15s with these latter two categories of use, it is easy to think of them essentially as weapons of war. I sympathize with their lament that the presence of AR-15s in civil society makes our public life feel like a battlefield.[8]

* * *

The story of the development of the AR-15 has been told so many times before that it is part of the oral tradition of contemporary gun culture. Of course, oral traditions are susceptible to selective memory, forgetfulness, distortion, and error. To wit: I have long known that the "AR" in AR-15 doesn't stand for assault rifle or automatic rifle, as its critics sometimes suggest. But I only recently learned that it doesn't stand for ArmaLite Rifle, as its defenders frequently assert. AR either stands for the first two letters in ArmaLite or for ArmaLite Research, depending on whether you believe the inventor's collaborator or his daughter. Beyond the oral tradition, the history of Eugene Stoner, ArmaLite, and the AR-15 has been written several times. I cannot do that history justice in one chapter, so some highlights will have to do.[9]

Like the Mosin-Nagant Sandy and I shot at her friend's farm event, or the M1 Garand used by U.S. forces in World War II and Korea, military rifles in the 1950s were burdened by "their heavy wooden stocks, blocky steel receivers, and preindustrial aesthetics." As America at mid-century was entering the space age, strong but lightweight materials like aluminum alloys and fiberglass promised to revolutionize firearms as well. By 1952, an amateur engineer and gunsmith, Eugene Stoner, had fabricated an aluminum receiver, the central component of a rifle. In combination with his "gas operated bolt and carrier system" (U.S. Patent 2951424 issued in 1960), Stoner had designed the key elements of what would become the AR-15.[10]

Today Eugene Stoner is placed alongside John Moses Browning and John Garand as one of America's greatest firearms designers. According to military historian Alexander Rose, Stoner's precursor to the AR-15, the AR-10 design, "perfectly reflected its era and the society that had given it birth.... A familiar form rendered startlingly modern, the high-style AR-10 ... resembled the jet-age, optimistic, newly affluent,

Tupperwareified America of the 1950s, a place where, having broken free from the traditional stiff constraints of wood, stone, and steel, designers molded, bent, and formed plastics and alloys into increasingly abstract shapes."[11]

The complex organizational politics of the military procurement process doomed the ArmaLite AR-10's bid to replace the M1 Garand as the U.S. Army's primary rifle, but Stoner and ArmaLite engineers Jim Sullivan and Bob Fremont were already working to update that platform to shoot a smaller, faster bullet. Again blurring the distinction between "civilian" and "military" firearms, the .223 Remington cartridge commonly associated with this military design was based on "a standard hunting round called the .222 Remington," according to McWhirter and Elinson. The AR-15 designed and engineered by Stoner, Sullivan, and Fremont was eventually adopted by the U.S. military as the M16 rifle in 1963.[12]

The line between the AR-15 as a selective-fire military weapon (which can be fired in semi-automatic, automatic, or burst modes) and as a semi-automatic rifle for civilians was blurred from the start. The same year the military adopted the Colt ArmaLite AR-15, Colt's Firearms ran print advertisements for its new AR-15 Sporter. Described as a "superb hunting partner," the rifle pictured in the ad was indistinguishable from the M16 in most ways: straight composite stock, pistol grip, detachable magazine, carrying handle above the receiver, and tall front sight. The advertised virtues for the civilian owner were its light weight (six pounds) and a muzzle velocity of 3,100 feet per second using a .223-caliber, 55-grain bullet. "If you're a hunter, camper, or collector," the ad read, "you'll want the AR-15 Sporter."[13]

The AR-15 Sporter was available at any Colt Registered Dealer for $189.50. It did not exactly set the civilian rifle market on fire, but whether it was a "flop," to quote McWhirter and Elinson, is a more subjective judgment. We know from their reporting that Colt's manufactured 2,400 AR-15 Sporters in 1964 and no more than 5,000 a year until 1973. McWhirter and Elinson put this in the context of thirty-five million or so civilian-owned rifles near the end of the 1960s. The AR-15 design was brand new—indeed, in many ways revolutionary—so resistance from consumers who had a very strong image of what a rifle is supposed to look like is not surprising. This applies to traditionalists and reactionaries in the gun industry as well. Even around the turn of the twenty-first century, the National Shooting Sports Foundation (NSSF) did not embrace AR-15s at its Shooting, Hunting and Outdoor Trade (SHOT) Show, and gun industry elites ridiculed civilians interested in AR-15s as "tactards" (an

The author shooting an AR-15 at a gun training course in Texas sponsored by the Liberal Gun Owners (photograph courtesy Yancy Faulkner).

offensive combination of "tactical" and "retard"), according to former Kimber firearms salesman Ryan Busse.[14]

The more recent history of the AR-15 is quite different. Hungry for profits and capitalizing on division sowed by the 1994 assault weapon ban, gun companies—first small ones, then big ones—leaned into manufacturing and selling AR-15s as a symbol of freedom and strength. The ongoing global war on terrorism and a growing fascination with special military units like Delta Force and Navy SEALS allowed gun companies to do what they have done forever: wrap their guns in the legitimacy of the military. The effect of exposure to AR-15s through the wildly popular *Call of Duty* first-person shooter video games is hard to underestimate. These developments also intersected with the ongoing evolution of Gun Culture 2.0, with AR-15s being sold as defensive firearms for civilians. A growing number of military veterans began offering training courses to civilians on the "defensive rifle," "tactical carbine," and "urban rifle." Notable among these were Travis Haley and Chris Costa of Magpul Dynamics, whose influential "The Art of the Tactical Carbine" course was released on DVD in 2008.[15]

It is in this same period following the expiration of the assault weapon ban in 2004 that big gun companies like Smith & Wesson and Sig Sauer started jumping into the civilian AR-15 market, both taking advantage of existing market demand and attempting to foster even greater demand. Whether one thinks of gun buyers as "cultural dopes" who simply succumb to industry marketing or affords them some significant agency in making consumption decisions, the dynamic relationship between supply and demand resulted in millions more AR-15s being manufactured and purchased in the following years. According to a 2022 survey by the *Washington Post* and the market research firm Ipsos, one in five U.S. gun owners and one in twenty U.S. adults—about sixteen million people—now own at least one AR-15. As many own more than one, the total stock of AR-15 rifles could realistically be 1.5 to 2 times the number of owners, or more.[16]

The AR-15/M16 and the AR-15 Sporter were specific rifles. The term "AR-15" now encompasses an entire family of firearms descended from Stoner's design. These are referred to by critics as "assault weapons" or "weapons of war" and by proponents as "modern sporting rifles" or "sport utility rifles." Following Cameron McWhirter and Zusha Elinson's lead in *American Gun,* I have been referring to all of the civilian rifles in this family as AR-15s (see endnote 1). More descriptive and politically neutral, if inelegant, terms are AR-15 pattern, AR-15 platform, or AR-15 style rifles. In protest of these designations, gun journalist Tom Gresham has tweeted, "It's time. Let's drop the silly 'AR-style rifle' and just call it what it is. A rifle. It's a design more than 50 years old. It's an action type more than 100 years old. It's a rifle. A popular, common, ordinary, regular, ergonomic, lightweight 'rifle.' That is all."[17]

AR-15s now dominate not only the military and law enforcement markets, but the civilian rifle markets as well. Although off-putting to some, it is not hyperbole to say the AR in AR-15 now stands for "America's Rifle."

* * *

Even before I was interested in guns, I would see signs for the gun shows held regularly at the Winston-Salem Fairgrounds Education Building. They were hard to miss because the venue is located near the complex housing Wake Forest University's basketball, football, baseball, and tennis facilities. The Winston-Salem events are run by C&E Gun Shows whose schedule for 2019 listed sixty-four show dates in North Carolina, Ohio, Pennsylvania, South Carolina, Tennessee, and Virginia. Most of their shows revisit the same locations several times a year. Before the Covid-19 pandemic, they typically held about five shows in Winston-Salem annually.

These days I only attend about one gun show a year. They are quite routine. Attendees walk up and down aisles looking at tables full of guns, ammo, and accessories, as well as knives, jewelry, food, books, clothing, collectibles, and the like. Some people buy things. More just like to window shop. An exception was C&E's final gun show in Winston-Salem in 2012, the weekend of December 22 and 23rd. I was excited to attend as it would be my first gun show following the invitational shoot in October and I anticipated seeing the products with new eyes informed by what I had learned and experienced.

It turned out that the show would be novel, but not for the reason I expected. The show fell just a week and a day after a depraved young man who professed "nothing other than scorn for humanity" killed twenty first grade children and six adults in Newtown, Connecticut.[18]

Like any normal human being, not to mention a father and teacher, I was sickened by news of the massacre. I could not even imagine what would possess someone to perpetrate such an evil nor begin to understand the grief families would feel at their loss. I was moved by President Obama's speech at an interfaith vigil in Newtown just two days after the event and recoiled from the tone-deafness of National Rifle Association executive vice president Wayne LaPierre's press conference the day before the Winston-Salem gun show. Although my beginner's mind could not grasp all of the complex dynamics of gun politics in 2012, this much I knew: tragedies lead to outrage, outrage leads to calls to do something, doing something means restricting or banning guns, and the specter of bans sells guns.

After murdering his mother at home with a .22-caliber bolt-action rifle, the twenty-year-old killer brought a Bushmaster XM15 .223-caliber semi-automatic rifle and ten thirty-round magazines to Sandy Hook Elementary School. He fired 154 rounds in under five minutes. In the anguished days that followed, pressure for greater gun control rose to levels not seen for years. Although he appointed a working group to study the issue of gun violence, President Obama at the same time signaled that he would seek to bring back the 1994 assault weapons ban.

The response of many gun owners and some of the gun curious was as expected: to buy as many guns and accessories as possible, especially the very rifles and magazines that they feared would be banned. Photos of empty shelves in gun stores soon began circulating on the web. Down the road in Charlotte, Hyatt Gun Shop reported doing one million dollars in business on a single day following the Sandy Hook massacre.[19]

When I arrived at 8:30 a.m. on the first day of the Winston-Salem gun show—thirty minutes before the doors opened and in thirty-degree weather—a line of over one thousand people had formed outside the education annex. I asked the person at the front of the line what time he arrived. He told me 7:00 a.m., some pride escaping through his layers of cold weather clothing. I took my place at the end of the river of people spilling out from in front of the building and flowing around the corners of the fairground's midway. Standing in front of a grandstand hundreds of yards away, I could hardly see the annex, much less its entrance.

By 9:00 a.m. when the show finally opened, I had rounded the corner but could still see several hundred people in front of me. They must have opened the doors early to accommodate the large crowd, I thought. Wrongly as it turns out. When I arrived at the ticket booth thirty minutes later I was told they began selling tickets at 8:30 a.m. and there was a separate line I had to wait in once I had my admission ticket. Even at 9:30 a.m. that line still had a couple hundred people in it.

"What are you planning to buy today?" I asked one twentysomething man in this second line.

"An AR," he said.

"Why?"

"Because I can."

Once inside the education annex I found a very different mood than a typical gun show. The feeling that gun and magazine bans were imminent permeated the building. Gun show attendees are typically happy spending time with people and things they enjoy. On this day they were all business. The only joking I heard was gallows humor about impending restrictions. People moved through the show with intent bordering on panic looking for ammunition, magazines, and AR-15s.

Thirty minutes in, I saw two people pulling hand carts each carrying 4,000 rounds of .223-caliber and 5.56 mm rifle cartridges. Many others were grabbing anything they could find. Uber-like surge pricing reflected the extraordinary demand. Thousand round cases of Federal XM193 5.56 mm cartridges were selling for $895, an eighty percent premium over the typical price. Still, by 11:00 a.m., all the bulk packs of the most common AR-15 cartridges were sold out at the show's two main ammunition vendors. There was also a run on thirty-round AR-15 magazines. Polymer magazines produced by Magpul Industries that typically sold for twenty dollars were selling for forty-five at one table. One shopper bought ten of them and the seller's entire lot was gone inside of two hours.

With supply fixed and prices high, the law of demand affected AR-15 purchasing somewhat more than ammunition and magazines. A couple of prospective buyers asked one vendor if he had any AR-15s for less than $1,000. His answer: Only .22-caliber models. Still, another vendor had 10 people standing at its booth with AR-15 purchase paperwork already completed just waiting to checkout.

One customer who was buying his first AR-15 for $1,700 lamented, "I could have gotten this same rifle for $1,100 a week ago." He then despairingly added, "But it could cost twice that much in January. If I could even get one."

I asked, "How long have you been waiting to check out?"

"20 minutes," he replied.

I passed by the booth again on my way out of the show and found him still waiting. "Do you know how long you've been in line?"

He replied with a wincing grin, "What day is it?"

The *Winston-Salem Journal* reported that 2,500 people had entered the gun show before lunch. When I left there was still a long line of people—perhaps 1,500 more—outside waiting to buy tickets. President Obama had only recently been elected to his second term when the Sandy Hook massacre took place. Although Covid-19 has since overtaken him as "the greatest gun salesman in U.S. history" (see Chapter 1), Obama's title was undisputed at the Winston-Salem C&E Gun Show in December 2012.

* * *

The inflated prices and shortage of ammunition following Sandy Hook did nothing to stoke my interest in buying an AR-15. I was not actively avoiding them. I just had no reason to buy one. I rarely shot the two .22-caliber rifles I already had in my gun safe and I did not need an AR-15 for home defense. Then one day in the spring of 2014, a friend pulled me aside at Wake Forest's tennis center and made an enticing offer. She worked for Remington Outdoor Company, which was having its annual employee discount sale. The sale prices were extended to immediate friends and family. Knowing I was into guns, she asked if I was interested.

Like most people, I associated her employer with the historic Ilion, New York, arms company Eliphalet Remington founded in 1816. Although it has produced many different types of guns over the years, when people say "Remington" two of the best-selling firearms in history come to mind: the Model 870 slide (or pump) action shotgun and the Model 700 bolt-action rifle. Even though I did not need either of those guns, I asked her to send me the order forms anyway just out of curiosity. It turns out that Remington Outdoor Company at the time also owned a dozen other brands, several of which were participating in the friends and family sale, including the AR-15 maker Bushmaster Firearms International.

As recounted in Chapter 3, by 2014, I was already a gun super-owner with twelve firearms in my arsenal. But I still did not own one of the most popular guns in America, an AR-15, which is akin to collecting trucks but not having a Ford F-150. Several Bushmaster rifles on the order forms caught my eye. Not knowing enough to distinguish between the different models, I picked the most expensive one, the Bushmaster XM15 PRE M4 VM 16" MOE Carbine in black. As the model's alphabet soup designation indicates, this is a PRE-ban rifle—meaning it had the very features that the 1994 assault weapon ban targeted: a bayonet lug, flash suppressor, pistol grip, and adjustable stock. It was patterned after the M4 Carbine adopted by the U.S. military. The V-Match (VM) upper receiver and 16" barrel are trimmed with Magpul Original Equipment (MOE) furnishings like the sights, buttstock, pistol grip, and trigger guard. The friends and family price was almost two-thirds off the $1,330 retail price, too low to pass up. I became the owner of a "military-style assault rifle."

I had no idea at the time that the Bushmaster XM15 I bought was a variant of the model used at Sandy Hook. I learned this six months later when relatives of nine people killed in the massacre filed suit against Remington for selling the AR-15 to the public. Lawyers for the plaintiffs argued that Remington specifically marketed Bushmasters to young men and linked "the AR-15 to macho vigilantism and military-style insurrection." Among the marketing efforts entered into evidence was an advertisement Bushmaster ran that showed the rifle with the caption: "Consider your man card reissued."[20]

If I had seen the "man card" advertising campaign, it did not register with me. But as a sociologist who studies American gun culture, I am well aware of the scholarly and popular view that guns are symbolic tools for socially privileged men to enact hegemonic masculinity. This is fairly evident in Bushmaster's immature ad campaign targeting younger men by placement in magazines like *Maxim*. But the connection between the "man card" campaign and "macho vigilantism and military-style insurrection" asserted in the lawsuit struck me as far-fetched. And the connection between the "man card" campaign and school shootings even more so. How many people saw the Bushmaster ad campaign? Probably in the millions. How many people owned Bushmaster XM15s? Probably in the thousands. How many people used a Bushmaster XM15 to kill schoolchildren? One.[21]

Having bought a Bushmaster XM15, I still needed to take delivery of it at a Federal Firearms Licensee (FFL). The obvious choice was Best Firearms & Ammo, one of the FFLs that contributed to Mocksville's top ranking in gun stores per capita in the state of North Carolina. Before it closed during the gun sales bust in 2019 known as the Trump Slump, Best Firearms was located on the lower level of a brick retail space just off the town square. Like many gun stores, it doubled as a community safe space where people could hang out and talk about guns. I would often swing by on my way to Sandy's parents' house just to say "hey" to the owner Brent Meacham and spend some time browsing, even when there was nothing I needed to buy.

After completing the required firearm transaction record paperwork (ATF Form 4473) and presenting my valid North Carolina driver's license and concealed handgun permit (in lieu of a background check), Brent presented the rifle to me in its large plastic case. Perhaps because I never had one in the first place, I did not feel my man card had been reissued in that moment. In fact, my dominant emotion was uncertainty because I had so little experience with AR-15s. The gun enthusiasts hanging around the store were far more excited. One of the store regulars, Ricky, stepped forward, picked up the rifle, and began admiring it. He told me to be sure to clean and oil the rifle well before using it. He must have seen the anxiety on my face because he proceeded to break the gun down and explain the process to me. After he was done, Ricky put the rifle back in its case and closed the lid. I paid the transfer fee, bought a couple of boxes of .223-caliber cartridges, and took the rifle home. I wanted to show it to Sandy, but she was at work, so I put two TSA luggage locks on the case and slid it under our bed. It spent four years there before I ever shot it.

So why did I buy an AR-15? I certainly did not have a gun industry-fueled insatiable desire to own one. I did not even feel I needed one. I was not a vigilante, insurrectionist, or insecure in my masculinity. I bought an AR-15 because the opportunity arose to get one of the most popular firearms available today at a very good price, and it filled a hole in my collection. This is a real, if admittedly not a profound, reason to buy a gun. Of course, I was also aware that the Obama administration could foreclose future opportunities to legally buy AR-15s. Echoing the words of the young man I met in line at the Winston-Salem gun show, I bought it because I could.

* * *

For their owners, AR-15s have many purposes. For their opponents, there is only one: mass public shootings, especially in schools.

AR-15s are not just the weapon of choice for the U.S. military, law enforcement, and millions of American civilians. They are also often found in the hands of the most heinous public mass murderers, especially in recent years as they have become America's Rifle. Four of the five highest-fatality mass shootings in U.S. history involved AR-15s or very similar rifles: Route 91 Harvest music festival on the Las Vegas Strip in 2017; Orlando's Pulse Nightclub in 2016; Sandy Hook Elementary School in 2012; and First Baptist Church of Sutherland Springs in 2017. Moreover, three of the five worst school shootings were perpetrated by individuals with AR-15s, including two at elementary schools, Sandy Hook and Robb Elementary School in Uvalde, Texas.[22]

These are horrific events, the trauma of which is felt well beyond those immediately affected. Fear of mass public shootings touches all our lives. We cannot go into a movie theater, grocery store, bowling alley, concert, bar, house of worship, or shopping mall without worrying about the possibility of these low-odds, high-stakes events. Many are truly acts of terrorism in this sense, violence purposely designed to strike fear in a population beyond the immediate victims to achieve political or ideological aims. This makes them all the more frightening and much harder to stop. We see the consequences of this terrorism in our reactions, like getting startled by a car backfiring, and over-reactions, like forcing students to do the poorly conceived active shooter drills in school that have become distressing rituals of childhood in America.[23]

In the face of this trauma and fear, I understand why people want to try to *do something*, anything, to make mass public shootings stop. So do I. But the frustrating truth is that there are no quick and easy solutions. Mass murder committed by civilians has a long history in American society and has been perpetrated with a variety of weapons. Sixty years before the AR-15 Sporter was brought to market, nine people were killed with a 12-gauge shotgun at a concert in Winfield, Kansas. Eighty-five years before Sandy Hook, the worst mass murder ever in a U.S. school—the 1927 Bath, Michigan, bombing that killed thirty-eight children and five adults—did not even involve a firearm. According to The Violence Project, even in the AR-15 era the third (Virginia Tech, 2007) and sixth (Luby's Cafeteria, 1991) worst mass shootings were executed with pistols. Despite the availability of AR-15s, Luby's was the worst mass shooting in the U.S. from 1991 to 2007 and Virginia Tech was the worst from 2007 to 2016. The 1966 University of Texas tower bolt-action rifle mass public shooting was the deadliest event from 1966 to 1984, and only fell out of the top ten in 2022. In 2017, one hundred seventeen people were killed in mass public shootings, the worst year from 1982 to 2019 according to a database constructed by *Mother Jones* magazine. This includes the Las Vegas and Sutherland Springs massacres with AR-15s, but those were the only two (out of 11 total) incidents in which AR-15s were used.[24]

This is a morbid accounting, to be sure. It is necessary, thought, to highlight that an Australia-style AR-15 ban and mandatory buyback would have tremendous social and political costs with very little payoff in terms of lives saved. The fantasy of safety from mass murders secured by an AR-15 ban would soon be revealed as a maladaptive coping mechanism.[25]

The legitimate fear we have of mass public shootings has unfortunately been amplified by a media and activist-fueled culture of fear around AR-15s. The website FiveThirtyEight highlighted this in a post called "The Phrase 'Mass Shooting' Belongs to the 21st Century." Their analysis of newspaper and newswire use of the phrase since 1978 revealed exponential growth beginning in 2012, well out of proportion to changes in the number or seriousness of mass public shootings. In addition to this old media carnival mirror, the proliferation of new media in the 2010s, especially social media on smartphones, has dramatically increased the immediacy of fear-inspiring news. This culture of fear, of course, cuts both ways. Fear of mass shootings *and* gun bans has been weaponized by the National Rifle Association and exploited by gun manufacturers, as well.[26]

There are many ways to slice the mass public shooting and AR-15 data pie, depending on your intentions. I have sliced the data enough ways to make an insomniac hibernate. My specific intention here is to address a fundamental question of whether ridding the U.S. of AR-15s would solve our mass murder problem, especially in schools. It is true that people with the serious intent to harm a large number of people have been choosing the AR-15 more in recent years. Still, history shows that highly motivated mass murderers—those who take the most lives in the most brazen manner—will not be deterred by their inability to purchase AR-15s. I find the work of those proposing comprehensive strategies to deter and defeat potential mass public shooters more promising. This includes, but is certainly not limited to, investigative journalist Mark Follman, student behavioral threat assessment specialist John Van Dreal, retired FBI agent Katherine Schweit, and the criminologists behind The Violence Project.[27]

* * *

Of course, from the perspective of critics like members of the *New York Times* editorial board, "It is a moral outrage and a national disgrace that civilians can legally purchase weapons designed specifically to kill people with brutal speed and efficiency." Ridding the U.S. of them is a necessary step forward even if the number of lives saved would be quite small. Doing so "would require Americans who own those kinds of weapons to give them up for the good of their fellow citizens." The implication is that failure to do so is immoral.[28]

From this widely-held perspective, there is no good reason to own an AR-15. Writing in the wake of the Las Vegas massacre, *New Yorker* staff writer Adam Gopnik followed his peers at the *Times* in targeting "the strange American fixation on the right to own military-style firearms." Without feeling a need to defend his position, Gopnik asserted,

> They don't have a *reason* for this fixation—no reason can be found. There's no *argument* for it—such weapons are useless in sport, except for the sport of using them; they play no role in hunting, or not hunting anything except helpless people; and they protect no one from a tyrannical government, since the tyrannical government, if it would ever come to that, is hardly in need of small-arms fire to assert its will.[29]

Setting aside the problematic distinction already highlighted between regular old civilian firearms and military-style firearms, it is patently untrue that there are no arguments for the right to own AR-15s. Just because I had no "good reason" to buy an AR-15 does not mean there are "no good reasons" to do so. Gopnik simply does not accept the legitimacy of the reasons that are routinely given.

Gopnik's first argument concerning sport is perhaps the most curious, because all sporting goods are useless in sport, except for the sport of using them. This includes golf clubs, tennis rackets, baseball bats, darts, bowling balls, stock cars, etcetera. Sport shooting is sport. Some even consider shooting a gun its *telos*. As political philosopher Timothy Luke has observed, "The purpose of guns is to shoot; and, to perfect that purpose in all respects before, during, and after the shot is 'experienced as intrinsically good.'" For those who own AR-15s primarily for recreation, the sport of using them is in fact a reason, whether Gopnik accepts it or not.[30]

Of course, some own AR-15s for serious leisure as well. As *Ars Technica* co-founder Jon Stokes wrote in *Wired* magazine back in 2013, Americans love ARs because they're gadgets. They are "the 'personal computer' of the gun world." Stokes continues,

> In the past two decades, the AR-15 has evolved into an open, modular *gun platform* that's infinitely hackable and accessorizable. With only a few simple tools and no gunsmithing expertise, an AR-15 can be heavily modified,

or even assembled from scratch, from widely available parts to suit the fancy and fantasy of each individual user. In this respect, the AR-15 is the world's first "maker" gun, and this is why its appeal extends well beyond the military enthusiasts that many anti-gun types presume make up its core demographic.

The people who like AR-15s in this way are like those who change their own spark plugs, read *Popular Mechanics,* and watch "Top Gear." People appreciate the AR-15 not only as shooters, but as everyday craftspeople.[31]

Gopnik next asserts that AR-15s play no role in hunting. I have not had the opportunity to hunt, though in my travels through gun culture I have met many people who do. Their experiences give me confidence in saying that *everything* about the AR-15 makes them useful for hunting certain game, varmints, or invasive species like feral hogs. They are light and compact, suiting them for extensive movement in diverse terrain. Their adjustable stocks offer flexibility to a single shooter or share-ability among different shooters (a parent and child, for example). Pistol grips and semi-automatic action allow faster follow-up shots than bolt action rifles with traditional stocks. They are sufficiently accurate and powerful at a sufficient distance to kill animals ethically. Their modular design allows them to be chambered in calibers effective for hunting larger game, such as the .450 Bushmaster. As noted, the AR-15's bigger sibling, the AR-10, was originally designed in the 1950s to take the .308 Winchester, the most standard of standard medium game hunting cartridges.

The third prong in Gopnik's argument holds that the government's superior firepower overwhelms civilian small arms as a check on tyranny. With heightened concerns about insurrection since January 6, 2021, I address this prong with trepidation about being misunderstood. So let me be as clear as I can from the start: Our government, though imperfect, is legitimate. It is not tyrannical. I do not advocate violently overthrowing it.

When he entered the 2020 presidential race as a Democratic candidate, California Rep. Eric Swalwell called for a ban on "military-style semi-automatic assault weapons." This was not a radical position considering that an assault weapon ban first appeared as a plank on the Democratic Party Platform in 1996 and was reiterated in 2020. Swalwell went further than his party, however, in advocating for a mandatory government buyback of existing rifles and criminal penalties for those who do not comply. Among the responses to this proposal was a tweet at Swalwell to the effect that the ban and confiscation would create a civil war. Swalwell responded by tweeting, "And it would be a short war my friend. The government has nukes. Too many of them."[32]

Although Swalwell later clarified that he was only joking, this idea underwrites Gopnik's and others' perspectives on government force superiority. Living more than half his life during the ongoing global war on terror has not tempered Swalwell's confidence in the U.S. government's capacity to win a short war against determined, unconventional resistance. But it should have. The ability of the U.S. military's superior firepower to quickly defeat such insurgencies has been disproven repeatedly, from Vietnam to Somalia to Afghanistan and Iraq; hence, the idea that we are living in an entirely new era of asymmetric warfare, sometimes called Fourth Generation Warfare (4GW).[33]

That personal firearms have a coercive power that can check military arms is a key element of the white paper written by the Executive Director of the Liberal Gun Owners, Randy Miyan, discussed in Chapter 2. In *The Liberal Gun Owner Lens,* Miyan distinguishes between force-superior and force-adequate weaponry. The nuclear warhead, fighter jet, and battle tank are all force-superior to hand-held firearms. But if a people have a force-adequate weapon that can be scaled up in number, it can become decisive in conflict. Miyan argues that the modern semi-automatic rifle is such a weapon, capable of defeating—or at least fighting to a stalemate—force-superior weapons. Thus, "'superior' weapons and delivery systems such as airplanes and missiles are not in the position of ultimate dominance, as the layperson may conclude."[34] Additionally, individuals with firearms are the gatekeepers of force-superior weapons; government control of those weapons is never ultimately assured. This does not even consider how members of the military might respond to commands to use lethal force against their fellow citizens.

Again: I am not advocating for domestic insurgency. But the notion that democratic ownership of force-adequate small arms cannot serve to check state-generated power is not true, as our own revolutionary war of independence from the British crown reminds us.[35]

Beyond sport, hunting, and resistance to tyranny, Gopnik omits one of the most common reasons civilians own AR-15s today: self-defense. According to *The Washington Post* and Ipsos, 65 percent of AR-15 owners give protection of self, family, and property as a major reason for ownership, followed closely by fun to shoot (63 percent) and target shooting (60 percent). These numbers track fairly closely with William English's 2021 National Firearms Survey, in which self-defense (61.9 percent) falls between recreational target shooting (66 percent) and hunting (50.5 hunting) as the most cited purposes for owning AR-15s.[36]

I do not personally keep a rifle at hand for everyday defense in my home, but I would not presume to tell others they cannot or should not do so. I would not tell Stephen Willeford that he did not need an AR-15 when he confronted the shooter at First Baptist Church in Sutherland Springs. I would not tell Dave Thomas that he did not need an AR-15 when he saved his apartment neighbor in Oswego, Illinois, from being stabbed to death. I would not tell the eight-month pregnant Florida woman she did not need the AR-15 she used to defend her husband who two home invaders were pistol-whipping while their 11-year-old daughter was in the house.[37]

Responding implicitly to Adam Gopnik and anticipating Chapter 6 of this book, gun trainer John Johnston addressed a question raised in my Sociology of Guns seminar about needing guns. "No one *needs* a gun," Johnston replied, "until they do. And if they need it, they *really* need it."[38]

* * *

Three days after the Route 91 Harvest music festival massacre in 2017, former Ronald Reagan presidential speech writer and current *Wall Street Journal* columnist Peggy Noonan made one of her regular appearances on MSNBC's "Morning Joe." During the segment, Noonan asked her fellow panelists, Why do people have AR-15s? It was a sincere question, in my judgment, and one widely shared in American society. It is a question that has been answered by AR-15 owners often over the years.

In this chapter, I try to answer this and the related question about civilian ownership of "weapons of war" authentically and transparently. In the end, I accept that some will hear my answers and still hold that no one *needs* an AR-15 for any of the purposes outlined, either because other suitable alternatives are available (for hunting and recreation) or the use cases are so improbable (for defense against tyranny and self-defense). *Good* is the operative term when people say there are no good reasons for a civilian to own an AR-15. On such value judgments, fellow citizens can disagree. I have learned to live with this, too.

5

Swept Up in the Concealed Carry Revolution

In June 2022, the Supreme Court of the United States handed down its most significant opinion on guns since the 2008 *District of Columbia v. Heller* and 2010 *McDonald v. City of Chicago* decisions. *New York State Rifle & Pistol Association, Inc. v. Kevin P. Bruen, in His Official Capacity as Superintendent of New York State Police* extends the court's thinking in these previous two cases. The *Heller* decision for the first time in U.S. history recognized an individual right to keep and bear arms for self-defense in the home. The *McDonald* decision found the right established in *Heller* is incorporated by the Fourteenth Amendment and, therefore, applies to every state. The *Bruen* decision held that the right to keep and bear arms for self-defense applies not only in the home but in public as well.[1]

The *Bruen* decision overturned New York State's law requiring applicants for unrestricted concealed carry permits to show "proper cause"—that is, a special need for self-defense greater than the general public. The Court held that the requirement "violates the Fourteenth Amendment by preventing law-abiding citizens with ordinary self-defense needs from exercising their Second Amendment right to keep and bear arms in public for self-defense." In doing so, it gives Constitutional legitimacy to a movement for concealed carry rights that has developed over the past forty years, a movement that dramatically reversed the historic pattern of restriction on carrying concealed weapons in public begun in the early 1800s.[2]

Being able to carry a firearm concealed in public without a permit ("permitless carry") is the frontier of this trend, but more liberalized ("shall issue") concealed carry laws are now firmly entrenched in a majority of states. The *Bruen* decision will likely force further expansion of public gun carry rights in the few remaining more restrictive ("may issue") jurisdictions. At the same time, the decision has also stimulated those jurisdictions to pass new laws regulating public gun carry. Even as I write these words, the situation remains very much in flux legislatively and legally.[3]

That said, when I decided to get a North Carolina Concealed Handgun Permit in 2011, I directly benefited from the past half-century's unprecedented expansion of the right to bear arms in public. As I was swept up in this concealed carry revolution long before the *Bruen* decision, the journey I recount here reflects this overarching historical trend and more settled aspects of the law, though it does point to some possible future developments.

* * *

North Carolina represents the national development of concealed carry permitting quite well. The state banned the carrying of concealed weapons in 1879, a ban that was upheld by the Supreme Court of North Carolina in 1882 and remained in place for 116 years. A 1995 revision in the state's concealed carry law now requires county sheriffs to issue permits to any person who meets the requirements specified in the statute. These include being legally allowed to own a firearm, undergoing a criminal and mental health background check, taking a state-prescribed concealed carry course, and passing that course's written exam and shooting test.

Sandy and I took the concealed carry course offered at Sportsman's Lodge Indoor Gun Range, the same facility where I bought my first gun and where we had subsequently become members. When we arrived on a Saturday morning in April 2011, we were greeted by a sign with simple red printing on plain white paper: "In 1776 the British Demanded we Surrender our weapons. We shot them." Although not a universally accepted interpretation of the Revolutionary War, there is a kernel of truth in this sentiment, one grounded in local history.

Sportsman's Lodge is located near the Shallow Ford of the Yadkin River, one of the major colonial wagon crossing routes through the Piedmont region of North Carolina. In October 1780, some five hundred British Loyalists were organizing in the area under the direction of brothers Colonel Gideon and Captain Hezekiah Wright, perhaps intending to join British General Lord Cornwallis who had advanced to Charlotte. Whig Major Joseph Cloyd rallied 350 North Carolina and Virginia militia members and confronted the Loyalists who had crossed the Yadkin River and were heading west. Although outnumbered by several hundred troops, the Whig militiamen killed Tory company commander Colonel James Bryan early in the brief skirmish, demoralizing the Loyalists and forcing their retreat back across the Yadkin River. The Patriot victory in the Battle of Shallow Ford foreshadowed and contributed to Cornwallis' eventual retreat from Charlotte.

Nearly 230 years later, Sandy and I were seated at a plastic folding table in a drab, fluorescent classroom at Sportsman's Lodge filled to capacity by sixteen other latter-day Patriots, ten men and six women. We were all there for an eight-hour course called "Concealed Carry Handgun Training." The class largely followed guidelines created by the North Carolina Criminal Justice Education and Training Standards Commission after the state passed its shall-issue permitting law in 1995. It included instruction in legal issues related to concealed carry and justifiable use of deadly force; handgun types, nomenclature, operation, and safety; and marksmanship fundamentals such as grip, stance, and using the sights.

Our instructor, Ray, was a tall, thin-haired New Englander with an Irish complexion. He taught in the matter-of-fact, borderline perfunctory manner of someone who has spent many Saturdays in this classroom teaching this course. Ray introduced his discussion of types of guns and ammunition by saying, "We have to talk about guns because the state says we have to talk about guns." This did not exactly convey the importance of doing it, but at other times, his experience shined through. He fielded questions about choosing guns for self-defense sincerely and well, which was impressive considering the diversity of backgrounds we brought to the class. I had been shooting for just a couple of months and Sandy carried a sidearm professionally in the Coast Guard. A younger mother of three was still deciding whether she even wanted to have a gun while an older couple had hunted their entire marriage.

Possibly betraying his gun ownership status, one student asked, "What is the best gun to buy?"

Ray revealed his wry sense of humor in answering, "I didn't help you pick your wife. I'm not going to help you pick your gun. How many did you go through before you picked your wife? Try as many as you want until you find the one you like."

Ray went on to debunk what he called the "little girl, little gun theory," noting the benefits of full-size handguns for both genders. He added, "Women, you should choose your own guns. You're the ones who are going to use them. Don't let your men choose them for you."

To receive the certificate necessary to apply for a North Carolina concealed handgun permit, we needed to pass a written exam on the legal block of instruction and a proficiency exam demonstrating our competence in firing a handgun. Our written exam was based on a video Ray gave us when we signed up for the course to view ahead of time. We took the test early in the day and Ray used grading as an opportunity to elaborate on and correct misunderstandings of the state's laws on concealed carry and the use of deadly force. We all passed the test, perhaps because the state statutes do not specify what a passing score is.

At the end of the day, we moved from the classroom at Sportsman's Lodge to its eight-lane indoor range for the shooting proficiency test. The North Carolina Administrative Code specifies "(a) The student shall fire 30 rounds of ammunition at a bulls-eye or silhouette target from three, five and seven yard distances; (b) At each yard distance the student shall fire ten rounds; (c) 21 of the 30 rounds fired by the student must hit the target." This is, by design, a minimal standard intended to select people in rather than weed them out. Still, I had trouble. We began the test facing a human silhouette target three yards away with our guns loaded and lying on the bench in front of us. Ray told us he would call out commands to shoot a certain number of rounds in a certain amount of time.

"Three rounds in six seconds," Ray instructed.

I picked up my compact .380-caliber Sig Sauer P238, pointed the gun at the target, and pressed the trigger. The gun fired but when I got on the trigger again it did not move. On my first shot, the spent casing was not thrown from the gun's ejection port. It got pinned in the firing chamber by the slide as it moved back toward its starting position. This prevented a new round from being pulled from the magazine into the chamber and rendered the gun inoperable.

As a new shooter, I had not yet learned standard operating procedures for clearing malfunctions like the "tap-rack," in which you tap the base of the magazine with the heel of your off hand to make sure it is seated properly then rack the slide of the gun to clear the malfunction and bring it back into battery. I sheepishly raised my hand to notify Ray that I had a problem. He came to my station, looked at the gun, and said flatly, "Stovepipe," invoking a commonly used term reflecting the appearance of the empty casing sticking up from the gun. He quickly removed the magazine, ran the slide a few times, set the gun down on my bench, and told me, "Load it back up." I did and, feeling the eyes of my fellow students on me, I fired again on his command. Another stovepipe. Ray came over again, looked at the gun, looked at me, and said, "You're probably limp-wristing it."[4]

Believing I had failed the shooting test, I gathered my things from the bench to give my spot to another student. Ray surprised me by asking if I had another gun I could use. I looked anxiously at Sandy who was planning to take the test with her Beretta 92FS, the civilian version of her Coast Guard M9 service pistol. The 92FS is a full-size duty pistol, making it much easier to grip and fire than the P238. I avoided further malfunctions using Sandy's gun and shot a perfect thirty out of thirty. With a passing score of just seventy percent, all the other students passed the test as well.

While Ray printed off the certificates of completion, we sat quietly back in our classroom, tired from the long day. We regained some energy when he returned. With characteristically reserved congratulations, Ray handed me and others the document we needed to submit along with our applications for North Carolina Concealed Handgun Permits. I thought our class might head over to the Broad Branch restaurant for a celebratory dinner, but our individual excitement never coalesced into collective effervescence. Instead, we all just filed out of the Sportsman's Lodge and went quietly into our Saturday nights.

A month later I completed the process at the same Forsyth County Sheriff's Office where I had earlier applied for my pistol purchase permits (recounted in Chapter 3). In addition to Ray's certification, I brought hard copies of four required documents: a list of my addresses for the previous twenty years, an application form verifying my qualification to receive a permit, an authorization for physical and mental health care providers to release my records to the sheriff, and an affidavit declaring my mental fitness to safely handle a handgun.

Applications are processed on a first-come, first-served basis, so I took a number and sat in an uncomfortably quiet waiting room along with a handful of other men. When my number was called, I approached the glass security window and greeted the deputy through the metal grate as I pushed my documents and ninety-five dollars in cash under the cutout in the glass. She looked them over thoroughly and then asked me to put my right hand on a raggedy Gideon Bible, raise my left hand, and swear that the information I provided on the application was true to the best of my knowledge. After taking my fingerprints, she told me it could take two months or more for the Sheriff's Office to complete the mental health and criminal background checks and approve my permit. As it turned out, just three weeks later I received a phone call notifying me that my permit was available to be picked up.

Just like that, I had joined the concealed carry nation, becoming one of eight million Americans at the time who also had public carry permits. That number has grown to over twenty million today, a truly

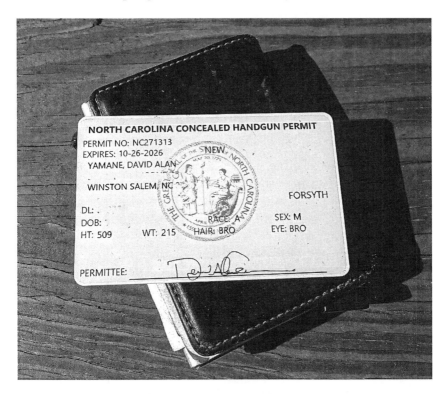

NORTH CAROLINA CONCEALED HANDGUN PERMIT
PERMIT NO: NC271313
EXPIRES: 10-26-2026
YAMANE, DAVID ALAN

WINSTON SALEM, NC

FORSYTH

DL: .
DOB: ·
HT: 509   WT: 215

RACE: A
HAIR: BRO

SEX: M
EYE: BRO

PERMITTEE:

The author's North Carolina Concealed Handgun Permit, with some identifying information removed (photograph courtesy Sandra Stroud Yamane).

revolutionary development in American society. My experience getting a concealed handgun permit in North Carolina reflects a national trend since the 1980s toward a dramatic liberalization in gun carry laws. We often think of laws as constraining what we can do, but laws also enable behavior. It is far easier for American citizens to legally carry concealed firearms in the United States today than at any time at least since the early 1800s.

* * *

When North Carolina banned the carrying of concealed weapons in 1879, it tread a path opened when the Commonwealth of Kentucky passed the nation's first law prohibiting concealed carry in 1813. Several other southern states followed in the ensuing two decades: Louisiana (1813), Indiana (1820), Georgia (1837), Arkansas (1837–38), Tennessee (1838), Virginia (1838), and Alabama (1839). After a hiatus for the Civil War, these laws spread to the rest of the South as part of Reconstruction, and from southern states to the rest of the country in the late nineteenth and early twentieth centuries.[5]

A highly influential model for the restriction of concealed carry in the North was New York's 1911 Sullivan Act, the same law overturned by the Supreme Court's *Bruen* decision. The Act required a government-issued license to possess and carry a pistol. To receive a license, the applicant was required to show evidence of "good moral character" and "proper cause." These highly (and intentionally) subjective criteria allowed sheriffs, police chiefs, or judges a great deal of discretion in deciding whom they permitted to carry legally. Among the states adopting Sullivan-style laws were California, North Dakota, New Hampshire, Michigan, Connecticut, New Jersey, Rhode Island, Massachusetts, Hawaii, and Oregon. In contemporary parlance, this class of laws is called "may issue," meaning the permitting authority is not required to grant a permit but *may* do so at its discretion.[6]

Although the *Bruen* decision targeted New York's "good cause" restriction, that is just one of two pillars of discretion in may issue permitting systems. The other is "good moral character." California's statutory language provides an excellent example. Penal Code Section 26150 reads in part, "When a person applies for a license to carry a pistol, revolver, or other firearm capable of being concealed upon the person, the sheriff of a county may issue a license to that person upon proof of all of the following: (1) The applicant is of good moral character. (2) Good cause exists for issuance of the license."[7]

With such highly subjective criteria, it is not surprising that California's decentralized system historically created extreme variation in permit issuance from county to county. Some issuing authorities have long interpreted "good cause" very liberally, such that anyone who wants to carry a concealed weapon for personal protection can get a permit. These jurisdictions, especially in the less populated areas of northern and central California, were *de facto* shall issue before *Bruen*. An example is Tehama County, which encompasses 3,300 square miles and whose county seat, Red Bluff (pop. 14,588 in 2021), is 130 miles due north of Sacramento. The Tehama County Sheriff's Office declares on its web page, "Sheriff-Coroner Dave Kain supports the right of law-abiding citizens to keep and bear arms. In this regard, all qualified residents of Tehama County are eligible to apply for a permit to carry concealed weapons." According to data released by the California Department of Justice, Tehama County issued 8,142 concealed carry permits from 2012 to 2021, accounting for some 12.5 percent of the population. Shasta County, to

Tehama's north, is another example. During the same time period, the Shasta County Sheriff issued 35,477 permits, one for every five residents in the county, the highest rate in the state.[8]

Other California counties are more conservative, requiring the applicant to establish a higher standard of good cause. These sheriffs look for some reason beyond simple personal protection, such as having been a crime victim, having a demonstrable credible threat of violence against you, carrying large amounts of money or valuables for work, or working late hours in a high crime rate area. My childhood home County of San Mateo is an example, with just 926 permits issued by the sheriff from 2012 to 2021, one for every 800 or so adult residents of the county. In fact, most of the counties in the San Francisco Bay Area, like San Mateo, and counties to the south, such as Santa Barbara, Los Angeles, and San Diego, have been very close to *de facto* no issue. Getting a permit in these jurisdictions was the exception rather than the rule. These are the most populous areas of the state, geographically arrayed along the coast from wine country to the border of Mexico.[9]

For most residents of may issue states like California, no character is moral enough and no cause is good enough to justify receiving a concealed carry permit. I discovered this myself while home visiting my parents in the Bay Area back in 2013. I decided to pay a visit to the San Francisco Sheriff's Department (which along with the San Francisco Police Department serves the geographically coterminous City and County of San Francisco). I wanted to see what it would take to get a concealed carry permit there.

Although there was no separate page of information about concealed carry on the San Francisco Sheriff's website, it was easy to find the address for the concealed carry office under the directory. Since I was staying in my childhood home south of San Francisco, I took the Bay Area Rapid Transit (BART) train into the city to the stop nearest the sheriff's office: 16th and Mission. After my trip, friends told me this BART station in "The Mission" is the worst in the city, and Yelp reviews repeatedly confirm this. A visitor from the East Village of New York City wrote, "WHOA, let's just say this is where I go when I want to picture what New York was like before Giuliani." The station is infamous for the "butt ass naked man" who for nearly ten minutes accosted people before police finally arrived, confirming the old saw that "when seconds count, police are just minutes away."[10]

Although blissfully unaware of this at the time, I was still happy to see a couple of City of San Francisco police officers at the top of the escalator when I exited the station.

"Excuse me, do you know how to get to the sheriff's office?"

"Yeah, go two blocks down Mission and turn right on 14th," one said, pointing me in the right direction. "The cross street is Shotwell," he added.

Pausing momentarily to process what he said, I responded, "Shotwell? Seriously?" We shared a brief laugh and I was on my way.

After walking a couple of blocks, I came to the intersection of 14th and Shotwell. To my right was a grocery store and to my left was an old Bartfeld Sales Co. warehouse building covered in ornate graffiti. Wondering whether I was in the right place, I continued slowly down 14th past Shotwell when I noticed a narrow parking lot with a fifteen-foot-high barbed wire-topped chain link fence running its one-hundred-foot length back to a nondescript two-story building. Although it was unmarked, I finally spotted what appeared to be a police car in the lot, so I jaywalked in that direction and made my way into the building.

I told the receptionist who greeted me in the lobby that I was interested in concealed carry and soon enough the Senior Deputy Sheriff responsible for permits met me at the front desk.

He asked politely, "How can I help you?"

"I live in North Carolina now, but I grew up in Half Moon Bay, and I'm thinking of moving back here. So I wanted to see what I need to do to get a carry permit. I have a North Carolina permit right now."

With a knowing though not dismissive smile on his face, he explained that I would need to do the following:

1. Establish residency, which would take 6 months.

2. Download the concealed carry permit application from the California Department of Justice. (Note: I spent fifteen minutes searching the DOJ website and was unable to find this document. I left a voicemail with the DOJ and never received a response.)

3. Submit the application along with a "good cause letter."

4. Pay a $20 application fee.

At that point, the sheriff would review my application and make a determination of my eligibility for a permit. If the sheriff gave me the go-ahead, I would then take the state-required training class, shoot the course of fire, and be instructed about authorized guns and ammunition.

I asked the Senior Deputy, "Is there anything in particular that would help my application in the eyes of the sheriff? Could I provide proof of classes I have taken like MAG-40?" (Referring to the Massad Ayoob Group's well-regarded forty-hour "Armed Citizens Rules of Engagement" course, which I discuss at length in Chapter 8.)

"That would be OK," he replied. "Turn in what you have with your application, but the biggest thing is the good cause letter."

"What sorts of things is the sheriff looking for there?"

"It would be helpful for you to get mugged a couple of times while you're establishing residency," he said, smiling.

"I don't think I would want to go out and get mugged just to get a carry license," I responded, smiling back at him.

"Well, just go a couple of blocks from here and you shouldn't have a problem," he assured me.

To wrap up, I asked, "Is it difficult to get a license in San Francisco?"

He nodded and explained, "The sheriff has not issued one in the two years I have been doing this job. This isn't North Carolina. Things are different here in San Francisco."

Different, indeed, I thought but did not say.

At the end of the day, not even being a Saint would qualify me as of "good moral character" and not even getting mugged a couple of times around the corner from the police station would be considered "good cause" in the eyes of the San Francisco County Sheriff. This was a perfectly legal level of discretion under California's may issue concealed carry statute at the time. As practiced in San Francisco, it was effectively an outright ban. According to a story on the Center for Investigative Reporting's *Reveal* website, there were only two active concealed carry permits in San Francisco in 2015, both issued by the City of San Francisco Police Chief. In the ten years from 2012 to 2021, only eleven permits were approved in the 800,000+ person county.[11]

Before the *Bruen* decision was handed down, may issue laws existed in California and eight other states: Connecticut, Delaware, Hawaii, Maryland, Massachusetts, New Jersey, New York, and Rhode Island. How much discretion authorities in these states exercise varies, but low permitting rates in may issue states today suggest they frequently deny permits to carry or create cumbersome processes to deter applicants in the first place. Nationwide, approximately 8.5 percent of the total adult population has a concealed carry permit. In shall issue states, 11 percent of American adults have a permit. In the nine may issue states, permitting rates range from a low of 0.00 percent in Hawaii and 0.02 percent in New Jersey to a high of 8.69 percent in Massachusetts and 11.29 percent in Connecticut. The average permitting rate of 2.93 percent in these may issue states is about one-quarter the rate in shall issue states.[12]

* * *

As a middle ground between complete bans and no restrictions on carrying, may issue laws in practice have tilted more toward bans;

hence, the *Bruen* decision. The alternative permitting system that leans more toward no restrictions is "shall issue" concealed carry. Shall issue permits still come with many regulatory strings attached. Legislative responses to the *Bruen* decision seeking to ensnare permit holders in a web of restrictions provide clear evidence of this. A week after *Bruen* was handed down, New York Governor Kathy Hochul signed the Concealed Carry Improvement Act (CCIA) into law. The CCIA severely restricts where those with concealed carry permits can exercise their right to carry by categorically banning firearms from some twenty "sensitive places" including but not limited to parks, protests, public transportation, entertainment venues, and even Times Square specifically. It also increases scrutiny of applicants' "good moral character" and requires completing a 16-hour state-approved training course.[13]

These efforts notwithstanding, in shall issue states the issuing authority has far less discretion in determining who is eligible to receive concealed carry permits. Any person who meets the statutory requirements *shall* be issued a permit. Prior to Florida's passage of shall issue concealed carry in the mid–1980s, only a few states made it relatively easy for an ordinary citizen to carry a concealed weapon in public legally.

Having adopted a Sullivan-style law in 1935, Washington became the first state to reverse course when in 1961 it "required that if the applicant for a concealed weapon permit was allowed to possess a handgun under Washington law, the permit had to be issued." For those who equate the State of Washington with the City of Seattle—the latter with its contemporary reputation for Starbucks-drinking, REI-wearing, Microsoft-rich liberals—this would seem an unlikely location for the nation's first shall issue permitting system. But the area's transformation into the "San Francisco of the Northwest" is fairly recent. Even today, one need not go far outside of Seattle proper to find a robust gun culture. Then, as now, much of the state was very rural, with strong hunting traditions and a substantial strain of libertarianism.[14]

Washington's change did not spark any broader movement for liberalization of concealed carry laws in other states. It was not until 1980, almost two decades later, that Indiana became the next state to go shall issue. By this time, major changes were taking place in the gun culture and the concealed carry movement was gaining strength. This created considerable momentum for passage of shall issue laws at the state level in the 1980s. Following Indiana in 1980 were Maine, North Dakota, and South Dakota, all of which adopted shall issue permitting systems in 1985. But the epicenter of the quake whose seismic waves would radiate across the country was Florida.[15]

Although Florida's 1987 law did not create shall issue concealed carry, it did open the floodgates for a massive expansion in the number of states with liberalized carry laws. Four other states passed shall issue laws in the three years following Florida—Pennsylvania in 1988, Oregon and West Virginia in 1989, and Idaho in 1990—for a total of thirteen with laws favoring the right-to-carry concealed weapons by ordinary citizens. (This includes Vermont, which has never banned or required residents to have permits to carry openly or concealed.) By the turn of the twenty-first century, more than half of the fifty states had liberalized their carry laws, and from 2001 to 2013, an additional twelve states followed suit.[16]

Just over one hundred years after New York passed the influential may issue Sullivan Law, forty out of fifty states had adopted shall issue concealed carry laws under which officials could not deny a permit to a citizen as long as that citizen met specific basic requirements. But within this overall trend toward liberalization, substantial diversity exists. All shall issue laws are not created equal. In fact, most concealed carry permit laws have many restrictions on who can carry what weapons where and when. Some states are more illiberal than others. As is often the case in regulatory law, the devil is in the details.

Illinois is on the high end of the shall issue regulation spectrum. Permit applicants must take a sixteen-hour course covering state and federal law, firearms safety and use, and marksmanship, with a minimum of four range hours culminating in a thirty-round live fire test. Illinois also has a particularly long list of "sensitive places" permit holders are prohibited from carrying, including (but not limited to) pre-schools and child care facilities, elementary and secondary schools, colleges and universities, hospitals and mental health facilities and nursing homes, public transportation facilities, bars and restaurants deriving more than half of their profits from alcohol, public gatherings or special events, public playgrounds and parks, casinos and racetracks, stadiums and arenas, public libraries, amusement parks, zoos, and museums.

As one exasperated recipient of an Illinois Concealed Carry License told me, "It seems like there are more places I *can't* carry than places I *can*." She has a point. Even with her license, this Chicago resident cannot legally carry her Smith & Wesson revolver when entering her downtown office building, having a drink after work at her favorite pub, visiting the Art Institute, walking through Grant Park, or riding the "L." Effectively, she has to leave her gun at home when she goes to work Monday through Friday, and many times on the weekends as well, depending on where she is going.[17]

North Carolina's concealed carry law is somewhat less restrictive than Illinois's. As we have seen, it requires an eight-hour course and has a live fire requirement. Prohibited areas for concealed carry in North Carolina include law enforcement and correctional facilities, state and federal government office buildings, and any private business that has posted a notice barring concealed carry on its premises. North Carolina's original law was amended in 2013 to allow concealed carry at parades and funerals, state and municipal parks, some educational properties, and bars and restaurants where alcohol is sold and consumed. The new law, however, retained the original prohibition on carrying concealed "while consuming alcohol or any time while the person has remaining in his body any alcohol or in his blood a controlled substance previously consumed." So, I can carry a concealed handgun at Fair Witness Fancy Drinks, my favorite craft cocktail bar in Winston-Salem, but I cannot drink, not even a drop, nor can I have consumed even a single drink for hours beforehand.

On the low end of the regulatory spectrum for shall issue states is Pennsylvania, which does not require applicants to complete any training course. Pennsylvania charges $19 for a permit, valid for five years, and requires only that the applicant meets certain qualifying conditions, most of which are required for legally owning a gun in the first place. The earliest state to go shall issue, Washington, is also still one of the most liberal. This was discovered by msnbc.com reporter Mike Stuckey when he was scandalized at being able to apply for a concealed pistol license from the King County Sheriff's Office in downtown Seattle in just twenty-two minutes.[18]

* * *

Whether those who apply for concealed carry permits should have to take a class, what that class should cover, and whether hands-on firearms training should be part of the required curriculum are among the most controversial issues surrounding the liberalization of concealed weapon laws. Those who oppose low regulation shall issue permitting systems often object that people should not be able to carry guns in public without "proper training." Jennifer Mascia, a reporter for the gun violence reporting initiative *The Trace*, reviewed the training requirements of the fifty states in February 2016 and found them about evenly divided in terms of a "live-fire" requirement. Twenty-four states and the District of Columbia have a shooting requirement like the ones in Illinois and North Carolina. Twenty-five states are like Pennsylvania and Washington State in not requiring any range time to receive a permit. (Recall that

Vermont does not issue permits to carry.) As the headline for Mascia's story declares, "25 States Will Let You Carry a Concealed Gun Without Making Sure You Know How to Shoot One." Moreover, existing recognition and reciprocity agreements between states create a situation in which it is possible for people, in Mascia's description, "to criss-cross the country toting concealed guns, without anyone having verified that their aim is true."[19]

But as my own experience makes clear, calling state-mandated concealed carry classes "training" is a bit of a misnomer. I learned some pertinent information about the laws governing the use of lethal force in self-defense, the rules of safe gun handling, and types of guns and ammo, but there was no actual hands-on training in how to use a gun, much less when. The live fire test at the end, which I passed using a gun I would never actually carry concealed, did not assess any particular gun training or my ability to draw from concealment and fire a gun safely and effectively in public. It is a minimal standard, as state-mandated standards tend to be. It is not unlike the driving test my kids passed for their North Carolina driver's licenses, which merely shows they can do a 3-point turn on an empty country road, but says nothing about their ability to handle a car under normal traffic conditions, much less when it hydroplanes on a busy freeway.

Gun trainer John Johnston passing the Texas License to Carry shooting test while blindfolded, with Chris Baker looking on (© 2019 Lucky Gunner, LLC. All rights reserved. Used with permission).

In reality, live-fire tests in mandatory concealed carry courses do not screen out many applicants. They cost time and money but do almost nothing to discriminate between those whose "aim is true" and those whose isn't. Everyone in my concealed carry class passed the live-fire test. No one has ever failed in any of the North Carolina concealed carry classes I have observed over the years. Alex Kogan, a Chicago-based gun trainer who runs Misha Tactical Arms, has taught the Illinois concealed carry class to over one thousand students since 2013. Only one of his students could not be coached to a passing level. Though Texas has one of the country's most challenging shooting tests for its license to carry, over one million Texans have passed since 1995. Karl Rehn of KR Training tells me that in twenty-plus years of teaching over 1,500 license-to-carry students, only a handful of students did not successfully complete the course. In a video for the online "lounge" of Lucky Gunner ammo, gun trainer John Johnston and lounge host Chris Baker demonstrate the low bar represented by mandatory live-fire requirements by shooting and passing the Texas course of fire *while blindfolded*.[20]

Many of those involved in the large and growing U.S. gun training industry take strong exception to the notion that the typical state-mandated concealed carry course is training in any meaningful sense of the term. "Concealed carry is a licensing class, not a training class," Arkansas gun trainer Rob Jennings tells me over drinks in Little Rock. "If gun training is a ladder, a concealed carry course is just walking up to the ladder." Karl Rehn offers a similar perspective in his book with John Daub, *Strategies and Standards for Defensive Handgun Training*. They argue that "state standards aren't realistic minimum performance standards" because they "don't include all the skills the average gun owner should be trained in" if they carry a handgun for self-defense. Perhaps most notably, no state-mandated concealed carry course requires students to draw from concealment, a necessary precondition of using a concealed handgun in self-defense. According to Rehn and Daub, those who teach the National Rifle Association (NRA) Basics of Pistol Shooting course, which satisfies the concealed carry training requirement in many states, are not even certified by the NRA to teach drawing from a holster if they want to go beyond the state minimum, as some trainers do in their concealed carry courses.[21]

The alternative to the present system, from the perspective of some gun trainers, is not to add more minimal state-mandated requirements where they don't exist or to increase them where they do. "The live-fire training requirement is a red herring," observes blindfolded shooter

Johnston. "It's unrealistic to think that I can give you an eight-hour class on a life-saving practice and think that class is going to be meaningful." Speaking as if he had observed my own concealed carry course in North Carolina, Johnston continues, "Nothing about those classes teaches you how to carry a gun on a daily basis and defend your life with a gun if the need arises. I would be fine if the state advocated meaningful training, but the amount of time and money that would cost is prohibitive."

I recently asked Karl Rehn how much time he would need to train individuals up to his minimum standard to carry a concealed gun in public safely. Being a deep thinker about gun training, Rehn did not immediately fall for my question. He instead responded, "It's not the number of hours that is important, it's meeting the standards of knowledge and shooting proficiency that is important." Someone with a great deal of experience with firearms might be able to demonstrate Rehn's minimum standards without any class time, while someone with no experience would require much more. When thinking about state-mandated requirements, we have to think in terms of what it would take to get the least qualified person up to the standard. So I asked Rehn, how much more? He suggested that 24 hours would probably be enough to take someone from no to basic competency. In terms of existing gun training curricula, this would be equivalent to taking both the eight-hour NRA Basics of Pistol Shooting and the sixteen-hour NRA Basic CCW (concealed carry weapon) courses.

A brief check of the NRA's online course directory reveals a number of these courses offered near my home in North Carolina. The Basic Pistol course costs $125 and Basic CCW $175 on average, not including any associated range fees or ammunition costs, which could easily add $100 to the bill. This is not to mention the cost of transportation and the opportunity costs of taking twenty-four hours over three days out of one's schedule. To be sure, I could afford $400+ and three days of my time if it were required to receive a concealed carry permit. I have spent many times that amount of money and time on becoming responsibly armed. But I am very privileged in this regard.

Rehn fully recognizes that requiring the training he suggests to get students to an acceptable minimum standard would have the unintended—or, perhaps for some, intended—consequence of creating a substantial barrier to receiving a concealed carry permit. One that discriminates especially against those who are more socially and economically disadvantaged. Rehn gives the analogy of voting rights. In his ideal world, "Everyone should pass a high school-level government test in order to be able to vote." Even a basic requirement that people are able to read ballots would be helpful. But Rehn recognizes that such limits on the ability to exercise one's rights are unconstitutional. I immediately grasp the connection Rehn is making between voting rights and gun rights. Especially under *Bruen*, socially and economically exclusionary requirements to get concealed carry permits could be considered unconstitutional for "preventing law-abiding citizens with ordinary self-defense needs from exercising their Second Amendment right to keep and bear arms in public for self-defense," to quote the Supreme Court decision.

These practical and legal considerations lead gun trainers like Jennings, Johnston, Rehn, Daub, and their peers to embrace and promote voluntary rather than mandatory defensive firearms training. In fact, the defensive gun training community established a standard for the trained armed citizen early in its development: a five-day, forty-hour course combining classroom and range work. Examples include the American Pistol Institute's 250 Defensive Pistol (now Gunsite 250) and the Lethal Force Institute's Judicious Use of Lethal Force/LFI1 (now MAG-40), about which I will have much more to say in Chapter 8.[22]

* * *

A convenient framework for summarizing the broad historical development of concealed weapons laws in the United States is this: The nineteenth century was the century of concealed weapons *prohibitions.* The twentieth century was the century of concealed weapons *permits,* with *may issue* permitting systems dominating early in the twentieth century, giving way to *shall issue* permitting by the turn of the twenty-first. Today, public concealed carry by average Americans is permissible, although not equally possible, in all fifty states and the District of Columbia. With the *Bruen* decision, it promises to become more equally possible everywhere.

A specter haunting proponents of restrictions on public gun carry is the twenty-first-century spread of what some gun rights advocates laud as "Constitutional carry." Not including Vermont, which has never regulated gun carrying, twenty-six states (including eleven in the 2020s so far) have adopted some version of permitless carry. Anyone who can legally possess a gun can carry it concealed in public without a license, although various other restrictions on who, what, where, and when still apply. My friend from Anchorage, Matthew Carberry, proudly calls these laws "Alaska carry" because Alaska was the first state (in 2003) to adopt a system in which the government issues but does not require concealed carry permits. In the post–*Bruen* era, it is certainly possible (if not probable) to imagine the Supreme Court allowing nationwide Constitutional carry on the Vermont model by ruling that permits themselves are an unconstitutional burden on a right to public carry.

Whatever the future holds, the present reality is that I am among the millions of Americans who have participated in this concealed carry revolution. Shall issue and permitless carry laws make carrying firearms in public by ordinary citizens like me much easier today than at any time in the past two centuries. Whether I should carry in public is a separate, though clearly related, question. Answering it requires me to conduct a serious analysis of the risks and benefits of keeping and bearing arms.

6

Pascal's Wager and Firearms

Why on Earth does someone need to carry a gun to get a gallon of milk at the grocery store? Aren't you more likely to get struck by lightning than to defend yourself with a gun? What are you so afraid of? People ask these questions, and more, when they find out I keep and carry guns for self-defense. I ask myself these sorts of questions. The decision to seek an armed solution to the problem of vulnerability I experienced in my apartment parking lot involved a complex—and ongoing—process of risk assessment.

I am a risk-averse person. When a friend from high school told me he was thinking of leaving his secure job with an established software company to join a startup, I thought it was too risky. He had a young family to worry about and the startup's business model was terrible. Why would anyone wait to receive DVD movie rentals in the mail when they could get them right away at the many Blockbuster Video stores on their way to or from work? Cryptocurrency? No, thank you. Apple stock? Overpriced. I don't drive fast, don't ride my bike without a helmet, don't jump out of planes or off cliffs, don't like boats or ATVs, don't drink to excess, don't pick fights. Whenever possible, I try to limit my exposure to unnecessary risk.

As a thoughtful risk analyst, I recognize that my place in history, socioeconomic status, and lifestyle make me unlikely to be the victim of a crime that would necessitate armed self-defense. I accept Steven Pinker's assessment in *The Better Angels of Our Nature: Why Violence Has Declined* that "today we may be living in the most peaceable era in our species' existence." In drawing this conclusion, Pinker looks at evidence for many forms of violence, including warfare, murder, slavery, sadistic punishment, rape, hate crimes, deadly riots, child abuse, and animal abuse. He finds that they have all declined over the course of human history. We also know criminal violence, especially involving guns, is like a blood-borne pathogen that travels through specific social networks enabled by specific social behaviors. I am outside those networks and do not engage in those behaviors, reducing my risk of exposure to violent victimization (see also Chapter 7).[1]

These facts notwithstanding, I cannot reduce my risk of criminal assault to zero. I travel to unfamiliar places for work and leisure. I give students bad grades. I shop at big box department stores. I enjoy walking around our city, eating out, and attending shows. Moreover, although it may be a low-odds event, if I should need to defend my life the stakes could not be higher. Before 2010, I had never witnessed a violent dispute in a parking lot and had a victim show up at my door. It has not happened again, but the fact that it happened at all—and could have gone much worse than it did—was enough to put the need to address low-odds, high-stakes events on my radar forever.

My approach to gun ownership for self-defense parallels the seventeenth-century French philosopher Blaise Pascal's approach to God. Pascal famously argued that a rational person should live as if God exists because the benefits of doing so, if God does exist, are much greater than the costs of doing so if it turns out that God does not exist. By contrast, living as if God does not exist and being wrong will bring a huge cost to the individual. Pascal's Wager translated into defensive gun culture holds that for a rational person, *it is better to have a gun and not need it than to need a gun and not have it.*

* * *

This approach to guns and risk could not be more different than that taken by my fellow social scientists, who operate according to a very different key assumption: no one really *needs* a gun for self-defense. This assumption is central to an approach that is coalescing in response to the rise of Gun Culture 2.0, what I call "The Standard Model of Explaining the Irrationality of Defensive Gun Ownership." At the heart of The Standard Model is the assertion that guns are rarely used (and not very useful) for self-defense and instead make gun owners less safe. Defensive gun ownership, therefore, is a bad bet.[2]

This argument has been made quite clearly by German social psychologist Wolfgang Stroebe. Writing with two colleagues, Stroebe observes, "There are strong arguments to be made that for most people, guns are neither needed for self-defense nor very useful when the need arises." Stroebe's assessment of the need for guns is based on what he calls the "objective risk of attack." Of course, there is no agreement among social scientists or risk scientists on what constitutes an *objective risk*. On the contrary, risk is a socially and culturally constructed variable. Nevertheless, Stroebe invokes as evidence for his argument the fact that homicide rates have been declining in the U.S. for decades. Constant concerns about the gun violence epidemic in some quarters be damned, Stroebe contends that the risk of being a homicide victim is very low, adding that the risk of being a homicide victim in a mass shooting is even lower. Needing a gun for defense against homicide is, therefore, not justified.[3]

Stroebe's fellow psychologist Nicholas Buttrick argues similarly when he states plainly that "gun owners rarely use their guns to prevent victimization." Here Buttrick joins others in citing data from the National Crime Victimization Survey (NCVS), specifically the 2015 article, "The Epidemiology of Self-Defense Gun Use." This analysis of NCVS data finds that guns are used defensively in just 0.9 percent of contact crimes reported by respondents. This statistic is popular among proponents of The Standard Model because it is the most limited way of defining defensive gun use (DGU).[4]

The NCVS only includes those who first report that they had been the victims of certain personal contact crimes. This excludes victims of other types of crimes as well as those respondents who did not see themselves as crime victims in the first place—perhaps because they successfully defended themselves with a firearm. "Refuse to be a victim" is a National Rifle Association slogan but it is not just a slogan. Moreover, given the correlation between low confidence in government and gun ownership, some NCVS respondents may feel uncomfortable disclosing a DGU to a U.S. Census Bureau employee. An assessment of scholarship on DGUs by the RAND Corporation concludes, "the NCVS estimate of 116,000 DGU incidents per year almost certainly underestimates the true number."[5]

In my view, any estimate of DGUs should include those who prevent themselves from being victimized, whether they discharge their firearm or not. I have met many people in my journey inside American gun culture who successfully defended themselves with their firearms without firing a shot, the mere presence of the gun acting as a deterrent to the threat they faced. So, when the Pew Research Center consulted with me about their survey of gun owners in 2017, I encouraged them to ask a simple but particular question about DGUs: "Have you ever used your gun for self-defense against another person, whether you fired the gun or not?" Pew did end up asking a DGU question close to mine on their survey: "Not including in military combat or as part of your job, have you ever used a gun to defend yourself, your family or possessions, either by firing it or threatening to fire it?" Pew's survey found that seven percent of all adult respondents answered this question in the affirmative, including seventeen percent of current gun owners. That was an estimated 17.5 million adults in the U.S. at the time. Perhaps DGUs are not so rare after all.[6]

Of course, Pew's question relies on respondents' subjective understandings of defensive gun use. Consider Andrew, an acquaintance of mine who drives a delivery truck. Andrew was sitting at the gas station one day waiting to go on his next run when he saw "this sketchy-looking guy" approaching his truck "yelling and acting crazy." When the man got on the truck's driver-side step and looked into the cab, Andrew held up his Ruger LC9 pistol. The man got down and left. Andrew considered this a successful defensive gun use. But what would have happened if he did not have a gun? It is impossible to say. As the RAND Corporation summary of research highlights, a major challenge in studying the utility of DGU is counterfactuals such as these. Would the outcome have been different? Not wanting to find out what might happen is a major reason for using the gun preemptively in the first place. This is why so many gun owners make Pascal's Wager. In Andrew's experience, it was better to display the gun when he may not have needed to than to wait and see if he needed to at which point it might be too late.

* * *

In June of 2016, I spent nearly two weeks working as the official racket stringer for a minor league professional tournament held at the Wake Forest Tennis Complex in Winston-Salem. On the Friday before the event began, I had one of my busiest days, stringing twenty-two rackets. That is not an overwhelming number for a professional tournament, except that I didn't start stringing until after I finished teaching that morning and many players did not drop off their rackets until after they finished practicing that evening. Consequently, I stayed at the tennis center until nearly 1:00 a.m. Saturday, five hours after the facility closed and the last person left.

Thankfully, I was perfectly safe (sarc.) because the tennis center is part of the Wake Forest University athletic complex and, as such, the university has signs posted at the entrances to the parking lots: "Private Property. NO CONCEALED OR OTHER WEAPONS PERMITTED. NCGS 14–269.2 NCGS 14–415.11(C)(8)." The tennis complex is in

"No Concealed or Other Weapons Permitted" sign posted at the Wake Forest University tennis and football complex (photograph courtesy Sandra Stroud Yamane).

a remote location, behind the football and baseball stadiums. It borders R.J. Reynolds Tobacco Company offices and warehouses, which border a higher-crime area of Winston-Salem. So, I am always extremely nervous and aware of my surroundings when I leave the tennis center building after hours. As usual, I made it safely to my car and home that night. I woke up the next morning, however, to an email from Wake Forest University's Office of Communications and External Relations notifying the campus community that a student had been shot in an armed robbery on one of the streets near campus.

Plato Collins "Lins" Barwick IV was enrolled in summer school at Wake Forest in June of 2016 to catch up on classes after taking the spring semester off for a pre-med internship at Cape Coast Teaching Hospital in Ghana. During his time in West Africa, Lins met Angel Komenda, an orphan with cerebral palsy who was discovered by pigs who rooted her out of a shallow grave on a farm outside Cape Coast. He later founded and helped raise over $25,000 for the Angel Komenda Fund. He is that kind of person.[7]

Lins is also the kind of young man who would offer to escort female friends home after Friday night flows into early Saturday morning. Although off-campus, Polo Road is an area where many Wake Forest students live and walk late at night, especially on the weekends. My son, who was a year ahead of Lins at Wake Forest, told me that he routinely walked from houses in that neighborhood back to his dorm room on campus, alone, at night. This particular Saturday morning, the unthinkable happened. Returning to his house after dropping off his friends, Lins was attacked by three young men in an SUV. They demanded his wallet. He complied. They shot him anyway. He stumbled, vomited, and fell in the street, the university water tower in clear view just a few hundred yards away. Lins tried to wave down passing cars, to no avail. He lost consciousness. Finally, an Uber driver stopped because she saw Lins lying in the street. In an equally improbable event, the car's passenger was a fraternity brother who comforted Lins while the driver called 911.[8]

The bullet entered Lins' abdomen, damaging his internal organs, and lodged near his spine. He recovered from 7.5 hours of surgery performed at Wake Forest Baptist Medical Center by the hospital's chief trauma surgeon and underwent a second surgery to remove the bullet. He was fortunate to survive and to have recovered from his injuries well enough to graduate from Wake Forest in December 2018.[9]

Lins Barwick's experience reminds us that an aggravated assault is sometimes just a failed homicide. One reason for the declining homicide rate in the United States—which Wolfgang Stroebe cites as evidence for declining objective risk of harm—is improvements in the treatment of gunshot victims. The murder rate in the United States in 2019 was 5 per 100,000 population, but the aggravated assault rate was fifty times higher, 250 per 100,000. One might still subjectively conclude that the objective risk of being shot in an armed robbery is very low. However, the low probability of being a victim of a violent crime is insignificant to those, like Lins Barwick, who become a crime statistic.

Reflecting on this experience, hours and years after the fact, reminds me that I should not be alone at a closed business in a gun-free zone (for those who follow the law) in the early hours of a Saturday morning. Lins Barwick was shot for no reason while walking down the street 1.27 miles away and 100 minutes after I left the tennis center. It could have been me.

* * *

The ability to defend one's life would seem to allow a person to take on more risks with greater confidence, like walking someone home early in the morning or working alone at one's business late at night. But I, like most gun owners I know, am much more interested in reducing than taking on more unnecessary risk. This contrasts starkly with the idea that people who own or carry guns for self-defense are itching for a fight. Critics of defensive gun culture seem to think that I, like Dirty Harry Callahan, want someone to "go ahead, make my day." To be sure, the idea of defensive gun ownership entails a willingness to use lethal force if necessary, but the goal of most is to set that bar of necessity very high. So high, in fact, that it is crossed, in Massad Ayoob's phrase, only "in the gravest extreme."[10]

Back in 2011 when I was thirstily consuming as much information about guns as possible, I discovered a world of gun-themed TV shows. I picked up a Time-Warner cable subscription with a premium channel package so I could watch the Outdoor Channel and Sportsman's Network for my "research." My most fruitful television field site became Wednesday Night at the Range on the Outdoor Channel, which still runs seven gun-themed shows from 6:00 p.m. Wednesday to 6:00 a.m. Thursday every week. In the same way that I marveled at the trick shot showdown on *Top Shot* when I first saw it, I would watch in awe as professional exhibition shooters like Bob Munden split playing cards and opened safety pins with bullets on the show *Impossible Shots.* Jim Scoutten's *Shooting USA* covered a variety of sport shooting competitions around the country. Michael Bane's *Shooting Gallery* featured gun culture in all of its various incarnations (hunting and sport shooting, self-defense and training) and all of the hardware that goes into these activities. But the show I most looked forward to watching weekly was *The Best Defense,* also co-hosted and produced by Bane.

The Best Defense often seemed tailored to my life situation. One of the first episodes I remember watching early in 2011 addressed security issues particular to those of us who lived in apartments, and the following week's episode covered parking lot confrontations. The heart of the show was self-defense scenarios. The parking lot confrontation episode runs through three variations of the same situation. Co-host Michael Janich pulls into a parking space next to another car whose driver, played by another co-host Rob Pincus, becomes irate thinking that Janich has hit his car. In the first variation of the scenario, Janich turns his back and walks away while chatting on the phone, only to be attacked from behind by a sap-wielding Pincus. This is a "worst-case scenario," as Pincus describes it in the post-event debrief. When they run through the scenario a second time, Janich hangs up his phone and gives his full attention to the agitated Pincus. He attempts to de-escalate the situation and maintain his distance, but when Pincus attacks this time, Janich recognizes the threat early enough to draw his concealed pistol and stop Pincus from attacking him.

This is the kind of self-defense shooting that is valorized in the "Armed Citizen" column in the NRA's *American Rifleman* magazine. But in his debrief, Janich says that although "in this case, I did a lot of things right…. I also had opportunities for escape." In the third and final scenario, Janich gets out of his car and is again confronted by an angry Pincus. This time, Janich gets off the phone and tries to de-escalate the situation by speaking with Pincus, but realizing it is not working, gets back in his car, locks the door, and drives off. In their final debrief, Janich notes that "keeping yourself safe is all about taking advantage of all your opportunities." To which Pincus adds in conclusion, "Just because you can defend yourself doesn't mean you should have to defend yourself. If you can get away, if you can avoid using lethal force … that is always going to be your best defense."

The tagline for *The Best Defense* has always been "avoidance, knowledge, awareness, preparedness." This was again very evident in the Season 5 premiere. This "neighborhood watch" episode was clearly based on the shooting of Trayvon Martin by George Zimmerman the previous year. In *The Best Defense* version, the head of a neighborhood watch program (played by co-host Mike Seeklander) notices an unfamiliar person walking down the street acting suspiciously. The unknown person, played by Michael Janich, walks across a neighbor's front lawn and begins looking in the windows of the house. At this point, Seeklander calls 911, has a very Zimmerman-like interaction with the operator, and then decides to cross the street to investigate further.

The scenario cuts off at this point and Michael Bane appears with Marty Hayes, J.D., head of the Armed Citizens' Legal Defense Network, to discuss what we have just seen transpire. Bane affirms Seeklander's decision to dial 911 and be a good witness, but questions his decision to cross the street. Hayes agrees that although he has a legal right to cross the street, it might not be the best choice compared to just waiting for the police to arrive. Transitioning to the next phase of the scenario, Bane observes, "It's America. You have a legal right to cross the street. But when you're carrying a gun, the situation starts changing."

As the scenario continues to play out, Seeklander confronts Janich on the front lawn of the neighbor's house. They exchange words and Janich begins to walk off. Seeklander puts his hand on Janich's chest to prevent him from leaving, at which point they start pushing each other. Seeklander then tries to break away from the conflict by throwing his hands up and walking away himself. As Seeklander walks away, Janich attacks him from behind, gets him on his back, and from a mounted position begins to slam his head against concrete landscaping blocks in the yard. At this point, Seeklander draws his concealed handgun and shoots Janich.

As in the parking lot confrontation episode I had watched two seasons earlier, the conclusions drawn from the neighborhood watch scenario are not what many would expect from a gun-centric self-defense program. George Zimmerman was vigorously defended by many in the gun community for being unjustly prosecuted, but he is less often upheld as a model armed citizen. Although some in gun culture are fond of the saying, "It's better to be judged by twelve than carried by six," *The Best Defense* makes clear that this is often a false choice. It was certainly a choice that the fictitious good neighbor Seeklander and the real neighborhood watchman George Zimmerman did not have to make. In his final reflections on the scenario, Janich concludes very simply, "The best defense was for the neighborhood watch guy to never cross the street in the first place. He never should have put himself into a situation that he didn't have to be involved in." Far from being a sheepdog protecting the flock, "If he wasn't duty bound, if he didn't have a badge, he had no business being there." I have argued the same about Kyle Rittenhouse.[11]

Although represented very well on his show, these perspectives are not limited to Michael Bane's *The Best Defense*. I also watched *Stop the Threat,* another program based on reenactments of actual self-defense situations. These scenarios were followed by a roundtable discussion of the incidents with various experts who emphasized awareness and avoidance rather than active involvement when unnecessary. This emphasis was so strong that that in an episode taped during the George Zimmerman murder trial in 2013, host James Towle began the show by reading an email from a viewer who was not happy that the message he was getting from the reenactments was "let the criminal run loose, stay in your house terrified." For a response, Towle threw the issue to gun trainer Kathy Jackson who said, "The first rule of a gunfight is …" and looked to her fellow panelist Marc MacYoung to finish her thought. Mac Young said, "…don't be there."[12]

Of course, my research on armed citizen risk mitigation strategies extends beyond just watching TV. I also read books about self-defense. Some address how to carry and use a gun, but the more interesting ones focus on how not to have to use a gun. Awareness and avoidance again play a big role in these books, like Gavin de Becker's best-selling *The Gift of Fear: Survival Signals That Protect Us from Violence.* De Becker emphasizes that fear can be a reasonable response to individuals or situations. We should trust our instincts to avoid the kind of violent encounters that would necessitate using a gun.[13]

Staying ahead of the violence curve does not mean you are ready to shoot first and ask questions later. It means not having to shoot at all by recognizing looming threats and preventing critical incidents from happening in the first place. At the 2016 NRA annual meeting, trainer Steve Tarani promoted what he calls preventative defense or *PreFense*®, the title of the book he gave away to attendees at his seminar. As the father of three children aged sixteen to twenty-one at the time, the idea of prefense over defense resonated with me. When my kids first started driving, I told them it did not matter how good and safe they are as drivers, because there are others out there who are bad and unsafe drivers. Because of these threats to their safety, they needed to be aware of the drivers around them and to anticipate what those drivers might do. Do not just respond to other drivers once they threaten you, I told them, but prevent yourself from having to react by being proactive. Basically, I was not telling them to drive defensively, I was telling them to act *PreFensively* when behind the wheel of a car, one of the situations that puts them as teenage drivers most at risk of injury or death. Colloquially, I could say with Steve Tarani that an ounce of prevention is worth a pound of cure, in driving as in life.

When I was taking ninth-grade Spanish, our teacher Sr. Fernandez would have us memorize colloquial sayings to learn the language. I still remember many of them today. The phrase I use most often—it appears on the syllabus for every course I teach—is *mas vale prevenir que lamentar*. It is better to prevent than to lament. This applies to my kids driving, students in my Introduction to Sociology classes, and armed citizens. A gun culture colloquialism attributed to defensive trainer John Farnam is known as the "Rules of Stupid":

Rule 1: Don't go to stupid places
Rule 2: Don't associate with stupid people
Rule 3: Don't do stupid things

To which Farnam later added a fourth: "Be in bed by 10 o'clock."[14] Of course, as a gun trainer, Farnam still recommends carrying a firearm whenever and wherever possible. But following the Rules of Stupid can mitigate the risk of harm for most of us most of the time.

There are those in the gun community who apply the Rules of Stupid very broadly, substantially curtailing their lives and activities. They do not go to certain big box stores because of "zombies" in the parking lot preying on shoppers, or attend art galleries, sporting events, or other venues that ban guns. They essentially treat public space as a minefield to be negotiated rather than a place to be enjoyed. I remember talking to respected self-defense trainer, Craig Douglas, about this after he guest lectured in my Sociology of Guns class at Wake Forest.

Craig and I were enjoying dinner together at the Katharine Brasserie in the former R.J. Reynolds Tobacco headquarters, a beautiful old art deco building in downtown Winston-Salem, when he commented, "Sometimes you just want to go enjoy a museum without having to worry about whether you have a gun or not." From there we walked to Bailey Park, an urban greenspace where I showed him the conversion of old Reynolds cigarette factories into a high-tech innovation district. We ended up meeting my wife Sandy at Fair Witness Fancy Drinks where we had a few of their specialty cocktails and many laughs. And we didn't have to yell at, eye gouge, punch, stab, or shoot anyone. It was a good day.

* * *

Although my night out with Craig Douglas was riskier than taking him back to his hotel after class, returning home for dinner with Sandy, and being in bed by 10:00 p.m., it was also more enjoyable. Risk management can sometimes lead to a myopic focus on limiting our exposure to risk. This orientation carries over into debates over guns, in which a strong emphasis is often placed on the *elimination* of risk. In his work on gun suicides, for example, medical doctor and sociologist Jonathan Metzl argues, "Risk helps people identify the possibility of peril in their loved ones and is something that we all want to avoid in our lives. Risk implies peril, hazard, and the possibility of loss…. As a doctor or as a researcher, I believe that a life with less risk is a life that is often longer, happier, and more secure. Risk is something that we should want to study, identify, and, ultimately, prevent."[15] On one level, this resonates with me as a risk-averse person. But there are two sides to the risk coin; the frequently neglected flip side is the reward.

Rather than thinking of risk as something to avoid, I think of it in the same way that gun trainer Will Petty does. "Risk is our currency," Petty says, "and we get to choose where we spend it." Consider this analogy: Risk can never be completely eliminated from sex, but we are willing to spend some risk to reap the rewards. The same is true with guns. There is safer gun handling and use in the same way there is safer sex. Although risk can never be eliminated entirely from gun ownership and use, we are willing to take on some of that risk in exchange for current and potential future benefits.[16]

Thinking of risk as a currency rather than something to be avoided at all costs also helps to keep risk in perspective. In November 2015, a coordinated Islamic terrorist attack at the Bataclan Theater in Paris, the Stade de France in Saint-Denis, and elsewhere killed 130 people and injured over 400 more. Following the attack, I received an email from my university's Office of Communications and External Relations reassuring our community that university officials "have not heard of any student who has been harmed or is in danger.... All are safe." Furthermore, there was no indication that any faculty or staff member "has been harmed or is in danger, either, in France."

Although it was good to know that no member of our university community had been harmed, I was surprised to read that the university also believed that they were all safe and none were in danger. The terrorist attack that created the need for the email itself suggested that no one in Paris, no one in France, no one anywhere is safe and out of danger. Although it would have been bad PR, a more accurate email would have read, "Students and faculty are probably, but not certainly, safe."

I was thinking about this in relation to my own life at the time because I was preparing to travel to Washington, D.C., for the American Society of Criminology annual meeting the week following the Paris attack. Washington, it seemed to me, would be a major target for terrorist activity and possibly a place to avoid so as not to incur that risk. Sandy and I considered canceling the trip.

In the end, we not only went to Washington but toured the National Zoo, the National Building Museum, The Phillips Collection art gallery, and the Lincoln Memorial. We ate out at Momofuku in Central City, Jaleo in the Penn Quarter, and the Jack Rose Dining Saloon in Adams Morgan. Not to mention all the meeting sessions I sat through in the Washington Hilton near Dupont Circle, where John Hinckley shot President Ronald Reagan. It was not all business as usual, though. When we attended the world premiere of the opera "Appomattox" at the Kennedy Center for the Performing Arts, the building's ornate interior was patrolled by law enforcement in tactical gear with bomb-sniffing dogs. Sandy also changed her wardrobe from a dress and heels to slacks and flat shoes in case she needed to run. Better safe than sorry.

Whatever concern I had about the risk of a terrorist attack was tempered by the reality that I was more likely to die in a car crash driving the 700-mile round trip to Washington. I was also more likely to be killed by the saturated fats and alcohol I consumed while I was there, the work-related stress of preparing for my presentation, and not exercising because of the conference.

The smart gun owners I know keep the risk of death from criminal assault in perspective. Aaron Haskins, for example, is a gun guy and risk management professional. His advice puts learning how to defend oneself far down the list of risk-reduction strategies (at #8), well behind getting in shape (#1), seeing a doctor once a year (#3), and taking care of your mental health (#5). "I've lost count of the number of patently unhealthy men and women I've met who don't wear seatbelts and don't carry medical equipment, but insist carrying a gun is what they need to do to protect themselves," Haskins writes. "Okay. You do you. There's an argument to be made that you don't want anyone else to kill you before you finish the job yourself, and that's fine. Your life, your decisions. But I suspect that gun will be small comfort when you're lying on the sidewalk dying from a heart attack or an arterial bleed that you could have prevented by focusing on actual risks versus carrying a gun-shaped safety blanket."[17]

* * *

Thankfully, I have never been forced to defend myself, my loved ones, or anyone else with a gun. So far. I hope I never do. I am not a defensive gun owner because I think it is likely that I will need to use a firearm in self-defense. I simply think it is possible. Recalling Pascal's Wager for firearms, gun trainer Massad Ayoob has written, "We can't base our choices on averages because the very fact that you need to fire a gun to survive means that you're already in a statistically improbable situation. There's no such thing as a 'statistically average aberration of the statistics.' Better to prepare for the worst case scenario." If the day comes when I need to use lethal force to defend myself or a loved one, I will be glad to be able to do so. The consequences of needing a gun and not having it are too high. As Brian Anse Patrick observed, "Concealed carry is a very modestly priced insurance policy with a priceless pay off in the event of a claim."[18]

Defensive firearms are sometimes compared to safety devices like fire extinguishers and seat belts. They are all forms of insurance in place to protect yourself from loss, even though you hope you never have to use them. Of course, the analogy between guns, fire extinguishers, and seat belts is not perfect. Fire extinguishers and seat belts are *designed* as safety devices, while firearms *can be used* as safety devices. Lethality is more inherent in firearms than in fire extinguishers. Indeed, the lifesaving potential of a firearm *depends* on its lethality. As defensive firearms trainer Tom Givens has said of guns, "These are deadly weapons. If they weren't they wouldn't be useful to us at all."

Guns are designed to propel projectiles in the direction they are aimed, with the projectiles damaging whatever they hit: pieces of paper or tin cans or birds or deer or human beings. The possibility of injury or death from firearms is much higher than with fire extinguishers and seat belts. Thus, the potential protective benefit of guns must be considered in the context of the potential for negative outcomes. I respect those who engage in their own risk assessment relative to guns and come to different conclusions than I have. This includes my lifelong friend Joel who disposed of his father's gun collection after his death because the risk of bringing them into his own home was higher than any perceived benefits. Another friend who is inside gun culture, John Johnston, warns, "Before you ever consider any 'good' you might do with a gun, consider all of the ways it can go 'wrong.'"

7

Guns as Risk Factors
for Negative Outcomes

If you have ever heard that people with guns in their homes are 4.8 times more likely to commit suicide or 2.7 times more likely to be murdered, you have Arthur Kellermann to thank—or blame. In the late 1980s and early 1990s, with the support of grants from the Centers for Disease Control and Prevention (CDC), Kellermann and colleagues reported these statistics in two landmark publications, "Suicide in the Home in Relation to Gun Ownership" (1992) and "Gun Ownership as a Risk Factor for Homicide in the Home" (1993). Although this research sparked an NRA backlash against CDC funding for firearms research (see: "Dickey Amendment"), understanding guns as a risk factor for negative outcomes such as injury or death remains the dominant approach among public health scholars.[1]

This scholarship also continues to be not only descriptive but prescriptive as well. Kellermann concludes his 1993 study of homicide by advising, "In light of these observations and our present findings, people should be strongly discouraged from keeping guns in their homes." Adopting the approach that there is no safe use of guns any more than there is safe smoking, Kellerman later hoped, "Perhaps, one day, fewer Americans will choose to keep or carry a handgun, and the rate of death from firearm-related injuries will decline."[2]

Although public health scholars today are usually more cautious in their pronouncements than Kellerman, the idea that gun abstinence is the best option is still sometimes spoken out loud. In 2012, the American Academy of Pediatrics declared, "The absence of guns from children's homes and communities is the most reliable and effective measure to prevent firearm-related injuries in children and adolescents."[3] With the exception of illegal narcotics, we rarely see this sort of "just say no" approach to other common risk factors for injury and death. I cannot imagine a professional medical association stating, "The absence

108

of swimming pools and cars from children's homes and communities is the most reliable and effective measure to prevent drownings and vehicle-related injuries in children and adolescents."

As someone who has chosen not to abstain from keeping guns in my home, how do I understand guns as a risk factor for the kinds of negative outcomes that rightly concern public health scholars? I became a gun owner, in part, to reduce my downside risk of violent victimization. But in insuring myself against catastrophe, am I actually introducing more risk into my family's life?

* * *

Recall that my introduction to firearms was motivated as much by fear as interest. Knowing how common guns were in North Carolina, I sought the opportunity to shoot for the first time because I needed a basic familiarity with how they worked in case I ever came across one. I especially want to know how to make a firearm "safe."

Safety has long been an important aspect of gun culture and continues to be part of the socialization process into gun ownership. This has often taken place in the context of families, especially between fathers and sons. But in many communities it was also taught in schools. Others learned in the Boy Scouts, at summer camp, or on shooting teams.

I was not so fortunate. Because my early education in firearms was largely self-taught, I know something about the consequences of not learning safe gun handling practices well enough. I wasn't far into my journey when I negligently discharged my gun at home.

A few months after I bought my first gun, I was safely storing my Sig Sauer P238 pistol in a lockbox at the end of the day. Trying to follow the rules of safe gun handling I had not yet learned well enough, I racked the slide, removed the magazine, pointed the gun at the floor a couple of yards in front of me, and pulled the trigger to drop the hammer on what I assumed was an empty chamber. The sound of even a small .380-caliber pistol firing inside a 120-square-foot bedroom pierced my ears. After I recovered from the shock of the gun going bang when I was expecting it to go click, I found that the bullet had nicked the edge of my metal bed frame and disappeared into the carpet. I lived in a ground-floor unit and so found the bullet lodged in the concrete foundation. I was lucky the outcome was not worse for such a serious mistake. The bedframe, carpet, and my ego were the only victims.

The concussive explosion of the gun and equally jarring realization of what I had done immediately shook the scales from my eyes so that

I could see with perfect clarity: Guns are dangerous. Of course, I knew this at some level from the start. Killing a bird with a BB gun turned me off from firearms for decades and their potential as self-defense weapons helped bring me back to them.

It is common today for gun owners to attempt to destigmatize guns by saying they are "just tools." I agree, in part. Guns are tools. Tools are technologies that allow us to get things done. They magnify our capabilities or give us capabilities that we don't otherwise have. Guns as tools allow us to hit targets at superhuman distances, harvest game, and defend ourselves against predation. They do this by propelling projectiles down a barrel at high speeds. This built-in capacity also makes firearms different from other tools. Recalling trainer Tom Givens' words from the conclusion to the previous chapter, "[Guns] are deadly weapons. If they weren't, they wouldn't be useful to us at all." Or as the tech industry brains behind Open Source Defense put it, "Guns are dangerous. That's a feature, not a bug."[4]

Although my kids were not at home at the time of my negligent discharge, it was not hard for me to envision how accidental gun injuries and deaths happen. Beyond my own direct experience, periodic news headlines highlighted them for me. "Jose Canseco shoots self in hand while cleaning gun." "Columnist M.D. Harmon died after gun he thought was unloaded went off." "CU-Denver accidental shooting: Now ex-staffer trying to unjam gun when it fired." "Boy dies after 'accidental shooting while play wrestling with his father.'" "FBI agent dancing in nightclub drops gun doing backflip, then accidentally shoots someone going to pick it up." "Man dies after dropping gun and accidentally shooting himself reaching to comfort crying baby." "Girl dies after four-year-old brother accidentally shoots her in the head."[5]

The combination of human fallibility and lethal weapons is not new, as Peter Manseau's book *Melancholy Accidents: Three Centuries of Stray Bullets and Bad Luck* attests. The book re-publishes short newspaper accounts of what were frequently called "melancholy accidents." These accidents are, in Manseau's words, "the perfect storm of bad judgment and misfortune." One of his many examples comes from *The Boston Post-Bay & Advertiser* on 3 July 1769:

> We hear from Milton, That last Friday a Man at that Place in striking Fire with his Gun, not knowing it to be loaded, it went off just as his Daughter was entering the Door from Milking, and shot her through both her Thighs, of which Wounds she soon after died.

Another is from *The Connecticut Journal* dated 19 June 1772:

We hear from Leicester that on Tuesday last a very melancholy Accident happened in that Town: A Son of Mr. William Henshaw, about 6 Years of Age, and another Lad being in a Chamber playing with a Gun, which they tho't not to be loaded. The Lad put the muzzle of the Gun to the Ear of Mr. Henshaw's Son, when it went off with a whole Charge of Partridge Shot, which tore his head to pieces, and killed him instantly.

Collectively, these stories highlight how guns historically "were as much a part of American life as the lake in which you might drown, or that draft horse that might run you over if you got in his way." Although Manseau suggests that guns ought to be as anachronistic as draft horses, even today guns continue to be as much a part of American life for many as a swimming pool in which you might drown or a car that might run you over if you got in its way.[6]

These events remind us that guns have no teleology, soul, or discretion. As such, there are as many bad things that can happen with them as there are bad decisions in handling or using them. And yet, of 225,000 people who died in accidents in the United States in 2021, only 549 (0.24%) were related to firearms. This continues a downward trend, even as handgun sales and gun carry have expanded with Gun Culture 2.0. The accidental gun death rate was twice as high in 1997 as in 2021. "Unintentional shootings have been declining for at least a century," observes Garen Wintemute, director of the Firearm Violence Research Center at the University of California, Davis, "and recent data just continue that trend." Increasing social concern over accidental shootings even as their prevalence has declined is yet another of the paradoxes plaguing the polarized debates over guns in America.[7]

Making a serious mistake with a firearm is a low-odds, high-stakes event, the consequences of which are not limited to death. One-third to one-half of all *nonfatal* firearm injuries are due to accidents, which is thirty to forty thousand people per year. Public health advocates like those at the Johns Hopkins Center for Gun Violence Solutions have attempted to reframe these events from blameless, melancholy accidents to *unintentional shootings*. This shift is meant to highlight the fact that playing with a gun or handling a gun while under the influence of alcohol or leaving a gun where it can be accessed by a child are preventable behaviors.[8]

Serious mistakes and negative outcomes, gun educator Claude Werner observes, "are rarely discussed openly in the gun community." They are typically kept behind closed doors because of the stigma many gun owners feel even when they use guns properly and because gun rights proponents do not want to make themselves vulnerable to attack by those seeking to regulate firearms further. This is unfortunate because the desire to reduce the number of unintentional shootings is an area of commonality between gun rights and gun violence prevention advocates that gets buried by politics.

* * *

I had no trouble spotting Claude Werner when we first met in a Sands Convention Center ballroom that had been set up for media covering the 2019 Shooting, Hunting and Outdoor Trade (SHOT) Show. SHOT is the firearms industry's annual trade show organized by the National Shooting Sports Foundation (NSSF). Bearing a resemblance to Peter Seller's Inspector Jacques Clouseau, Werner stood out from the crowd of tattooed military vet bros and Millennial social media influencers. Although he served in the U.S. Army in various capacities from 1972 to 1995, he looks more like a college faculty member at this point than the paratrooper, Ranger, and Green Beret he once was.

The intellectual curiosity and analytical ability Werner cultivated as an Army intelligence officer followed him into his civilian career in real estate research. A Master of City Planning from Georgia Tech with a thesis on automating real estate development led to work as research director for three commercial real estate firms and eventually the position of National Director of Real Estate Research for the U.S. branch of the global consulting firm Deloitte. This civilian work is not as distant from his military service as it might appear at first glance. "The Army and real estate business have certain parallels between them," Werner reflects. "They're both involved in acquiring property. In one case you use tanks and soldiers and in the other you use money."

While at Deloitte, Werner began participating weekly in shooting competitions sponsored by the International Defensive Pistol Association (IDPA). Through IDPA, Werner learned about a shooting school run by Bill Rogers in Ellijay, an hour and a half north of Atlanta where he lived. The Rogers Shooting School is no ordinary gun training outfit. Its five-day pistol course is considered one of the most elite and challenging in the world, training everyone from military special operations units to high-level civilian shooters. Beginning in the late 1990s, Werner attended classes so often that Rogers told him to stop paying the tuition. When the chief instructor stepped aside in 2005, he recommended Werner assume the role. The first class Werner helped teach was a three-day course for a special forces unit from Fort Bragg that was preparing to deploy to Iraq.

Werner's work as a gun educator today combines his analytical skills with his knowledge of shooting and tactics. As "The Tactical Professor," Werner specializes in "things people don't want to hear." This includes the preventable downside risks of gun ownership. He literally wrote the book on the topic: *Serious Mistakes Gunowners Make.*[9] Serious mistakes can lead to any number of negative outcomes, in Werner's accounting, including:

- Shooting yourself
- Shooting someone you shouldn't have, either intentionally or unintentionally
- Getting needlessly arrested
- Getting shot by police officers responding to a call for help
- Leaving guns where unauthorized persons can access them, resulting in tragedies
- Frightening innocent people around you
- Endangering innocent people needlessly

"The Tactical Professor" Claude Werner explaining his work on firearms and personal protection to the author (photograph courtesy Sandra Stroud Yamane).

Examples abound. Tatiana Duva-Rodriguez received eighteen months of probation and lost her concealed carry permit after shooting at a fleeing shoplifter's car at a suburban Detroit Home Depot. Michael Dunn was convicted of first-degree murder for shooting Jordan Davis at a Jacksonville, Florida, gas station in a dispute over loud music. Another Florida man, Richard Dennis, shot and killed his son-in-law Christopher Bergan who jumped out of the bushes at Dennis' home to surprise him for his birthday. Good Samaritan Johnny Hurley, who had intervened to stop an active shooter in Arvada, Colorado, was shot and killed by a police officer responding to the situation. Veronica Rutledge was shot in the head and killed at a Hayden, Idaho, Walmart by her two-year-old son who accessed the handgun she kept in her purse.

To be sure, data is not the plural of anecdote and these cases are the exception not the rule for legally armed Americans. But, as Werner frequently reminds us, the cost of these mistakes is high. Jordan Davis, Christopher Bergan, Johnny Hurley, and Veronica Rutledge were people, not merely statistics.

As we enjoy a free continental breakfast provided by the NSSF to SHOT Show media, Werner tells me he used the two thousand mile drive from his home in Georgia to Las Vegas as an opportunity to do some research along the way. I was particularly intrigued by his stop in Abilene, 150 miles west of Fort Worth, Texas, to explore the site of what he calls the "duel at the dumbster" (not a typo, as we will see).

A few months prior to our meeting, Johnnie and Michael Miller, a father and son, had a dispute with their neighbor, Aaron Howard, over the discarding of a mattress near a dumpster in an alley behind their homes. A cell phone video taken by Howard's fiancée shows the final two minutes of the confrontation leading up to the Millers shooting and killing Howard. For Werner, the video shows "two minutes of monkey dancing between two prideful fools and a man with mental health issues." The serious mistakes made by all four individuals involved are legion.[10]

In Werner's analysis, all of the individuals involved were "emotionally hijacked," turning the mere disposal of a mattress into a test of honor. Both sides ignored the primary option for personal security: "a lifelong commitment to avoidance, deterrence, and de-escalation." The main partners in the dispute, Aaron Howard's fiancée and Johnnie Miller's son, "fanned the flames" rather than de-escalating the situation. The ridiculousness of the event was highlighted in a quote from Werner's friend Lars Smith: "We aren't supposed to kill each other over who is king of the landfill until *after* society collapses."

But the seriousness of the negative outcomes here is anything but laughable. Most significantly, thirty-seven-year-old Aaron Howard lost his life, his fiancée lost her future husband, and Tim Howard lost his father. The cost of killing is also high, Werner observes, "whether it is righteous or not." In the end, a jury convicted seventy-one-year-old Johnnie Miller of murder in 2023 and sentenced him to fourteen years in prison, probably all or most of the rest of his life. Although the same jury exonerated Michael Miller, he too suffered negative outcomes. The combined bond for the Millers was in the hundreds of thousands of dollars, meaning they likely had to pay a bail bondsman tens of thousands of dollars to stay out of jail during the years between their arrest and trial. Not to mention the high cost of a defense attorney, which Werner spitball estimates at $200,000 or more. Photos Werner took of the alleyway dueling ground during his site visit suggest the Millers had modest means to begin with.

As Werner meticulously breaks down the "duel at the dumbster," he constantly highlights the many ways in which these negative outcomes could have been avoided. The extended title of his *Serious Mistakes Gunowners Make* book is *and the Bad Decisions That Led Up to Them.* A highly proficient shooter and elite shooting instructor himself, The Tactical Professor's educational motto is: "More than weapons manipulation." Making good decisions, especially with a gun present, is an essential difference between being a mere gun owner and being a responsibly armed citizen.

* * *

"Guns killed more young people than cars did for the first time in 2020." This headline appeared in *The Washington Post,* but many news outlets picked up on analyses of newly released CDC data published in the *New England Journal of Medicine* by public health scholars from Harvard and the University of Michigan. The analyses highlighted the historic crossing of the mortality trend lines for motor vehicle crashes—long the leading cause of death per capita among younger Americans—and firearms-related injuries. From 2000 to 2020, the rate of car-related deaths among those twenty-four years old and younger declined from 13.6 to 8.3 per 100,000, while the rate of gun-related deaths increased from 7.3 to 10.3 per 100,000. Looking just at those nineteen years old and younger, reveals a similar pattern, though with a lower level of prevalence.[11]

These stark facts give me pause as a husband and father thinking about the presence of cars and firearms in my home and the risks they entail. From age 16, all three of my children had unsupervised access to motor vehicles, but not to any of my firearms. Although I worried about the dangers of my teens driving, I did not go out of my way to ensure their safety from cars. By contrast, I always made sure my guns were locked in a safe or completely under my control at home. Recall that my negligent discharge happened as I was unloading my gun so I could "safely store" it.

The differences in my approach to cars and firearms led me to think more about the meaning of these statistical averages on the ground. Looking at death rates for those aged one to twenty-four or one to nineteen aggregates children, adolescents, teenagers, and young adults. A more fine-grained analysis of the 2020 CDC data paints a somewhat different picture. From ages one to twelve, traffic-crash-related deaths exceed firearms-related deaths. From ages thirteen to nineteen—the vast majority of deaths examined—gun deaths exceed car deaths.[12] Why? Because of a crucial, but frequently unnamed, difference between gun deaths and car deaths: Most of the former are intentional and most of the latter are accidental (even if they often include elements of negligence).

Data compiled by the Bill & Melinda Gates Foundation-funded Institute for Health Metrics and Evaluation (IHME) shows the risk of dying from a car accident in 2019 was 8.61 per 100,000 population as compared to 0.21 per 100,000 for firearms accidents. So, the relative risk of dying from a car accident is forty-one times greater than dying from a firearms accident. This excludes what the IHME calls "road injuries" (including pedestrian, cyclist, motorcyclist, and other injuries) that alone have a rate of 4.00 per 100,000—a nineteen times greater risk than firearms. If we add all "road injuries" together, their relative risk (8.61 + 4.00 = 12.61) is sixty times greater than that of firearms accidents.[13]

These data highlight the fact that most gun deaths in any given year are not accidents but are the result of intentional acts of criminal violence or self-harm. Even broadening our focus in this way presents a paradox: The United States has higher rates of gun violence than many other developed nations, but most gun owners will never be victims or perpetrators of gun violence.

Using the Pew Research Center's conservative estimate of 30 percent personal gun ownership in the United States, 77.5 million American adults own guns. The CDC recorded 20,958 firearm homicides and 26,328 firearm suicides in 2021, a total of 47,286 intentional firearm deaths. Therefore, the rate of intentional firearms deaths per gun owner in the U.S. is 0.0006, or 0.06 percent. Put the other way around,

99.94 percent of firearms owners are not involved in these fatal firearms injuries (recall my similar calculation for 2019 in Chapter 1). Of course, this only looks at these negative outcomes on an annualized basis. What about the cumulative risk of firearms death over a lifetime? According to an estimate by Dr. Ashwini Sehgal of the Case Western Center for Reducing Health Disparities, the lifetime risk of death from firearms in the U.S. is 0.93 percent. This is essentially the same as for motor vehicle accidents (0.92%), but substantially less than drug overdoses (1.52%).[14]

* * *

The fact that Americans own more guns per capita than any other people in the world seems logically connected to the fact that we have higher rates of gun-related deaths than many of our peer nations. The total homicide rate for the United States in 2019 was 5.4 per 100,000, which puts us at #85 out of 204 countries in the Global Burden of Disease (GBD) database constructed by researchers affiliated with the IHME. But do I really care that our homicide rate is well below that of #1 El Salvador (48.71), #10 Haiti (28.38), or #25 Panama (15.02)? Better to compare the U.S. to other high-income, high human development index, nations such as the 38 members of the Organisation for Economic Co-operation and Development (OECD). Here we find the U.S. has the fifth highest homicide rate of all OECD member nations. We are substantially lower than Colombia (35.71), Mexico (24.55), Costa Rica (10.66), and Latvia (7.08), and on par with Lithuania (5.38)—not exactly a feather in our national cap. Our high overall rate of homicide is driven by firearms homicides (3.96 per 100,000 in 2019), which is the fourth highest among OECD nations. Here we leapfrog Latvia, where killing people with weapons other than guns is rampant.[15]

At a basic level, this makes sense. People cannot drown where there's no water. People cannot die in car accidents where there are no cars.[16] The presence of a firearm is a precondition of firearm homicide. But is it really as simple as that?

Not from my perspective.

Gun violence—like the violence that "has been ubiquitous in human history"—is culturally motivated, socially organized, and unequally distributed.[17] It is an intersectional health disparity. While aggregating data for the entire country into an overall homicide rate helps us see some things, it blinds us from others.

In 1973, statistician Francis Anscombe highlighted what I call *the problem with averages*. Anscombe created four data sets that have the same summary statistics (mean, standard deviation, correlation coefficient, and regression line). Simply put, the same "averages." But the underlying distribution of cases in each of "Anscombe's quartet" was very different. Set 1 showed a roughly linear relationship between the two variables, Set 2 was curvilinear, Set 3 was linear with a single outlier, and Set 4 showed no clear relationship.[18]

The lesson here is that averages are good because they give us an idea of the central tendency in a variable (e.g., annual homicide rate) or tell us something about the relationship between two or more variables (e.g., gun ownership and homicide rates). The problem with averages, however, is that they can mislead by concealing underlying differences and ignoring outliers.

Averages blind us from the unequal and uneven distribution of gun violence in the United States. According to a review of 2020 data by the Johns Hopkins Center for Gun Violence Solutions, men were five times more likely to be murdered than women, Blacks twelve times more likely than whites, Black women five times more likely than white women, and Black men fifteen times more likely than white men. At the intersection of this health disparity, we find Black males aged fifteen to thirty-four with a 17.9 times higher rate of firearm homicide victimization than the national average. Similarly, recall that the lifetime risk of firearms death in the U.S. is 0.93 percent. But for Black males it is 2.61 percent while for Asian American females it is just 0.08 percent. An Asian American male like myself has a 0.38 percent lifetime risk of firearms death, which is less than one-third the lifetime risk for a Native American male.[19]

To properly understand guns and homicide in America, we must consider not just the demography but also the geography of "murder inequality." No one lives in "The United States." We live in fifty different states, some with higher rates of homicide (e.g., Mississippi, 17.9; Louisiana, 17.1) and some with lower rates (Idaho, 1.55; Massachusetts, 1.93). But we do not just live in one of fifty states, we live in one of over three thousand particular counties or county-equivalents. Some of these counties, both rural and urban, have rates of homicide higher than the national average (e.g., Phillips County, Arkansas, 55.4; Lowndes County, Alabama, 48.4), and as many as half of counties, mostly sparsely populated, register no homicides in any given year.[20]

But we don't just live in one of three thousand-plus counties. We live in one of tens of thousands of cities, towns, villages, and unincorporated areas. Homicide rates in some localities are well above the national average (St. Louis, 88.1; New Orleans, 51.0; Detroit, 49.7; Memphis, 44.4), and even during the especially violent Covid year of 2020, there were cities in gun-rich parts of the U.S. that had lower than average homicide rates, like Scottsdale (Arizona) and Lincoln (Nebraska) at 2.7, and Plano (Texas) at 1.0. If the entire country had Plano's homicide rate, the United States would rank #175 out of 204 countries in the world, rather than #85.[21]

Those of us who live in cities also live in particular neighborhoods. The gun violence reporting organization *The Trace* explored this in St. Louis, the U.S. city with one of the highest homicide rates in recent years. "The homicide rates in several neighborhoods in the city are so high," *The Trace* reports, that "they exceeded those in Honduras, the deadliest country in the world." At the same time, in other neighborhoods in St. Louis, "the risk is negligible." The city of St. Louis is one of the murder capitals of the U.S., but some parts are as dangerous as San Pedro Sula and some as safe as Geneva. It is not surprising that we see these differences underlying the national average because economic inequality is strongly related to homicide rates cross-nationally. Some neighborhoods in the U.S. are like the developing world socio-economically and others are like the developed world.[22]

Violent crime is so endemic that even neighborhoods can be too geographically broad to use as a unit of analysis. Criminologists today study "micro-geographic places": particular street segments in particular neighborhoods. For example, one study found that fifty percent of crime in New York City takes place on just over four percent of street segments.[23]

Researchers from the Centers for Disease Control have observed that "firearm violence is not evenly distributed by geography or among the populations in these communities. Rather it is highly concentrated in specific 'hot spot' locations and often occurs within high-risk social networks." Andrew Papachristos utilizes the complex mathematical tools of network analysis to uncover these patterns of gun violence in communities. Papachristos shows that gun violence, while tragic, is rarely random; like a blood-borne disease, it travels within social networks. In Boston's Cape Verdean community, Papachristos found that eighty-five percent of gunshot injuries occurred in a network of just six percent of the population. In a high-crime neighborhood in Chicago, forty-one percent of homicides took place in a network of just four percent of the population.[24]

This highlights the fact that even in high-crime micro-geographic places, most residents are not directly involved in gun violence. This is not to say that gun violence in communities where it concentrates is not a significant problem. About eighty percent of people shot in criminal assaults survive. Beyond the physical and psychological traumas they directly suffer is the broader trauma experienced by their family, friends, and communities. As sociologist Patrick Sharkey has documented, being in a violent neighborhood has many negative indirect effects, including PTSD, depression, decreased cognitive performance, and diminished attention and impulse control. That these disproportionately affect young people is even more reason for concern.[25]

My concern about the risk of these negative outcomes is actually more for others than myself and my loved ones. I judge our risk to be quite low compared to many others. An analogy offered by Open Source Defense was very helpful for me in putting these risks in perspective. Speaking of funding given by the startup accelerator Y Combinator, co-founder Paul Graham noted that their two percent acceptance rate does not mean that any individual applicant has a two percent chance of getting in. "It means that 2% of applicants have a near–100% chance, and 98% of applicants have almost zero chance." Like applicants to Harvard. Or individuals being victims of criminal violence.[26]

* * *

As concerning as it is, Americans generally misunderstand how homicide fits into the big picture of gun death in America. A 2019 survey reported by NPR's Heath Druzin found that thirty-three percent of U.S. adult respondents named murders and twenty-five percent named mass shootings as the most common form of firearm death. Only twenty-three percent correctly identified suicides as the most common, even though they exceed murders by a two-to-one margin and mass killing victims by nearly seventy-to-one. In fact, in 2021 suicide was the eleventh leading cause of death in the U.S. overall and the second leading cause among those ten to thirty-four years old.[27]

Here again, complexity is key to how I understand the risk of this negative outcome with firearms. While guns are a constant in American society, the annual rate of suicide has fluctuated considerably over time, with higher rates in the first half of the twentieth century than in the second half. From the 1970s to 2000, the suicide rate showed an overall pattern of decline, but from 2000 to 2018 it increased almost every year. Rates fell in 2019 and 2020 but increased again in 2021.[28]

On a global scale, the United States ranks #49 out of 204 countries in terms of overall suicide rate, with about 14 per 100,000 population.

So, we are in the top quartile of countries, but not particularly exceptional. Even within the OECD, the U.S. falls in the high middle of the pack (#14 of 38), alongside the Czech Republic and Germany. Gun-free havens like South Korea (#2 in OECD) and Japan (#8) rank well above the gun-saturated United States, having 1.97 times and 1.4 times the overall U.S. suicide rate, respectively.[29]

Where we stand apart globally is in our rate of firearm suicide. We have the second-highest rate in the world (7.12), well behind Greenland (16.36) but well ahead of Uruguay (4.74). Firearms play a particular role in suicide due to their lethality. The overall ratio of suicide attempts to suicides is twenty-five-to-one (a four percent case fatality rate), but for suicide attempts with firearms, there is an eighty-five percent case fatality rate. Even though there are far fewer suicide attempts with firearms, just over half of completed suicides involve guns (54.6% in 2021).[30]

Like criminal gun violence, there are clear social markers of suicide vulnerability, though the markers for suicide are considerably different than for homicide. Suicide concentrates among older, white and Indigenous men in the rural South and West, though rising rates among younger people and sexual/gender minorities are causes for additional concern. Geographically, suicide clusters in states with strongly individualistic cultures, laxer gun restrictions, and higher rates of gun ownership. The 2021 suicide rate in Montana was 31.7 compared to 7.4 in New Jersey.[31]

Establishing a clear causal link between gun ownership and suicide is methodologically challenging. Although it seems logical on the surface that removing access to a firearm from someone intending self-harm would prevent suicide, the issues of intentionality and replacement must be considered. Do people who are highly motivated to kill themselves opt for firearms, while people who are less motivated engage in cutting or taking pills (intentionality)? If so, they could simply substitute other methods of self-harm that also have high case fatality rates like drowning or hanging/suffocation (replacement). One study by Michael Siegel and Emily Rothman of the Boston University School of Public Health, for example, suggests that substitution of another mechanism of suicide for firearms is likely for women, but only partial replacement of firearms by other means is likely for men.[32]

Like Kellerman's pioneering work, most studies of guns and suicide are empirically correlational not causal. This is not a criticism of these scholars but a methodological limitation inherent in research on guns and negative outcomes. When trying to identify the causal factor that explains an outcome of interest—for example, the effect of vaccination on contracting polio—a researcher will run experiments in which individuals are randomly assigned to an "experimental" group (that is exposed to the treatment) and a "control" group (that is not exposed to the treatment). Random assignment to experimental and control groups is designed to ensure that the only systematic difference between the two groups is the causal factor of interest. Therefore, if differences in outcomes are observed after the experiment, the researcher can conclude with some confidence that the treatment caused the outcome. This is how Jonas Salk and his team established the efficacy of vaccination in preventing polio.

This randomized, controlled trial (RCT) as an experimental method is often called the "gold standard" for making causal inferences because it is best able to isolate the causal factor of interest.[33] Obviously, it is both unfeasible and unethical to do such experiments to establish the causal effect of gun ownership on suicide more precisely. We cannot randomly assign individuals to treatment (gun-in-home) and control (no gun) groups.

When randomized assignment to treatment and control groups is not possible, researchers use various quasi-experimental designs, including what are called "cohort studies." Cohort designs mimic the logic of the RCT gold standard. In a cohort study, participants begin the study period without being exposed to the causal mechanism of interest (e.g., a gun in the home), are followed over time, and are divided into "experimental" and "control" groups according to exposure to the suspected cause (e.g., acquiring a gun vs. not). The incidence rates for various outcomes (e.g., the suicide rate) can then be calculated for the experimental and control groups, with exposure to the "treatment" (gun-in-home) being presumed to play a causal role in the outcome.

A recent cohort study led by Stanford Law Professor David Studdert using data from California offers some significant insights into the relationship between handgun acquisition and suicide. Studdert's study found that individuals who acquired a handgun (the experimental group) had considerably higher rates of suicide by any method than those who did not (the control group). The relative risk of suicide was 3.34 times higher for males and 7.16 times higher for females. These rates certainly give gun owners like me pause.

As Studdert's study demonstrates, when assessing how much risk firearms pose to members of a household, public health scholars typically examine the relative risk: compared to households with no firearms, how much additional risk do firearms-owning homes have? Examples abound, beginning with the landmark studies of "gun ownership as a risk factor" by Arthur Kellermann and his associates. But in my personal risk assessment process, I always look not just at the relative risk of negative outcomes, but also at the absolute risk. Relative risk compares the likelihood of something happening between two groups (e.g., smokers vs. non-smokers developing lung cancer), while absolute risk measures the likelihood of something happening at all, either in a particular group (smokers developing lung cancer) or in the population as a whole (anyone developing lung cancer).

I could write an accurate headline with respect to firearms: "Rate of accidental gun deaths in U.S. twice as high as Italy." This would be true since the rate of accidental gun deaths in the U.S. is 0.21 per 100,000 and the rate in Italy is 0.11 per 100,000. The relative risk of accidental gun death in the U.S. is two times that of Italy. But absolute risk tells a different story than relative risk in this example. The absolute risk of dying from an unintentional firearms injury in Italy is one in a million and in the U.S. it is two in a million. That is, the absolute risk of dying in either case is very small.

Although Studdert and his colleagues found that adding a handgun to a home increases the likelihood of a completed suicide, their data also shows the probability of *not* dying by firearm suicide among handgun owners and nonowners over the study period. Over the twelve years of the study, just over 99.6 percent of those in the handgun-acquiring treatment group had not committed suicide by firearm, compared to over 99.9 percent of the handgun nonowners in the control group.[34] The relative risk of dying by suicide is higher among handgun owners than among nonowners, but the absolute risk of dying by suicide for both groups is quite low.

Knowing the elevated risk for suicide due to guns means I take precautions to prevent unauthorized access to my arsenal. But it does not lead me to disarm myself completely as some public health scholars suggest I should. The reality is that most gun owners and those they live with will not experience self-harm with their firearms. Of course, this does not diminish the significance of firearms as a risk factor for suicide or the trauma that suicide entails for survivors.

In fact, suicide is one of the most promising areas for collaboration between gun owners and gun violence prevention advocates. A growing number of groups exist that seek to reduce the toll of suicide on the firearms community, none more interesting than Walk the Talk America, founded in 2018 by "the most un-gun gun guy" in the firearms industry, Michael Sodini.

* * *

Karl Lagerfeld's short book of photos, *Escape from Circumstances*, reproduces nineteen nude photos of a single male model around the grounds of his French estate, Elhorria Le Domaine. The legendary designer for Fendi, Chanel, and his own label explained, "Clothes reflect human conditions, lifestyles and positions. Young and beautiful bodies have no social connotations." That body belonged to Michael Sodini, to whom Lagerfeld dedicated the book.[35]

Appearing nude in Lagerfeld's photobook was nothing new to Sodini. He broke into the modeling business soon after graduating from Arizona State University in 1998 when a stranger approached him in a New York City nightclub and asked if he would consider appearing in *Playgirl*. After receiving his mother's blessing—she told him, "If someone asks you to do *Playgirl*, you do it!"—Sodini flew to Miami for a photoshoot. He not only appeared as the centerfold in the September 1999 issue but also full frontal in *X-Ray*, a book of portraits by makeup artist François Nars'—alongside celebrities like Boy George, Anjelica Huston, RuPaul, and Alanis Morissette.[36] Sodini also amassed an impressive portfolio with clothes on, working internationally as a fashion model on runways and in advertising campaigns for three years.

This background alone would make Michael Sodini the most interesting man in gun culture today. But it just scratches the surface.

Sodini's biological father was Arthur H. ("Artie") Stock, whose central New Jersey nightclub empire was so vast in the 1970s that the state's Division of Alcohol Beverage Control charged him with having a monopoly on bars. Art Stock's Royal Manor in Wall once hosted a fight between Victor the Wrestling Bear and professional boxer Chuck Wepner, who became famous for inspiring Sylvester Stallone's "Rocky" when he lost to Muhammad Ali by technical knockout with nineteen seconds left in the fifteenth round. An eighteen-year-old Lynn Sodini worked as a record girl and bartender at the Royal Manor and became Art Stock's "side-chick," as Michael describes the relationship.

Art Stock, Jr., was born in October 1975. Within hours the first name on his birth certificate was changed to Michael and the family name to Sodini, after his mother. When Artie and Lynn's relationship deteriorated, a custody battle ensued, even though Artie had a wife and children at the time. When a court ordered Lynn to surrender Michael to Artie,

Lynn's father George said she had two choices: fight in court and likely lose, or take the child and run. So she ran. First to Chicago then Canada, briefly, and eventually to Spain where George Sodini had business connections. Mother and son eventually returned to the United States under the assumed names Denise Ferguson and Mike Saunders, settling in San Francisco's Mission District.

Mike's ability to relate to different people and points of view was profoundly shaped by these travels. Racial and economic diversity was part of his everyday life as the child of a single mother who had little money. Denise befriended a gay man, George, who took Mike to San Francisco 49ers and Giants games, became a hero to the boy, and in the process demonstrated the normality of homosexuality. Mike's childhood musical tastes were shaped by the Bay Area's version of West Coast hip-hop, especially rappers like E-40, Too $hort, and Rappin' 4-Tay.

As an eighth grader, Mike moved to Singapore for a year because Denise married a man who was in the shipping industry. They were later transferred to Seattle where Mike spent his first two years of high school. When his stepfather was transferred back to Singapore, Mike wanted to stay in the U.S. Although the Sodini and Stock families were "like the Hatfields and McCoys" of the Jersey Shore, Mike's Uncle George said Art Stock was old at that point and unlikely to act on his custody claim. So Mike returned to Asbury Park and changed his name from Saunders back to Sodini.

When he left for college in 1994, Michael Sodini had no intention of going into the family business. Founded by his grandfather George Sr. and uncle George Jr. in 1988, Eagle Imports rose to prominence by importing value-priced international firearms brands like Llama and S.P.S. from Spain, Bersa and Comanche from Argentina, and Metro Arms from the Philippines. After graduating, Michael reluctantly joined Eagle Imports as "head sandwich getter," learning the business by doing a little bit of everything. Having grown up outside of gun culture in Spain, the West Coast, and Singapore, Michael knew little about firearms technically or as a lifestyle. His first stint at Eagle Imports lasted only six months, ending when he signed with the elite Click modeling agency. Wanting to start a family and live a normal life after three years of full-time modeling, Michael hinted to his Uncle George that he was looking to get back into the family business, but was told they didn't have a position for him at the time. The man who replaced Michael when he quit, Bill "Stroh" Strohmenger, was doing just fine. "I think they wanted me to beg for my job back," Michael recalls. "But I wasn't going to do that."

After four productive years in exile, Michael returned to Eagle Imports. At this point, George Jr. was "the king" as George Sr. had stepped away from the business, though "he still came in every day to read the paper and mess up the bathroom." Michael's replacement, Bill Strohmenger, was now his boss. The two developed a close relationship during weeks-long road trips to call on clients. When George Jr. died of a stroke at age fifty-two in 2006, Strohmenger was promoted to President of Eagle Imports and Michael's role in the company grew.

Three years later, Michael received an early morning phone call that would eventually propel him in yet another new direction in life. "Did you hear about Bill?" his friend Barry asked. Michael immediately thought he had been in a car accident. Or was it a stroke like the one that took his uncle's life?

"He's dead," Barry continued. "He shot himself."

With just over four years of experience working in the gun industry, in 2009 the thirtysomething former male model Michael Sodini took over as President of Eagle Imports, "the death seat" vacated first by his Uncle George and now by his close friend Stroh. The timing was fortuitous. He took over the business just months after "the greatest gun salesman in U.S. history" Barack Obama was sworn in as President. Although he still didn't know much about guns, Michael "was like a surfer that caught a wave."

The wave propelled the gun business to new heights but only took Michael so far personally. He recalls telling himself, "I don't want just to sell guns for the rest of my life. I never wanted to be here anyway. I know there's more to life than this." Entering his forties, Michael started thinking more and more about the role the firearms industry should play in addressing negative outcomes with guns. He recalled conversations with Stroh about people who visited the Eagle Imports booth at the SHOT Show or NRA annual meeting one year and were gone the next. He thought about how after mass shootings like the one at Sandy Hook Elementary School, one side would blame guns, the other side would blame mental health, and nothing would get done. As the president of a gun company, he had to admit, "We in the firearms industry do a horrible job of addressing these things."

In 2018, Michael Sodini founded Walk the Talk America (WTTA), a 501(c)(3) nonprofit, to bridge the gap between the firearms industry and those seeking to reduce gun deaths. Sodini initially funded WTTA by donating one dollar for every gun sold by Eagle Imports. He first thought he could just find organizations with proven programs and have gun companies like his "throw money at them." But at the 2019 SHOT Show

Walk the Talk American founder Michael Sodini (far right) on a gun violence panel at the Aspen Ideas: Health Conference in 2023 (photograph by Leigh Vogel. Property of the Aspen Institute, used with permission).

in Las Vegas, gun educator Rob Pincus told his fellow WTTA board members, "Anyone can donate money to mental health. How are we going to be different?" The question set WTTA on its current course.

Sodini has since partnered with Mental Health America to make free, anonymous mental health screenings available through the WTTA website. He put cards in the boxes of the gun brands Eagle Imports represented that sought to destigmatize mental health struggles and direct buyers to WTTA's online screening tools. When he received positive feedback from some of his consumers, he approached his old friend Charlie Brown who agreed to put the WTTA cards in Hi-Point Firearms boxes. He went to Armscor to ask the same of Martin Tuason, whom he had also known for years. "That makes sense," Tuason said. Later the firearms giant Ruger signed on.

Sodini then connected with Jake Wiskerchen, a therapist and founder of Zephyr Wellness, an outpatient mental health counseling practice based in Reno, Nevada. With Rob Pincus, they developed introductory, intermediate, and advanced "cultural competence" classes for mental health professionals who can get continuing education credits for learning about guns, gun owners, and gun culture. Financial support from the United States Concealed Carry Association (USCCA), Ruger,

Armscor, Chattanooga Shooting Sports, and the National Association of
Sporting Goods Wholesalers is helping WTTA to develop a public directory of firearm-competent mental health professionals. It currently lists
eleven providers who are licensed to practice in thirty-seven states.[37]

One of the few systematic studies of firearms training curricula,
published in 2017, found that only ten percent of the twenty basic firearms classes studied covered suicide and prevention.[38] In collaboration
with WTTA, the USCCA is adding online video modules on mental
health and suicide prevention to its firearms training curriculum. The
videos feature Sodini, Wiskerchen, and two USCCA staff members who
specialize in the topic.

In 2018, Michael Sodini sold his stake in Eagle Imports and resigned
as president to work on WTTA full-time. After burning through a considerable portion of his savings to support his wife and adolescent daugh-
ters, he realized he needed to get another job. Needing flexibility to build
WTTA, he began delivering food for DoorDash in 2020. That lasted all of
three days before he switched over to Uber. Sodini drove Uber for a year
and a half until WTTA was receiving enough donations that he could
draw a salary, albeit a fraction of what he made as a firearms executive.

"It's challenging to your ego, your pride," he tells me of his stint as
an Uber driver. "You're making 25 bucks an hour, going backward in life,
working harder and making less money." But, he adds, "People want to
see you give a shit."

Michael Sodini certainly walks the talk himself.

I find Sodini's history and work fascinating because, like me, he has
one foot inside and one foot outside American gun culture. His diverse
childhood and adult experiences traveling the world and crossing cultures clearly influence his approach to addressing negative outcomes
with firearms. Positioning Walk the Talk America at "the intersection of
guns and mental health," as their slogan proclaims, takes advantage of
Sodini's ability to act as an ambassador, mediator, translator, guide, and
conduit between these two worlds. He demonstrated this on a gun violence prevention panel at the prestigious and influential Aspen Institute's
2023 Aspen Ideas: Health Conference, exemplifying the kind of thinking we could use more of in today's polarized and polarizing debates over
guns in America.

* * *

"Everyone who is *opposed* to gun safety, please raise your hand."
In the many years I have made this request to students in my Sociology

of Guns course at Wake Forest University, no one has ever raised their hand. From the purest Second Amendment supporter to the staunchest gun abolitionist, people on all sides of America's great gun debates agree that "gun safety" is important. But what do we talk about when we talk about gun safety? I see two different views of what constitutes gun safety, driven by fundamentally different underlying views of the role of guns in American society and Americans' lives.

Those who view guns as having a net negative effect on American society and focus on harmful gun owner behaviors are concerned about safety *from* guns. Viewing guns primarily as a risk factor for injury or death, from this perspective the safest approach to guns is to avoid them altogether. This orientation shapes many medical, public health, and violence prevention approaches to guns and has for some time.

Those who view guns as having a net positive effect on American society and recognize the normality of firearms for tens of millions of gun owners are concerned about safety *with* guns. The emphasis of parents, firearms trainers, and gun groups is on how to safely handle and use guns. This is evident in the gun culture's well-known "rules of gun safety," hunter education and other firearm training courses, Range Safety Officer certifications, and so on.

Assuming the normality of gun ownership works against abstinence-only approaches to firearms. This is in line with managing other risky behaviors people routinely engage in, from swimming to driving to having sex. The best approach is not to counsel avoidance of these behaviors altogether but to suggest how to do them more safely. Not safely, mind you, as that is an illusion, but in ways that reduce risks of negative outcomes. The gun-owning community is a resource not an impediment to this end.

Consider an area of agreement between gun rights and gun violence prevention organizations: safe storage of firearms. Both the NRA and Brady, the NSSF and Everytown agree that firearms should be safely stored when not in use. But those who adopt a safety *from* approach are more likely to counsel—and advocate for laws that require—gun owners to store their guns locked and unloaded with the ammunition stored separately. Those on the safety *with* side recognize that many responsible gun owners do not want to store their guns unloaded, but instead seek ways of storing or staging their loaded firearms in ways that prevent unauthorized access.[39]

As the handgun editor for *Shooting Illustrated* magazine Tamara Keel argues, unnecessary administrative gun-handling or "futzing around with the pistol" increases the odds of a negligent discharge.

In a similar vein, Mike "The Gun Guy" Weisser is fond of borrowing a phrase from the novelist Elmore Leonard, "Don't fool with guns in here, okay? The goddamn piece's liable to go off." Had Tam Keel observed me unloading my sidearm before storing it when I shot my bed frame and floor back in 2011, she no doubt would have screamed her cautionary refrain, "Stop touching that!"[40]

Promoting safety *with* guns does not deny that firearms introduce risk into the lives of their owners. On the contrary, it signals an understanding that guns are tools that are by design dangerous, so gun owners assume a certain amount of risk for themselves and their loved ones when they bring firearms into their homes and lives. The key is to be thoughtful in understanding and mitigating risk. In some circumstances and for some people, Pascal's Wager is a bad bet (cf. Chapter 6). Sometimes it is better not to have a gun.

"Avoiding Negative Outcomes is a goal of all training," Claude Werner observes. "Although I may have coined that particular phrase, it has been the goal of the training industry from the beginning. Trainers don't want you to shoot yourself, your family members, people around you, and we don't want you to have to interact with the legal system because you made a mistake. Knowing what you're doing and knowing the rules goes a very long way to avoiding Negative Outcomes." Some gun owners are liabilities and some are assets; some are merely gun owners and some are responsibly armed citizens. Serious gun training helped me move from one category to the other in my maturation as a gun owner.[41]

8

Being Responsibly Armed

There is an old saying in the gun training community, *"You are no more armed because you are wearing a pistol than you are a musician because you own a guitar."*[1]

As I learned early in my career as a gun owner, wearing a pistol and being a responsibly trained armed citizen are two different things. Although serious gun training has helped me develop from one to the other over the years, when I read critiques of civilian defensive gun training, I often feel as though gun owners are damned if we don't and damned if we do. Recall the complaint that shall issue and permitless concealed carry laws allow people to carry guns in public without sufficient training (see Chapter 5). But when people do take defensive firearms classes, we are frequently condemned for what is allegedly taught and learned.

In an entry on his *Psychology Today* "Ethics for Everyone" blog, for example, philosopher Michael Austin considers the relationship between guns and virtue. He begins by drawing on my argument that the center of gravity of American gun culture has shifted over the past fifty years from hunting and recreational/sport shooting (Gun Culture 1.0) to personal protection and concealed carry (Gun Culture 2.0). So far, so good. But Austin goes on to suggest, "To the extent that the Gun Culture 2.0 instills in people a willingness to kill, it can be harmful to their character. My claim is not that owning and using a gun necessarily compromises character. But if one does so, and adopts much of what Gun Culture 2.0 involves, it can have a negative impact."

Austin maintains that human beings have "a deep psychological resistance to killing other people" and that one of the outcomes of defensive firearms training is to overcome that resistance by conditioning people "to fire a gun at another human being without really thinking about the action that is being performed." By weakening our resistance

131

to killing, firearms training reduces our empathy. Because "empathy is important for good character," it ultimately harms us ethically.[2]

But the harmful consequences of defensive gun training are not limited to individuals. In May 2023, my fellow sociologist of guns Harel Shapira published an opinion essay in the *New York Times* whose headline grabbed my attention: "Firearms Taught Me, and America, a Very Dangerous Lesson." In the essay, Shapira recounts lessons he learned from observing forty-two firearms training classes in four states and immersing himself in firearms schools in Texas. Shapira concludes that the "primary lessons" of defensive gun training courses "are about if and when to shoot someone on purpose. And this is where the trouble begins."[3]

Shapira's concerns both echo and extend Austin's. Rather than feeling safer and more confident, people who take defensive gun training courses "end up feeling more afraid than before." Even worse, the courses "prepared us to shoot without hesitation and avoid legal consequences." Fear and a hair trigger are a toxically lethal combination.

But assaults and homicides at the hands of trained gun carriers are just part of the problem. Ultimately, defensive gun training courses are harmful because they "instill the kind of fear that has a corrosive effect on all interactions—and beyond that, on the fabric of our democracy." Shapira concludes that defensive firearms classes are "training [people] to not be citizens."[4]

That civilian defensive gun training erodes both individual character and democracy are serious charges. They are especially disturbing for me as there is no part of contemporary gun culture that I have traveled more extensively. From 2011 to 2023, I participated in or observed more than 500 hours of formal training classes in ten states from California to Virginia, Texas, to Minnesota. Although Michael Austin, Harel Shapira, and I have covered some of the same ground, my experiences in the gun training community have taught me very different lessons.

* * *

Massad Ayoob is a pioneer in the civilian defensive gun training business. In 1980 he published a landmark book, *In the Gravest Extreme: The Role of the Firearm in Personal Protection,* and a year later began teaching classes through his Lethal Force Institute. Thirty years and a name change later, I enrolled in the Massad Ayoob Group's flagship course, "Armed Citizens' Rules of Engagement." The course is better known as "MAG-40" for the forty hours of instruction it entails over five days. Although I had previously taken short gun classes like the North

Carolina concealed carry course and an NRA "First Shots" course, this was the first major training school I attended.

In November 2012, Sandy and I spent part of four days on the range at the Phoenix Rod and Gun Club with nineteen other MAG-40 students learning and practicing the fundamentals of marksmanship. The fourth day brought all of the instruction together in a sixty-round qualification course of fire. Standing on the four-yard line facing a brown cardboard torso target, I focused hard on the "A" zone—the 6-inch wide by 11-inch tall center of the target. I had not felt so nervous in years. My heart raced and my breathing shallowed. I was about to test all of the marksmanship and gun handling skills I learned over the previous three days.

In retrospect, this was not an extremely challenging course of fire. But having shot a gun for the first time less than two years earlier, the abilities tested were mostly new to me. My mouth was as dry as my hands were wet with perspiration. I tried to use visualization techniques to ease my nerves and focus my attention on the target. Picturing myself hitting the "A" zone with all sixty rounds for a perfect score of 300, I instead jerked my first shot into the "C" zone. This was worth only four points, so after just one trigger press I was already "one down" from a perfect score. Missing relaxed me and I did fine in the end, putting fifty of sixty rounds in the "A" zone, and ten in the "C" zone for a total score of 290. This score put me in the top five of the class and one point ahead of Sandy's 289. Though Sandy earned the high lady title for the class, I still brag a little about being the top shot in our household.

How does this relate to Michael Austin's critique that firearms training in Gun Culture 2.0 harms people's character by weakening the human resistance to killing by conditioning them to fire reflexively at human-shaped targets? Having shot and observed others shooting tens of thousands of rounds in MAG-40 and other gun training courses across the country, I find Austin's perspective too simplistic. It is true that human or humanoid targets are frequently employed in civilian defensive gun training courses. Some of these targets are quite graphic in depicting the brain, heart, spinal column, and other vital organs. But shooting these targets during the drills and course of fire at MAG-40, for example, is not tantamount to Pavlovian operant conditioning to kill.

At least not according to Mike Pannone, a retired member of the 1st Special Forces Operational Detachment-Delta who is currently a full-time gun trainer. Shooting drills, Pannone tells me, are designed to exercise component gun handling and marksmanship skills like drawing a gun quickly, shooting accurately, reloading efficiently, and managing malfunctions skillfully. In his essay, Austin gives two examples of a drill called "rolling thunder." This drill requires shooters to coordinate their actions with the person next to them in a line, adding some stress and complexity to the underlying component skill being exercised. Drills like rolling thunder and the ones I shot at MAG-40 allow us to practice certain skills with purpose. They do not, as Austin contends, create "a quick-shot reflex which can weaken the natural resistance to killing another human being."

On the contrary, as gun trainers like John Johnston and his Citizens Defense Research instructor cadre regularly highlight, the more mastery an individual has of the component skills of shooting, the less "cognitive load" that person bears when it comes to managing actual defensive situations. That is, not having to worry as much about the physical details of gun handling and marksmanship frees the mind to make good tactical and ethical decisions about the use of force in self-defense should the need arise.

Although I have spent time recreationally at gun ranges blasting away at targets without thinking, such mindlessness has not been part of any gun training course I have taken or observed. On the contrary, as I graduated from basic to more advanced courses, I moved from simple skill development drills to more complex situational drills designed to test my ability to think with a gun in my hand. Gabe White's "Tactical Success with Technical Skills" course is a good example. White is a rising star in the gun training community, known for his technical proficiency (i.e., he shoots fast and well) and for shooting competitions using his everyday carry gun and gear. I took a four-hour version of White's course at the 2018 Rangemaster Tactical Conference in Little Rock, arriving at the Direct Action Resource Center training facility before dawn to ensure myself a spot in the first-come, first-served 8:00 a.m. class.

The course was advertised as "covering the core technical skills of drawing, ready position, presentations, and shooting," but also added a tactical dimension in applying the fundamental skills under different circumstances. For example, if confronted with a lethal threat three or five yards away, I might need to draw and shoot as quickly as possible. If that threat is fifteen to twenty yards away, I might need to draw and issue commands before shooting. If the threat is armed with a knife, that is one thing; if armed with a gun, another; and if armed with a phone, yet another. On the range, rather than just issuing commands to "shoot" our targets, White specified different distances from the threat and called out "gun" or "knife" or "phone" to disrupt any tendency to shoot without thinking. Or he would call out "gun" then switch to "phone," or vice-versa, requiring us to assess situations rather than mechanically shooting at a perceived threat in front of us.

Similarly, a common drill in basic firearms courses to exercise the fundamental gun handling skill of reloading quickly is shoot-reload-shoot. In Rob Pincus's Combat Focus Shooting course, students are quickly asked to go beyond this component skill by adding an ongoing assessment of the situation to the process. When I took the course during his instructor development conference outside Minneapolis in 2017, I was told not to shoot-reload-shoot but to determine after reloading whether or not to continue shooting. Did I think the attacker was still a threat? Was there a second attacker that needed to be addressed? In a real-life situation, I could empty my gun shooting at an attacker and while reloading the attacker might surrender. Continuing to shoot could constitute criminal homicide. Or I could empty my gun at one attacker, reload, then shoot at the attacker's accomplice who I saw initially but who has since turned to run away. This could be one justifiable homicide and one criminal homicide. Or any number of other scenarios in which just reloading and automatically shooting again would be problematic in terms of claims to lawful self-defense.

* * *

Although he does not elaborate the point in his *New York Times* opinion essay, Harel Shapira alleges that defensive gun training courses not only teach students to shoot without thinking but also "to avoid legal consequences." In no class I have ever taken or observed, from the most basic concealed carry course to the most advanced training school, has any instructor ever taught students how to avoid the legal consequences of using lethal force in self-defense. Rather, attention is paid to laws that govern the use of lethal force so that in the unlikely and unfortunate event that I must defend myself, I do so within the law. If I use lethal force in self-defense within the law, there are no legal consequences to avoid.

Early in 2021, I received a letter from Forsyth County Sheriff Bobby Kimbrough saying it was time to renew my North Carolina Concealed Handgun Permit. I first got the permit in 2011, did a five-year renewal in 2016, and needed to renew again in 2021. I set the letter aside and by the time I unearthed it on my desk in August, it was too late. My permit had expired. As a consequence, I had to take the state's required concealed carry course again to re-apply for a permit. In September 2021, I paid eighty dollars for the eight-hour course at Apache Solutions Firearms Training in Yadkinville, just down the road from Sportsmen's Lodge where I took the concealed carry course I described in Chapter 5.

The primary content of the North Carolina concealed carry course is determined by statute and the North Carolina Criminal Justice Education and Training Standards Commission. Among the minimum standards for the course is that at least two of the eight hours must be the legal block of instruction. Like many North Carolina concealed carry courses I have observed, the course at Apache Solutions followed the required curriculum closely. Each student in the course received the actual book on "Concealed Carry Handgun Training" produced by the North Carolina Justice Academy, and our instructor marched us through a PowerPoint with quotes from the book, having me and my six classmates alternate reading sections aloud.

Legal issues were the first substantive topic covered, and justified self-defense was the first legal issue. Here we learned the quite limited circumstances under which a citizen "is legally justified in using deadly force against another." Several conditions must *simultaneously be* met ("if and only if") to qualify:

> a. Imminence: "The citizen actually believes deadly force is necessary to prevent an imminent threat of death, great bodily harm, or sexual assault and...."
> b. Reasonableness: "The facts and circumstances prompting that belief would cause a person of ordinary firmness to believe deadly force was necessary ... and...."
> c. Innocence: "The citizen using deadly force was not an instigator or aggressor who voluntarily provoked, entered, or continued the conflict leading to deadly force, and...."
> d. Proportionality: "Force used was not excessive—greater than reasonably needed to overcome the threat posed by a hostile aggressor."

Although self-defense law varies from state to state, these four requirements are often considered universal elements. As one leading legal expert observes, if even one element is missing, "the best your attorney can do is get you a good plea bargain."[5]

A fifth condition, avoidance, is made more complex by the existence in North Carolina and many other states of so-called "Stand Your Ground" laws. These laws have been subject to considerable misunderstanding and derision, and often both. These are expressed clearly by Everytown for Gun Safety: "Shoot First laws—also known as Stand Your

Ground legislation—are deadly, reckless, and extreme. They give people a license to kill, allowing them to shoot first and ask questions later, then claim self-defense."[6] In Shapira's words, they allow people to kill and "avoid legal consequences."

This is simply incorrect.

The North Carolina Red Book clearly states: "A citizen faced with an imminent threat of death or great bodily injury generally does not have a duty to retreat prior to using deadly force, *when all of the other elements of deadly force are satisfied*" (emphasis added). Far from empowering armed citizens to use lethal force recklessly, the law of self-defense creates a framework that specifies the many, many instances in which lethal force is not justified, and the rare occasions when it is. In my concealed carry course at Apache Solutions, I learned that deadly force may not be used to stop a simple assault, in response to violent language, because a trespasser refuses to leave, to prevent a criminal's escape, or to protect property.[7] This is not to say that people never attempt to use the law of self-defense to shield themselves from criminal prosecution and conviction. But just because criminals invoke the law of self-defense does not make self-defense itself criminal.

Beyond what is legally allowable, many courses address what is practically advisable. My concealed carry instructor at Apache Solutions, Frank Horvath, observed that even though there is no duty to retreat in North Carolina, "It's probably a good idea to flee the fight." The National African American Gun Association's Basic Pistol course I sat in on in July 2023 also addressed the conditions that must be met before a person can lawfully resort to lethal force in self-defense. It concluded this section of instruction with a reminder: "You win EVERY fight you avoid." The idea is not novel. As noted already in Chapter 6, it is a defensive gun culture cliché that "the first rule of gunfighting is don't be there."

* * *

These practical considerations apply not only to Stand Your Ground in public, but also to self-defense in one's home. During the review of Castle Doctrine in my Apache Solutions concealed carry course, instructor Horvath observed, "Just because you have a right to shoot someone in your home, doesn't mean you should." He gave examples of mistaken identity shootings to support his point. I cannot count the number of times I have heard variations of this same idea from gun trainers over the years.

It is certainly possible to find people, usually on social media, boasting that they will kill anyone who breaks into their house. These are often the kinds of people who post "I Don't Dial 9-1-1" signs on their front gates. But rather than giving undeserved attention to keyboard commandos, I place more credibility in what actual military operators involved in civilian gun training teach about home defense.

Approaching the entrance to the Combat Shooting and Tactics (CSAT) building in February 2019, I was greeted by a sign with "GOOD AMERICANS WELCOME" printed below an image of a waving American flag. I traveled to the south side of Nacogdoches, Texas, to interview Master Sergeant Paul R. Howe (U.S. Army, Retired). I prepared by staying up late the night before re-watching his training DVD, *Make Ready with Paul Howe: Combat Mindset*. In the video, Howe draws on his experience as a member of Delta Force during the "Battle of the Black Sea" in Somalia, famously recounted in Mark Bowden's book and dramatized in the movie *Black Hawk Down*. *Combat Mindset* is the only video from Panteao Productions that comes with a warning on the cover: "*This video contains graphic content, which some viewers may find disturbing.*"

The graphic content is disturbing enough that I will not describe it here, but to say MSG Howe is intense in this video understates his demeanor. I was surprised when a mild-mannered, soft-spoken gentleman greeted me at the door. With graying hair long enough to comb, a baggy untucked button-up shirt, and cargo pants, Howe was just as he describes himself in his book *Leadership and Training for the Fight*: "a 'kinder-gentler' middle-aged ex-action guy."[8]

What does an ex-action guy have to teach ordinary armed citizens? In terms of basic shooting mechanics and skills, the lessons are the same for civilians, military, and law enforcement. The students in Howe's Tactical Rifle 1 course I observed that weekend ranged from a game warden to a novice rifle shooter. On the morning of the second day, students practiced "breaking angles," working barriers, stepping out to the right and left, and taking 75-yard shots, both standing and kneeling. Basic skills.

In the arena of tactics, by contrast, the same skills are applied differently based on context. In our conversation before class, Howe explained that the way he would use these techniques differs if he is clearing houses in combat as compared to investigating a problem at his home. He gave me the scenario of an unknown person showing up on my doorstep. "Is it a drunk neighbor or someone in the wrong place? This needs to be determined." Howe explained how he would approach such an uncertain situation tactically: "I'm not going out the front door. Go out the back door and work to the front, assess, give verbal commands, give yourself cover and distance. Maybe the police get there and then the gun goes in the pine straw." Combat mindset notwithstanding, at the end of the day, "You don't want to take a life unless you have to." Spoken from more experience than most of us will ever have.

Howe's perspective is not unique. Although Travis Haley's prior experience as a Force Recon Marine and Blackwater contractor in Iraq was considerable, he became well-known in the gun culture more broadly because of his Magpul Dynamics "Art of the Firearms" training videos with Chris Costa. That the complete set—which includes "The Art of the Tactical Carbine," "Dynamic Handgun," "Dynamic Shotgun," and "Precision Rifle"—is hard to come by today pleases Haley. "I'm glad the Magpul videos went away," he told me when I visited him at the headquarters of Haley Strategic Partners in Scottsdale, Arizona. "Because my training has developed and evolved since then."

When I asked Haley how he developed his thinking about training, he immediately responded, "A lot of failures." To illustrate, he goes back to a key moment in his military career, one involving an AK-47 he displays in his office today, on the wall directly across from his desk where it is always in view. That he told the story—the details of which were off the record—with halting speech and glassy eyes suggests the ongoing burden of the bad decision-making that got him into a situation he could have avoided. He also recognized that in getting himself out of the situation, "My brain drove the fight, not the gun or the technique." This helps explain a motto prominently displayed on the wall leading to the Haley Strategic Partners training lab: Thinkers Before Shooters.

When Haley landed in North Carolina a year later to teach his 3-day Disruptive Science (D5) Handgun course, I saw his motto in action. He began the final day with a classroom presentation on cultivating the attitude necessary to take on the "massive responsibility" of owning a defensive firearm. Haley echoes Paul Howe in asserting, "Shooting is shooting. Whether you're in a cave in Afghanistan or a stay-at-home mom." But being responsibly armed requires much more than the ability to pull a trigger.

Haley stressed the need for emotional control and open-mindedness in the face of perceived threats. He applied this lesson to defense against a home intruder. "Maybe it's just a drunk guy stumbling in the wrong house," Haley suggested. "That's happened four times in my neighborhood, in a gated community in Scottsdale." He then gave a hypothetical example of a fourteen-year-old breaking into his house to steal something on a bet with some neighborhood kids. "Do I sit him down and have a word with him versus blasting him in my house because 'I can shoot anybody I want because of fucking Castle Doctrine'? That is not how it works in America. And if you think that, you're a liability." With the entire class's full attention, Haley continued, "Especially because if I did shoot that 14-year-old kid.... Anybody in this room killed somebody? You have to live with that for the rest of your life."

For Haley, as for Howe and many other defensive gun trainers, the issue goes beyond the technical question of *how* to use lethal force and the legal question of whether one *can* use lethal force to the deeper ethical question of under what conditions *should* one use lethal force in self-defense.

* * *

Which brings me back to Massad Ayoob. Few in the gun training community have thought more about the ethics of armed self-defense. Although easily the most stressful part of the class, the shooting portion of "Armed Citizens' Rules of Engagement" (MAG-40) is not the most important. The description of the course reads: "An intensive 40-hour program encompassing the legal and ethical parameters of the use of lethal force and deadly weapons by private citizens in defense of themselves and others within the mantle of their protection, including the use of the defensive handgun under stress with an overall emphasis on safety and fast, accurate shot placement." My summary as a MAG-40 alumnus is: You spend sixteen hours on the gun range learning how to use lethal force to stop threats, and twenty-four hours in the classroom learning why you want to avoid this at all costs.

Although MAG-40 has a final session that Ayoob describes as "the mandatory ethics part," in fact the entire class centers on ethics. He has been teaching versions of this course since 1981 and during that time some things have changed, like hardware and shooting techniques. But the fundamental principles endure. Ayoob's humanitarian approach to armed self-defense insists from the start that life is precious and the use of lethal force is a cosmic decision that is not to be made lightly. His well-known deep baritone reinforces the seriousness of his admonishment that responsible armed citizenship is not simply a matter of knowing when you *can* legally use lethal force; it is fundamentally about understanding what you *should* and *should not* do.

Like the Marvel Comic universe's *Spiderman*, Ayoob reminded us that the gun carries with it great power and society rightfully expects armed citizens to exercise a proportional level of responsibility. In choosing to carry firearms in public, armed citizens are held to a "higher standard" in understanding both the legal and ethical parameters of their use. "Ask yourself," Ayoob instructed us, "Why are you carrying a gun in public? Because you anticipate that you may need to shoot someone in public. That is an awesome responsibility."

One of the major goals of MAG-40 is to teach us when we can and cannot do this from a legal perspective. "Any time you draw the gun, you are walking on ice. We are going to teach you to walk where the ice is thick." This reflects a very realistic perspective on the use of lethal force. Ayoob was mentored by Bill Jordan, known in some gun circles for his book, *No Second Place Winner.* The title is taken from the idea that, unlike in a shooting competition, where second place gets a trophy, in a gunfight only first place "wins." In Ayoob's view, "Bill Jordan was an optimist." In a gunfight, "there is no first-place winner either." This echoes the sentiments of real-life military gunfighters Paul Howe and Travis Haley. To be sure, Ayoob acknowledged, the way you handle the aftermath of a shooting could make things better. And if you are truly in a life-threatening situation, pulling the trigger means losing less than you would have otherwise. But surviving a justifiable self-defense shooting is not victory but damage control. Hence, Ayoob's bottom line is that the only true victory for the armed citizen is deterrence.

The power to deter, however, comes only with the willingness to kill. Ayoob gave the analogy of toxin-antitoxin therapy in which you use a poison to counter another poison. For example, using chemotherapy to fight cancer. You do not want to use the poison, but the alternative—death—is worse. So, even though deterrence is very powerful, Ayoob insisted we should not carry a gun just to scare somebody. If you confront a life-threatening situation, the reaction time is one to three seconds. That is not enough time to make a decision as cosmic as taking another human being's life. You need to have made "The Decision" ahead of time so you can act if and when the time comes. And you must understand that The Decision is an ethical one.

Willingness to kill is not the same as a desire to kill. Ayoob challenged the view that "when you kill a man, your beer tastes colder, your bed feels warmer, and your jokes are funnier." According to Ayoob, the *Diagnostic and Statistical Manual of Mental Disorders* used to have a term for these people: "psychopaths." (It has been replaced by "antisocial personality disorder.") In his typically blunt fashion, Ayoob declared, "This is bullshit. Killing another American citizen is not going to make you feel good. It is a larger-than-life act. The shooting of a criminal is still the death of a citizen."

Ayoob concluded with a poignant story. In November 1967, his sister and only sibling Elizabeth died from Hodgkin's disease. She passed in his arms at twenty-six years of age, when he was nineteen. After Elizabeth's death, their mother suggested Massad go deer hunting to get out from under the pain. Near the end of his day in the field, Ayoob saw a nice year-old deer. He put the crosshairs on him, looked at him for some time, and then decided to let him live. In tears, he realized the power in the choice not to kill.

In the end, Ayoob reminded us that we have a lot to fight for—a lot of debts, loved ones, and people who rely on us. The willingness to live and help others live is more important than the willingness to kill. "The gun gives you the power to kill. The ultimate power you have, however, is the choice not to kill."

* * *

Early in my journey inside American gun culture, I learned that the armed citizens' ideal toolkit not only goes beyond guns; it goes beyond physical objects themselves. Having taken his course, I read more deeply into Massad Ayoob's writing, including his awkwardly named book, *Combat Shooting*. (The seventh edition of the book adds a clarifying subtitle: *An Expert's Guide to Defending Your Family, Your Home and Yourself.*) The book begins not with what gun to use or even how to shoot but with a chapter on "Mindset." Ayoob opens with the observation of John Steinbeck in his posthumously published book, *The Acts of King Arthur and His Noble Knights*: "The sword is more important than the shield, and skill is more important than either. The final weapon is the brain, all else is supplementary." The passage is actually spoken by Steinbeck's character Lyne, a sixty-year-old woman who goes on a quest with one of the noble knights, Ewain, and teaches him how to fight along the way.[9]

As someone who has spent my entire adult life in the comfort of exclusive universities, it is no surprise that I am both drawn to an emphasis on the brain and repelled by the idea of fighting. How is a middle-aged professor supposed to understand the intersection of the two in what Paul Howe and others call the "combat mindset"? How can I mentally embrace a willingness to fight when my daily life is so peaceful? The need to fight is largely lost on comfortably upper-middle-class professionals like me who typically outsource our violence to others serving in the military and law enforcement. In fifty-five years of existence, my martial experience is limited to one short and poorly executed fistfight with a schoolmate at our bus stop back in 1980.

As a sociologist, I lean toward the nurture side of the nature vs. nurture question, and so certainly believe a combat mindset can be learned. What better place to cultivate it than at the shooting school founded by a man characterized by sociologist James William Gibson as "preaching what he called a 'philosophy of violence'"?[10] John Dean "Jeff" Cooper founded the American Pistol Institute at Gunsite Ranch in 1976, spawning the entire civilian defensive gun training industry in the process. His goal was to train military, law enforcement, and civilians side-by-side in "The Modern Technique of the Pistol." As Cooper elaborated it over time, The Modern Technique is composed of three parts known as the Combat Triad: gun handling, marksmanship, and mindset. Although gun handling and marksmanship are central to The Modern Technique, mindset is the foundation.[11]

By emphasizing the curriculum taught rather than the person teaching it, Cooper's school is unique in having survived his retirement. To this day, civilians can travel to the desert of Northern Arizona for Gunsite Academy's 250 Defensive Pistol Course to learn The Modern Technique of the Pistol, as I did in the summer of 2017. The 250 Pistol course is now referred to as "The Gunsite Experience" because the school is a destination location for gun training. During my visit, I met guys on "brocation" (guys vacation), retirees crossing an item off their bucket list, a husband and wife, an uncle and nephew, and a mother, father, and daughter attending together. Ken Campbell, the chief operating officer of Gunsite, realizes this. As he told me, "We want to give you dinner and a show." Gunsite being Gunsite, the cost of the experience is steep: $1,695 tuition plus $450 for enough 9 mm ammo to cover the five-day course (travel and accommodations not included). Today, Campbell refers to attendees as "clients." Using language reminiscent of those in the competitive airline industry, he told his clients, "We know you have choices and we appreciate your spending your training time and dollars with us." He expressed his appreciation, in part, by making daily appearances at the 100+°F range with Otter Pops for the students.

The Gunsite I observed almost thirty years after James William Gibson embodied a much less martial ethos. A protégé of Jeff Cooper and a controversial figure himself in the gun training world, Gabriel Suarez explains, "The challenge that Gunsite faces is that it is so tied to its own legacy, which creates expectations on the part of the people who go train there. Some of the martial elements of Cooper's teaching about mindset are lost in the translation." Certainly some 250 Defensive Pistol students are looking to become civilian warriors. But during my week at Gunsite

Ranch, I didn't see many who wanted to be what Suarez tells me Cooper wanted: "People with blood on their boots."

I first noticed this when Rangemaster Steve Hendricks emphasized to his class that Gunsite "is a fighting school not a shooting school." As they performed marksmanship drills on the range, he reminded them, "This is a fighting school. If you are shooting tiny groups, you are not fighting." When practicing threat assessment after shooting, Hendricks implored the students, "You need to search after [shooting] like you're fighting. More and more bad guys are coming in groups of two and three. Tactical mindset folks. This is a gunfight." In one of his mini-lectures during water breaks on the range, Hendricks expressed frustration at having to repeat himself: "I have discovered through my life the world is a dangerous place. I know for a fact it is. I don't mean to yell at you, but that is what we're here for. The mechanics of shooting are easy. The difficult part is fighting. Please enjoy yourself while you're here. Have fun. But we're here to learn how to fight with a handgun." Hendricks' emphasis on the combat side of the Combat Triad made more sense when I learned later that he has the distinction of being the last Gunsite instructor personally chosen by Jeff Cooper himself.

I think of Hendricks imploring his Gunsite students to adopt a fighting mindset over two years later when talking to Paul Howe about civilian gun training. In our conversation, Howe described combat mindset as the "willingness to push forward" in the face of danger. Specifically, "We're talking about you pushing forward against another person with a gun and taking their life." At this point, Howe asked me as someone who has watched his *Combat Mindset* video twice, "Are you going to surrender now to somebody if you have a gun and the ability to fight?"

"I hope not," I answered truthfully. But part of me wondered, am I going to be the one who runs forward or not?

"And that's what I want to know," Howe responded. "I have friends that would never run forward. They're still my friends. They're just not the right person."

Feeling perhaps a bit too comfortable speaking to a retired Delta Force operator, I recounted a dinner conversation I had with my friend and gun trainer, John Johnston, and his friend, Green Beret Chris Cypert. We were talking about who we would take with us if we had to go fight. John and Chris found easy agreement in one choice: "Honestly, David, if we're going to a fight, you're not coming with us." Upon hearing this story, kinder-gentler ex-action guy Paul Howe reassured me, "I don't have a problem with that."

I left Nacogdoches thinking about different applications of the combat mindset. The instinct to protect my children that swelled up after my apartment complex parking lot incident showed I have a fighting impulse inside of me, even if it did not coalesce into a coherent mindset and I lacked the tools to fight effectively at the time. But fight I would. Unlike Paul Howe or Chris Cypert, however, as a civilian, I am never obligated to run forward, to put my life at risk for a stranger.[12]

I recognized my need to cultivate tools, including a mindset, specific to what gun trainer and dentist Dr. Sherman House calls "the civilian defender." Crucially, House begins with the understanding that the civilian defender does not "replace the kind of help that our standing army, fire departments, police departments or emergency medical staff provide to our society." Quite the contrary. The civilian defender simply wants to "survive situations they may encounter when the aforementioned public servants won't or cannot be there to swoop down and save them from whatever perils they encounter." The distinction he makes between the proactive nature of first responders and the defensive nature of civilians is essential.[13]

Where Jeff Cooper defines combat mindset as "that state of mind which ensures victory in a gunfight," the civilian defender's mindset should also include the attitude expressed by my friend and gun writer Tamara Keel: "Can't lose a fight you're not in."[14] A mindset oriented toward avoiding situations that require fighting centers on awareness and avoidance, two attributes I touched on already in Chapter 6. The importance of these qualities of mind is stressed even by gun trainers who come from military backgrounds. Retired Navy SEAL Jeff Gonzales trains civilian gun carriers through his business Trident Concepts, served on the National Rifle Association's Training and Education Committee, and writes extensively about self-defense with firearms. In a training video on *Concealed Carry TTPs* (tactics, techniques, and procedures), he begins by stressing the importance of detecting and defusing before defending. Similarly, former Delta Force operator Mike Pannone teaches his students "always to avoid and evade first" before fighting.

Detecting, avoiding, defusing, and evading are essential to a civilian defensive mindset, but they are also skills to be learned. They are an important part of a diverse and robust defensive toolkit designed to maximize the power of choice.

* * *

Former undercover narcotics officer Craig Douglas (a.k.a., "Southnarc") exemplifies a more holistic and integrated approach to self-defense training that goes beyond the gun itself. His "extreme close quarters concepts" (ECQC) course focuses on "aggressive problem solving during a life or death struggle at arm's length or closer." Although the class is sold as "building functional, combative handgun skills at zero to five feet," the problem-solving taught goes well beyond handgun skills. ECQC's interdisciplinary approach also seeks to "give every student the empty-hand skills of an MMA fighter." But even more fundamentally for my purposes, ECQC begins by teaching students how to avoid needing to solve problems with a gun or mixed martial arts in the first place.

Sitting on the mats at Chapel Hill Gracie Jiu-Jitsu in March 2019, my fellow students and I listened as Douglas began our class by observing, "A good self-defense course should begin with not letting it get shitty."

We learned how to do this by practicing what Douglas calls "the high art of victim de-selection" and conflict de-escalation. Many self-defense trainers emphasize the importance of situational awareness. Douglas maintained that "awareness is not a verb. It is not something you can do. You cannot *aware*." Rather, he operationalized awareness in terms of expanded or restricted fields of awareness. For example, we need to avoid task fixation that restricts our fields of awareness, especially getting lost in our cell phones in public. This allows us to detect potential threats early and make ourselves less vulnerable to ambush attacks by bad guys who prefer unaware targets.

Early detection of potential threats also gives us more time to "manage unknown contacts" (MUC) in public space, again allowing us to avoid having to fight in the first place. Using our words is a key first line of defense. Most of us will not achieve Douglas's ideal of having "the verbal agility of a stand-up comic." But he insisted that everyone needs at least to develop a "playlist" of concise, repeated phrases representing a range of verbalizations from asking to telling. Before an unknown contact is even within a couple of arms-length from us, a clear request should be made like, "Hey, man, can you hold up right there?" If the request is not met, verbal escalation to a clear command like "Back up!!!" is warranted. Along with these verbalizations, the hands should be brought up in a high, compressed "fence" position. This reinforces the command, gives a visual signal to someone who may not understand the words, and gets the hands in a defensive position if necessary.

We paired off and did various role-playing improvisations to practice "not letting it get shitty" through verbalization and movement. Alternating between being the defender and the unknown contact allowed us to imagine the many different situations in which we might find ourselves—some potentially threatening, many others not. This alone can help shift the initiative from a potential attacker to us as defenders in real-life encounters.

From this starting point, the course dedicated two full days on what to do if things do get shitty. Rather than focusing solely on guns, ECQC also emphasizes empty-hand fighting. Douglas's curriculum centers on Greco-Roman wrestling while standing and jiu-jitsu-based ground fighting. This part of the course featured short bits of instruction and long stretches of application. Repeated one-minute rounds of grappling on my feet with younger, stronger, fitter partners exposed my physical limitations. By the time we were fighting on the ground, I had to quit. Although he was not addressing me specifically at the time, I could not help but be stung by Douglas saying mockingly to the class: "I carry a gun because I'm not into this wrasslin' shit." I realized that physical fitness itself is an important part of a robust defensive toolkit.

I left ECQC fully understanding the importance of ensuring my self-defense strategy included options "between a harsh word and a gun," to quote gun trainer Chuck Haggard. One tool that Haggard himself teaches is pepper spray. In ECQC, Craig Douglas taught the eye jab as a defensive tactic. Pepper spray is "an eye jab in a can." Haggard not

The author (right) grappling in Extreme Close Quarters Concepts (ECQC) course with instructor Craig Douglas (far left) coaching (photograph courtesy Sandra Stroud Yamane).

only teaches how to use pepper spray, but why. Writing in the magazine *RECOIL Concealment,* he observes, "You can't shoot every threat you run into—pulling or using a gun on a less-than-deadly-force threat can get you put in prison. The old saying 'If all you have is a hammer, every problem gets treated like a nail' is in play here." Haggard uses a high-profile example to reinforce that this is not just a matter of avoiding run-ins with the law. "In my class lectures on this subject," he writes, "I often refer to the case of George Zimmerman. Change the dynamics of the case a bit; if George had sprayed Trayvon Martin in the face with OC spray when he was confronted, would we even know who George is? The answer is likely not, because this would've very likely ended the confrontation right there. And everybody involved would've been better off for it."[15]

* * *

In the months following ECQC, I sought out further opportunities to learn from trainers who integrate a variety of defensive toolkit options—from harsh words to guns—into the same course. This quest took Sandy and me on a road trip to Kennesaw in the northern suburbs of Atlanta for The Complete Combatant's 1.5-day "Force Readiness" course. The course's stated objective is auspicious. According to head coach Brian Hill, Force Readiness attempts "to cover the entire personal protection process from beginning to end." The class is book-ended by a single idea: choice. Hill began the course stating: "This is a class about the power of choice." He concluded by reminding us, "The more robust your skillset, the more choices you have."

Here the mascots of The Complete Combatant—Joe and Jane, the "Combat Ants"—are instructive. The Combat Ant has a diverse defensive toolkit and hence the power of choice. It is no accident that Joe and Jane are armed not just with guns, but also knives, flashlights, phones, and martial arts skills. The Hills note that an updated Combat Ant would need a couple of extra tools on its skill belt, including pepper spray and a tourniquet. And probably some Nikes to emphasize the defensive value of what their friend John Correia calls "Run Fu." The Combat Ant reflects the overarching vision of Brian and Shelley Hill's defensive training company. As Brian told our class, "It's not about guns or martial arts, it's about you." The Complete Combatant's motto expands John Steinbeck's idea: "You are the weapon."

Brian Hill maintains that having and knowing how to use a gun only solves one percent of the average person's safety problems. Force

Joe the Combat Ant, mascot of The Complete Combatant, Brian and Shelley Hill's defensive training company (photograph courtesy the Complete Combatant).

Readiness does address gun use in part, but the bulk of the class was oriented toward solving the other ninety-nine percent of problems we face in everyday life. As in medicine and ECQC, an ounce of prevention is worth a pound of cure. Force Readiness began with not letting things get shitty in the first place. If they do, we learned some basic elements of defensive and offensive fist-fighting and grappling. As we sparred with our fellow students, Hill reminded us that "the goal here is not to win a martial arts match." We want to buy ourselves time and space to escape. Hill implored us: "You must give yourself permission to run away. It does not make you a coward."

Both pepper spray and flashlights expand our choices in self-defense situations. We practiced for a minute or two deploying pepper spray one-handed, with a flashlight in our other hand—just long enough to see how it felt and to assess where we were with the skill. Flashlights are boring but essential tools, we were told, not just for when we are under attack, but for determining if we are under attack. The "Tactical Professor" Claude Werner repeatedly highlights the "serious mistakes gunowners make" (like shooting one's own child) that could have been prevented if a flashlight (or pepper spray) had been drawn before a gun.[16]

Force Readiness wrapped up by having us apply our learning in dynamic scenarios. As Hill described our scenarios, "This is not real, but this is the realest fake stuff we can do" under the circumstances. Each scenario was tailored to the greatest extent possible to specific students. They included a car accident followed by road rage, getting jumped in the rental car area of an airport, an armed robbery, a mass shooting in a shopping mall, a drunk guy accosting someone, and more. Reflecting the broad skillset we covered in Force Readiness, the "solutions" to these scenarios varied and infrequently involved shooting the attacker. The student resolved the mass shooting incident, for example, by using the Nike Defense and running away. Pepper spray ended the rental car ambush. Sandy is a nurse practitioner and her scenario entailed a hostile patient in a behavioral health unit. She used her cell phone to call hospital security to handle it.

Each of the scenarios highlighted how self-defense is a problem-solving genre. The challenge is that self-defense problems are not like math problems where (except in extremely exceptional cases) there is a single correct answer. Those less familiar with self-defense are often like Sheldon from *Big Bang Theory*, looking for invariant, universally applicable laws of behavior. They want a mathematically-based physics of self-defense where $E=mc^2$ every time. But self-defense is not so formulaic. There is no $F=ma$. Self-defense is fluid and interactive. The problem we think we are solving may turn out to be something else altogether, and the problem changes as we engage it.

Craig Douglas and Brian Hill taught me that self-defense while armed is more art than science. Of course, just because there are no mathematical formulas we can use to solve self-defense problems, does not mean that chaos reigns. When practiced at a high level, every form of art is a discipline. It involves techniques that are cultivated over time through practice. When done well, defensive gun training cultivates a diverse toolkit so we students can avoid hammering screws.

* * *

Underlying both Michael Austin's and Harel Shapira's criticisms of gun training courses is the belief that they encourage people to "shoot first and ask questions later." News headlines regularly highlight incidents that seem to justify this fear. In April 2023, sixteen-year-old Ralph Yarl was shot and injured after approaching the wrong house in Kansas City while trying to pick up his siblings. Two days later, twenty-year-old Kaylin Gillis was shot and killed after a car she was riding in pulled into the wrong driveway in upstate New York. The following month, a fourteen-year-old was shot and injured by a homeowner in Starks, Louisiana, while playing hide-and-seek in his backyard. And so on.

These are terrible events. But as noted earlier in this chapter, nothing in the law allows a person to shoot someone and get away with it merely by claiming self-defense. This is why I dislike politically charged rhetoric that refers to Stand Your Ground laws as "shoot first" laws. I fear this may unintentionally mislead people into thinking that self-defense laws actually give them a blanket license to kill with impunity. They do not. While some self-defense shootings get attention when they are ultimately ruled justifiable—think George Zimmerman and Kyle Rittenhouse—many other claims of self-defense have been found wanting in court. Among those now incarcerated for homicide are the killers of Jordan Davis in Jacksonville, Renisha McBride in Detroit, and Ahmaud Arbery in Georgia.[17]

That Davis, McBride, and Arbery are all Black and their killers all white gives life to claims that a racialized culture of fear animates some gun owners, if not gun culture itself.[18] But the question here is whether gun training courses are complicit in these negative outcomes. I have seen no evidence to suggest that the actions of the shooters in these cases were motivated by anything they learned in gun training courses. If anything, it seems to me that these gun owners would have benefited from more training like what I describe above.

Harel Shapira, of course, disagrees. He maintains that gun training takes its toll not only on individuals, but on society as a whole. Shapira alleges that it instills fear in students, leading them to avoid "the kind of public interactions that make democracy viable.... It's training them to be suspicious and atomized, learning to protect themselves, no matter how great the risk to others. It's training them to not be citizens." While this is no doubt true for some, I question the generalizability of this claim. My observations and personal experiences certainly differ.

I have come a long way from being a well-intentioned but naïve Good Samaritan to my neighbor who was being accosted in our apartment complex's parking lot in 2010. Although the work is never done, becoming responsibly armed has better equipped me to handle such situations today. I understand more about when and how to detect, avoid, and evade trouble. I know more practically and tactically about how and when to shoot (and not to shoot), legally when I can shoot, and ethically if I should shoot. I have a diverse defensive toolkit that maximizes my choices.

Becoming a more capable weapon owner allows me to enjoy all of the benefits of living life to the fullest without fear, even in an uncertain world. Beyond engaging in the kind of everyday public interactions that make democracy viable, my training actually makes me more comfortable reaching out to people I may encounter in public—welcoming the stranger, offering food to the hungry and drink to the thirsty, and looking after the needy. I know I am not the only defensive gun owner who feels and acts this way.

This is not to say there are no limits just because I am armed with a full range of tools and skills in my defensive toolkit. As a civilian defender, I am not obligated to push forward in the face of threats. Even with over a decade of education, training, and reflection on self-defense under my belt, I would be lying if I said I knew with certainty how I would handle a violent confrontation involving a neighbor today. But if I did choose to intervene, I would do so more aware of the potential dangers and better prepared to defuse and defend. Most importantly, I would do so as the kind of person John Correia implores his 3+ million Active Self Protection YouTube channel subscribers to be: "good, sane, sober, moral, and prudent." That is, as a good citizen.

Conclusion:
What the Professor Learned

What B. Bruce-Briggs called "the great American gun war" in 1976 has only intensified as our political system has grown increasingly polarized and guns have become a wedge issue in our worsening cultural divide. One consequence is that dichotomous thinking dominates what are complex and multifaceted realities. Guns are seen either as the salvation or destroyer of democracy. We can either have gun rights or public safety. To borrow an image from my friend Randy Miyan, we find ourselves in a Chinese finger lock over whether guns are good or evil.

If there is a single overarching lesson I have learned in my search for the truth about American gun culture, it is the importance of understanding that guns are not one thing, but many—and paradoxical at that. They are fun and frightening, dangerous and protective, diffuse and concentrated, unifying and divisive, attractive and repulsive, interesting and controversial, useful and useless, good and bad, and neither good nor bad. This is to say, guns are not inherently anything. They take on different meanings according to the various purposes to which people put them. Which is a long-winded, professorial way of saying that the meaning of guns is their use in society.[1]

This book reflects my personal and sociological curiosity as I seek to understand this complex reality. It is difficult to summarize all that I have learned about guns, gun owners, and gun culture in America over the past thirteen years. Each chapter of this book offers some of my insights. Rather than seeing guns exclusively from the perspectives of criminology and epidemiology, I understand how guns are normal anthropologically and culturally. Rather than gasping in shock at gun super-owners hoarding weapons, I demonstrate that different guns in a vast personal arsenal serve different purposes. Rather than condemning AR-15s as weapons of war that have no business on our streets,

I question the bright line drawn between military and civilian weapons and explore the many different reasons people own them. Rather than making oversimplified generalizations about guns as risk factors for negative outcomes, I highlight more complex ways of viewing and managing risk from the perspective of gun owners. Rather than seeing defensive gun training as teaching people to "shoot first and ask questions later," I highlight ways in which it does exactly the opposite.

In this concluding chapter, I stand back from these specific insights and offer five major lessons I have learned from my surprising journey inside American gun culture. I hope they move us away from the heat of polarizing disagreement and toward the light of a more nuanced understanding of this fundamental reality of American life today.

* * *

Lesson 1: Shooting Is Fun

For the past nine years, I have been taking Wake Forest University students enrolled in my Sociology of Guns seminar on a field trip to the gun range prior to our first in-class session on campus. Although shooting is not required, in recent years every student has opted to try each of three semi-automatic firearms I bring: a .22-caliber pistol, a 9 mm pistol, and an AR-15 pattern rifle. The purpose of the field trip is not to convert students to gun ownership but simply to give them firsthand experience with the object whose complicated role in society we will discuss for the following fourteen weeks. Most students have never fired a gun before or have only limited experience.[2]

As expected, student responses vary. Some dislike it. Most enjoy it. In their field trip reflection papers, many students echo the feelings I had the first time I shot a gun:

> I was surprised at the amount of joy I felt when I first hit the target.... I almost felt as though I was on an adrenaline rush after a long run. Therefore, in contrast to my fear and uneasiness based on my prior knowledge of guns, I really enjoyed myself and had fun not only shooting but especially hitting the target.

> The part of the field trip that surprised me the most was how much I truly enjoyed it. I walked away feeling a sense of exhilaration and as if I had been relieved of the day's tension and stress. I immediately contacted my family to tell them how great of a time I had with the different types of guns.

> I was surprised by how much I enjoyed the feeling of consistently hitting the target, and I definitely did not expect it to be so fun! I walked out of the range

that day thinking that I was pretty cool for getting at least some shots on target and even exclaimed that I would consider doing it again.

When I compare my first-time gun range experience to my prior understanding of guns in the US, I am met with cognitive dissonance and discomfort from the enjoyment I received from firing a gun.

Especially in contrast to their prior understandings of guns as instruments of crime and violence, many students come to the same conclusion as comedian Trae Crowder's *Liberal Redneck Manifesto*: "The simple fact of guns is that they're fun as shit."[3]

"Shooting is fun" was one of the three lessons I shared in my lunchtime lecture at the National Firearms Law Seminar in 2019. My takeaway from this lesson for the audience was the importance of introducing people to shooting. I always enjoy getting a gun in people's hands and helping them have a safe and fun experience, regardless of their reason for wanting to shoot. I am not sure who said it first, but I always attribute a memorable line about this to Jon Hauptman of PHLster Holsters: There is no such thing as an anti-gun gun range.[4]

I sometimes get so caught up in my research on defensive gun ownership and culture that I forget this essential point. My scholarship focuses on the shift in the center of gravity of gun culture from hunting, target shooting, and collecting to self-defense—from Gun Culture 1.0 to Gun Culture 2.0.[5] But this conceptual framework is a two-edged sword. It is insightful, but also limiting. In a simplistic reading, it can obscure the reality that American gun culture has always been and continues to be internally diverse, with multiple thriving recreational subcultures. This can be seen in dead tree and social media, in stores and on ranges, in personal collections and museum galleries, and in exhibitions from the smallest local gun show to the National Rifle Association's annual meeting. Participation in these subcultures is not mutually exclusive. Many who find my work describe themselves as belonging to Gun Culture 1.5.

"Unlike a specific new flu virus strain," writes political philosopher Timothy Luke, "there is not just one gun culture in America. There are many, not all involve shooting, and not all shooting is violent."[6] Although I think of myself primarily as a defensive gun owner, my point of entry into gun culture was recreational. I first went to the range because I was afraid of guns and I came away from the experience realizing that shooting is fun. To this day, I mostly use my guns for pleasure.

Few challenge innocuous reasons for gun ownership like hunting, target shooting, and collecting. Concerns about guns and gun culture center on defensive gun ownership and use.[7] This suggests the problem is not really guns themselves but something even more fundamental: the potential for violence guns embody.

* * *

Lesson 2: Violence Can Be the Answer

When I was in second grade, I made a drawing for a class assignment. It hung on my bedroom wall through high school and, thanks to my mother, I still have it. The rudimentary pencil and crayon artwork depicts the Rev. Dr. Martin Luther King, Jr., standing on the steps of the Lincoln Memorial speaking to a gathered crowd. My mom's neat handwriting around the picture gives the assignment's prompt and my response:

> *I have a dream that one day…*
> *I can do what Martin Luther King did.*

Although I have fallen far short of realizing this dream, Martin Luther King's quest for social justice informed my liberal sentiments and continues to inspire me.

I still keep photos of King near the computer monitor in my office as a reminder that the cause for which he fought is still a cause and the dream for which he died is still a dream. One of them has these words above his image: "Nonviolence…. Our Most Potent Weapon." The political practice of nonviolent civil disobedience was central to my understanding of King's work. But in time I learned that nonviolence and pacifism are not equivalent. After the bombing of his Montgomery home in January 1956, King applied for a concealed carry permit from the local sheriff. Because the concealed carry revolution I discuss in Chapter 5 had not yet begun, he was denied a carry permit under Alabama's may issue regime. But King still kept a gun at home for self-defense—or, rather, "an arsenal," as one of his advisors characterized it.[8]

Although our lives and impact on the world differ dramatically, what both King and I have in common is a belief in the importance of fundamental rights. Most basically a right to life itself. Because of this, the right to defend our lives is fundamental. King recognized this, writing in his final book that "the right to defend one's home and one's person when attacked has been guaranteed through the ages by common law." This right to self-defense gives rise, in eighteenth-century English jurist William Blackstone's view, to an auxiliary right of having arms

Drawing by the author of Martin Luther King's "I Have a Dream" speech at the 1963 March on Washington, completed for a second grade class project in 1976 (photograph courtesy Sandra Stroud Yamane).

because they are a good and accepted means of self-preservation. Not the only means, but good and accepted ones.[9]

An old adage, among conservatives at least, is that a conservative is just a liberal who has been mugged by reality. I am still a liberal, but the incident in my apartment complex parking lot back in 2010 (recounted in the introduction) fundamentally altered my perspective on many things. Especially violence. A desire to protect my children swelled up inside me and I envisioned myself defending them by any means necessary. The experience triggered the survival module in my ancient Hominin brain. In Randy Miyan's words, I "had the switch flipped" and continuing involvement in gun culture holds the self-preservation switch in the "on" position (recall Chapter 2).[10]

Looking back on intervening in my neighbor's dispute, I try not to think about what might have happened if the assailant had turned his attention from her to me and my kids. I was wholly unequipped to deal with violence at the time, but I was not about to leave it that way. My journey inside American gun culture has better equipped me to deal with the reality of interpersonal violence, not just with guns but with a different mindset concerning violence and a range of tools, from my words to lethal force (see Chapter 8). A few years after taking Extreme Close Quarters Combat (ECQC) with Craig Douglas, I visited a knife-fighting course he was teaching at the Fit to Fight gym in Charlotte. In the class was a petite but tenacious Christun Erwin wearing a shirt with "Give Violence a Chance" in bold letters across the front. I knew exactly what she meant.

The fact that I responded to my parking lot confrontation by becoming a defensive gun owner certainly bothers many of my liberal friends and colleagues. Many will see it as allowing me "to identify with hegemonic masculinity through fantasies of violence and self-defense," to quote my fellow sociologist Angela Stroud. Some of this resistance is certainly due to discomfort with guns. But I think it masks a more fundamental reservation about the capacity for violence guns represent and, indeed, about violence itself. As the authors of the scholarly treatise *Virtuous Violence* declare, "We ourselves judge violence to be repugnant."[11]

Even the use of violence in acts of justifiable self-defense is often seen as something to be avoided. This underwrites opposition to Stand Your Ground laws. "Not many people confront the reality that lethal force sometimes is, in fact, unavoidable, necessary, or imperative," observes Timothy Luke. In certain cases, violence is something liberals should support, even if reluctantly. In their theory of virtuous violence, anthropologist Alan Page Fiske and psychologist Tage Shakti Rai identify the use of violence for "protection in the form of defense" as "almost universally recognized as morally acceptable, justified, and even obligatory." Beyond mere self-preservation, "when humans violently defend their children, spouses, family, buddies, or allies this defense is virtuous violence. It is virtuous because protecting partners is the core of the relationship. It is a moral obligation to protect one's partners."[12]

As I argue in Chapter 6, avoidance and making good life choices will insulate most people from being victims of violence and preempt the need to engage in defensive violence in response. Many of us are fortunate to live, as Harvard professor Steven Pinker argues, during "the most peaceable era in our species' existence." Self-defense expert Tim Larkin seems to have me in mind when he writes, "For most of us, violence is an anomaly—a black swan event whose likelihood is as predictable as its consequences, which is to say *not very*. Most people will go their entire lives without experiencing serious violence." Because black swan events are rare, Larkin explains, "they're relatively cheap to hedge against, but they're so unlikely that most people don't bother to hedge at all." Here's the catch: "those who do [experience violence] will feel firsthand its power to drastically change, or even end, lives. It only has to happen once."[13]

My heart and mind tell me that I do not ever want to hurt anyone I do not have to hurt to protect myself or my loved ones. Going back to my childhood worship of Martin Luther King, Jr., and his ethic of nonviolence, I believe with Tim Larkin that "violence is rarely the answer." But Larkin maintains, and I think King would agree, "when it is, it's the only answer."[14]

I recognize that violence is often morally repugnant. This is not a call for the civilian defender to become a citizen-vigilante. Unlike the "shoot first" ethic that critics erroneously attribute to defensive gun culture, my instincts have been formed by my training to distinguish between the black swan events when violence is the answer and the normal circumstances when violence is not the answer. Echoing gun trainers Massad Ayoob, Brian Hill, and others, choice is the ultimate power we have (see Chapter 8). This includes the power to choose violence, or not.

In truth, most liberals are not really opposed to guns or violence altogether. We simply prefer to outsource them to the police. Where I differ from many of my peers is in my recognition that there may come a day when I must give violence a chance.

* * *

Lesson 3: Gun Culture Is Inclusive (But I May Never Feel Fully at Home There)

This book begins with me standing at a podium in downtown Indianapolis in April 2019 speaking to the NRA's National Firearms Law Seminar about my experience of becoming a gun owner. Literally at the same time, a short distance away, President Donald Trump stood at a podium speaking to the NRA Institute for Legislative Action Leadership Forum confirming the organization's support for his reelection bid. Not two years later, my work on an essay about "Understanding and Misunderstanding America's Gun Culture" was interrupted by a text message from a friend: "They are storming the capitol." It took me a moment to figure out who "they" were, but I soon made the connection. They were people wanting to "Save America" by overturning Trump's defeat in the November 2020 presidential election.

I was sorry but not surprised to see countless images from that day of a Confederate battle flag with an AR-15 and "Come and Take It" superimposed on it flying alongside all manner of Trump MAGA flags. Every stereotype of gun culture was on full display at that moment. Aggrieved white men firmly rooted in a racially unequal past flying the flag of their totemic emblem and rallying cry. In the crowd, Oath Keepers and Three Percent militias shared their NRA-fostered gun rights "insurrectionist fever dreams" with Proud Boys, Nick Fuentes's Groyper Army, and QAnon conspiracists. If there is a swamp that needs draining, I thought, here it is.[15]

I also argued in the essay that was disrupted by the Capitol riot that blaming gun culture as a whole for the events of January 6 "makes a causal connection that does not reflect the broader reality of guns and gun ownership in America." Tens of millions of gun-owning Americans hear the exhortations of the NRA and other (even more fervent) gun rights groups, are exposed to gun industry advertising, and engage in other social activities around guns, but are not infected by the insurrectionist virus.[16]

My two responses to January 6 highlight the duality of repulsion and attraction I experience relative to gun culture. I have lived more of my life outside gun culture than inside it and most of my days are spent in my faculty office and classroom at an elite private university. But at least part of every day I spend either directly or indirectly in contact with gun culture. My hybrid identity as a liberal professor gun owner in theory means having two tribes to call my own; however, I often instead feel homeless, "betwixt and between" different social worlds.[17]

My worst experience in gun space was when I told a guy working at a gun range that Sandy and I were planning to go to Memphis for the Rangemaster Tactical Conference in 2014. He responded, "Why would you want to go to Memphis? The only thing they got there is [N-word] and the Navy, and the Navy is pulling out." Gun culture certainly has no monopoly on racists, but it is the case that I had lived forty-five years before someone used the N-word in a conversation with me. Although this was thankfully a one-time occurrence, racist dog whistles sound too often when discussions among gun owners turn to the causes of gun violence. I recognize that even a knitting group can have assholes in it, to paraphrase something Michael Bane said to me on this issue. But I could do with less casual and not-so-casual racism. And do not get me started on misogyny, like the Quentin Defense POTUS-45 AR-15 lower receiver that has the following selector switch options: "Build Wall—Drain Swamp—Grab Pussy."[18]

At the same time, as I have gotten more into gun culture, I have felt less than fully at home among my fellow academics. Liberal professors, especially sociologists, are my people. But when they talk about guns and gun culture, I often feel a profound sense of alienation from my own experiences and understanding. I vividly recall attending a session on guns at the annual meeting of the Association for the Sociology of Religion in Philadelphia in 2018—the same year Jonathan Metzl declared "guns are bad" at the American Sociological Association meetings being held concurrently (recounted in Chapter 1). One of the panelists said that self-defense gun culture in America is essentially the province of white men and that guns are "a totem of white masculinity." This is certainly true as far as it goes, evidenced by the work of Quentin Defense. But it does not go far enough. I thought about guns as totems of white masculinity for the entire thirty-minute Uber ride I took after the session to meet up with Annette Evans at a gun range she was working to open at the time. Annette is a first-generation American, the daughter of immigrants from Hong Kong, an attorney, a competitive shooter, and an advocate for women's self-defense under her "Own Her Own Life" brand.[19]

During breakfast at a different academic conference, a colleague I knew before studying gun culture asked me, "Are you a gun owner?" This is a surprisingly difficult question for someone who owns thirteen guns to answer. My reluctance to say yes is similar to when people ask me, "Are you a golfer?" I always offer a canned response, "No, but I play golf." I deny the label golfer because of the heightened expectations that come with it. In the same way, I resist the gun owner label because of the lowered expectations that come with an identity that is stigmatized, especially on university campuses, but also in parts of the gun control movement and among cultural elites in media, publishing, and other liberal enclaves. I am wary of efforts to do to gun owners what was done to smokers and drunk drivers: make us public health pariahs.[20]

The master scholarly narrative of guns holds that America's original sins of racism and misogyny are constitutional features of gun culture. Guns were inextricably woven into the fabric of Settler Colonialism in the Americas from the start; the Second Amendment was created to allow Southern states to police enslaved people; and armed self-defense represents "white hetero/cis-masculinity." But there have always been alternative narratives of guns in America, just as parts of gun culture today rally for diversity and inclusion. The National African American Gun Association, A Girl & a Gun Women's Shooting League, Pink Pistols, the Liberal Gun Club, and other groups representing diverse gun owners come immediately to mind.[21]

I have long argued that Gun Culture 2.0 has the potential to be more inclusive because self-defense is a universal concern, and some people will respond to that universal concern with firearms. This was nowhere more evident than during the Great Gun Buying Spree of 2020+ recounted in Chapter 1. This buying spree, which continued into 2021, is remarkable for how clearly it reflects the ongoing shift in American gun culture toward self-defense and the changing face of gun ownership that accompanies it. Amidst social uncertainty and social unrest, it makes sense that a broad swath of the American population would respond by buying guns, including many new gun owners from non-traditional backgrounds. Many of these new gun buyers were gun curious individuals motivated by the circumstances to get off the fence. According to the 2021 National Firearms Survey conducted by researchers from Harvard and Northeastern Universities, 1.5 percent of all American adults (3.8 million people) became new gun owners in 2020. Compared to existing gun owners, they tended to be younger, more female, more Black and Hispanic, more urban, more likely to have children, and less likely to have ever been married. They were also more likely to own only handguns, suggestive of their self-defense orientation. These new gun owners reflect a movement away from the *Duck Dynasty* gun owner stereotype of older, politically conservative, white, cisgender men from the rural South. They represent an important part of the future of American gun culture.[22]

I was a new, non-traditional gun owner myself when I began this journey in 2011. Every year I become more comfortable in gun culture, though there are still aspects of it that make me feel less than fully at home. This is a moment of opportunity and challenge for gun culture. The opportunity is to embrace new and non-traditional gun owners in all their diversity. The challenge is embattled conservative culture warrior gun owners who make some diverse gun owners feel unwelcome. My liberal tragic optimism ultimately brings me back to Martin Luther King, Jr. I believe that the arc of gun culture history is long, but it bends toward inclusion. And if it doesn't, we need to bend it.[23]

* * *

Lesson 4: Gun Owners Are (and Should Be and Can Be More) Responsible

In the wake of the Great Gun Buying Spree of 2020+, *Atlantic* staff writer David Frum made a particularly strong, if not exceptionally unique, argument that "responsible gun ownership is a lie."[24] I appreciated his forthrightness in saying what he really thinks, because I sense many in the gun violence prevention movement believe this in their hearts but soften their public stances for political purposes. They perhaps remember too well what happened in the 1990s when Arthur Kellermann said out loud what he really thought about gun ownership (see Chapter 7).

At the heart of the lie for Frum is the distinction between responsible gun owners and trouble-making others. In his words, "Drawing a bright line between the supposedly vast majority of 'responsible,' 'law abiding' gun owners and those shadowy others who cause all the trouble is a prudent approach for politicians, but it obscures the true nature of the problem. We need to stop deceiving ourselves about the importance of this distinction." Those of us who legally own guns are also part of the problem, in Frum's calculus, because gun ownership increases our risk of negative outcomes from accidental injury to death. We are "falling victim to bad risk analysis" (a criticism I take up in Chapters 6 and 7).

Frum accepts the usual incremental regulatory solutions to this problem, but his vision for the future goes well beyond mere legislation. When his essay ran online, it had a different but still telling title, "How to Persuade Americans to Give Up Their Guns." He implores his readers, "You want to be a protective spouse, a concerned parent, a good citizen, a patriotic American? Save your family and your community from danger by *getting rid of* your weapons, and especially your handguns. Don't wait for the law. Do it yourself; do it now." Frum argues that "progress can be made against gun violence, as progress was once made against other social evils: by persuading Americans to stop, one by one by one." His illustrative case: Drunk driving.

The example of drunk driving hits home for me. My dad was of the generation of Americans who would play golf, have several beers, and drive home, sometimes not remembering the time between leaving the course and arriving in the garage. As a 16-year-old rising senior in high school in 1985, I was swept up in the Mothers Against Drunk Driving cultural revolution and helped organize an initiative called Safe Rides in my area. We gave peers a free, anonymous ride home to avoid driving drunk or riding with someone who was. These efforts were not enough to save our small high school from the sins of our elders. In December 1985, David Gorton, a 16-year-old Half Moon Bay High School sophomore, was killed by a drunk driver while riding his bike close to home. So, I fully agree with Frum that drunk driving is a social evil.

But guess what? We did not stop drinking and we did not stop driving.

As a society, we have certainly tried treating alcohol itself as a social evil given the known individual and social problems attached to it (recall Chapter 1). Prohibition did not go well. Most of us also do not see driving itself as a social evil, either, although the negative externalities of driving cars might warrant such a view.[25] We accept that people can drink responsibly, including by not driving, and drive responsibly, including by not drinking.

Responsible gun ownership is no more a lie than responsible drinking and responsible driving. As I elaborated in Chapter 7, most gun owners will not shoot themselves or others, accidentally or intentionally, nor will most guns be used to injure or kill people.

Of course, gun owners *should be responsible and can be more responsible.* Many work toward this goal, including Claude Werner and Michael Sodini whom we met in Chapter 7. In my experience, no one in the gun community has pushed responsible gun ownership more consistently than Rob Pincus. Although he is best known as a gun trainer through his I.C.E. Training and Personal Defense Network brands, I think of Pincus as a gun educator. That is, an educator about guns, both outside the gun community in his frequent media appearances and as a gadfly inside of it. A case in point is his 2018 "Gun Rights and Responsibilities Manifesto." The gun rights side is fairly obvious, but his argument concerning responsibility merits being quoted at length:

> In our successful efforts to expand gun ownership and gun rights, I fear that we ourselves have not done enough to educate and promote gun responsibility. I fear that we have not policed our own assertively enough when it comes to issues such as gun storage, gun use and general firearms education around the best practices when it comes to defensive firearms carry and the defensive use of firearms in or around our homes, families and businesses. Too many children have been shot accidentally. Too many teens have completed suicide or committed murders with their parents' guns. Too many veterans have taken their own lives. Too many guns have been stolen and used violently by criminals. We have worried about "the other side" using these facts against us for too long. These tragedies are taking place within our community and it is time for us to redouble our efforts to prevent them by working within our community. I have come to the conclusion that a nefarious Anti-Gun Agenda is not the biggest threat to our rights; the perception that we cannot exercise them responsibly is a greater threat to our future.

Pincus's point here is not that gun owner responsibility should be advocated for pragmatic reasons—let's regulate ourselves before the government does. His point is normative—it's the right thing to do. Pincus rightly points out that he is identifying a common ground that should bring gun owners together with those outside the gun community: "We are *all* Pro-Gun-Responsibility."[26]

Pincus has guest lectured several times on the topic of gun owner responsibility in my Sociology of Guns seminar, especially in connection with negative outcomes like suicide. In advance of his visit in fall 2023, he offered to send me one of the PD-10 9 mm pistols his company, Avidity Arms, recently brought to market for my students to use during our field trip to the gun range. I was pleased when I opened the case to find a Walk the Talk America guns and mental health information card and sticker. I was even more impressed when I took the gun out and saw a phrase laser cut into the case's custom foam: "Rights Come with Responsibilities."

Although I disagree with David Frum's conclusion about the possibility of responsible gun ownership, I join Rob Pincus and others in full agreement that there is room for improvement. As Frum worries, "The mass gun purchases of 2020 and 2021 have put even more millions of

"Rights Come with Responsibilities" laser engraved in the custom foam for the Avidity Arms PD-10 pistol (photograph courtesy Sandra Stroud Yamane).

weapons into even more hands untrained to use and store those weapons responsibly."[27]

I disclosed in Chapter 7 that when I was a new gun owner, I negligently discharged a round into the floor of my apartment. Two years later, TSA agents at the airport in Greensboro found a loaded pistol magazine I forgot was in the satchel I was carrying. Thankfully, those have been my only two serious mistakes, and I have worked hard to become a more responsible gun owner over the years (see Chapter 8). Because "eternal vigilance is the price of liberty," gun owners should always work on being more responsible themselves and building a culture of responsible gun ownership by encouraging others.

Guns should be responsibly stored or staged. Responsibly means not accessible by those who are "untrained, unable to control firearms owing to strength/age, unable to understand risks, [or who have] altered judgment or perception." Although definitions of "safe storage" vary from study to study, the best available evidence suggests that gun owners are getting better but still have room for improvement. Data from the 2021 National Firearms Survey found that 44.1 percent of gun-owning households with children stored all of their firearms locked and unloaded, up from 29 percent in the 2015 National Firearms Survey. In 15 percent of households with children, at least one firearm was kept loaded and unlocked. This could be an accident waiting to happen. Of course, room for improvement is an admittedly unscientific term. I am influenced here by Derek LeBlanc, a gun safety educator whose Kids S.A.F.E. Foundation's motto is the aspirational "ZERO firearms accidents is the only acceptable goal."[28]

Stolen firearms have long been a problem, but with more new gun owners and more public gun carry, theft of guns from cars is becoming a bigger concern. In a recent study of vehicle firearm storage among a (non-random) sample of male gun owners, forty percent of respondents said they at least occasionally stored firearms in their cars and fifteen percent of those stored them unlocked and loaded. In my old neighborhood in Winston-Salem, people frequently roam the streets at night pulling door handles in the hope of finding an unlocked car. They will take anything they find—like loose change and N95 masks from Sandy's car one night—but if they are lucky, they might get an iPad or laptop computer. And if they are very lucky, they will get a gun. This is why I hear more and more gun people shouting on social media to any gun owners who will listen, "Your car is not a holster!"[29]

Because scholars studying firearms have focused so intently on guns as risk factors for negative outcomes, we know little about what gun owners do to mitigate risk beyond storing their firearms. One of the only national surveys to investigate how much firearms training the average gun owner has found that sixty-one percent of firearms owners in 2015 reported receiving formal firearm training, roughly the same proportion as an earlier 1994 study. Reflecting informal firearm training during childhood socialization into gun ownership, those living in rural areas had the lowest rate of formal training (54.7%). More concerning was that two of the least trained demographics were those with less than a high school education (44.7%) and those with an annual household income of less than $25,000 (48.8%). This suggests that cultural and economic capital requirements can be barriers to gun safety education and training.[30]

Because gun owners are, should be, and can be more responsible, I would like to see both the government and non-governmental organizations do more to promote responsibility, instead of always seeking to punish irresponsibility. This is especially true for the neediest among us who always suffer the most from punitive regulations. Why not offer gift cards or other material incentives to attend gun safety courses or purchase gun safes? This would do more to promote public safety than gun buyback programs. Why not have mandatory firearms safety courses in schools? Even those who will never personally own guns benefit from understanding gun safety. As my occasional writing coach Brendan O'Meara's observed, "Being gun literate is a civic responsibility in a country with so many guns."

Responsible gun ownership is, after all, about safety *with* guns rather than safety *from* guns.[31]

* * *

Lesson 5: Reclaiming Conversation with Fellow Citizens About Guns

In June 2023, I participated in a public panel sponsored by the Vail Symposium called "Conversations on Controversial Issues moderated by Clay Jenkinson." The topic was gun violence. The other panelist was Josh Horwitz, long-time Executive Director of the Coalition to Stop Gun Violence and, since 2022, Co-director of the Johns Hopkins Center for Gun Violence Solutions. He actually recommended me to the organizers as a potential panelist with a different view of guns. I am grateful to him for the opportunity to discuss our differences and, more importantly, our similarities in understanding and addressing gun violence.

In just two hours we could not begin to solve what social planners call a "wicked problem"—that is, a complex problem that not only cannot easily be fixed but which resists straightforward solutions. Of course, solving the problem was not the point. The point of the event was to have a *conversation*. I think this framing is vital because, unlike a debate, no one wins a conversation. Conversations are geared toward mutual understanding and, sociologist Sherry Turkle reminds us, help to build empathy. Concern for the experiences and feelings of others is crucial to building a stronger democratic culture from the ground up. It helps us to see other people as fellow citizens. The moderator of the Vail Symposium conversation, Clay Jenkinson, is a noted public humanities scholar and first-person historical interpreter of Thomas Jefferson. He modeled recognition of the dignity of others when he met individuals before and after the event with the greeting, "Hello, citizen."[32]

Prior to the Vail Symposium, I had participated in enough face-to-face dialogues that I was convinced we need to reclaim conversations about guns from the unfortunate information silos of social media and the uncompromising world of partisan politics. I have been doing this on a small scale in my Sociology of Guns class since 2015. Although the course is best known for its gun range field trip, the work we do in class is equally important. The course seeks to approach the issue of guns in society through "reasoned discussion based on the best available information," to borrow a phrase from gun studies scholars Philip Cook and Kristin Goss.[33]

In addition to encouraging students to think like social scientists, I also want them to better understand their personal beliefs about guns. Ideally, their scholarly understanding will inform their beliefs so they can make informed choices about the place of guns in their own lives and the lives of their communities in the future. In reality, I do not delude myself by thinking that the best available information will persuade students or anyone else to change their fundamental views of guns. This was a lesson I learned the very first time I taught Sociology of Guns.

At the end of the course, I had the students reflect on their personal views of guns in light of their coursework during the semester. A very consistent theme emerged from their essays:

A full semester's worth of learning and I still draw the same conclusion.

I came into this semester very strongly anti-gun.... The material I have studied in this class has made me more passionate in my convictions.

Even though I came across such interesting perspectives on what role guns should play in American society, I still firmly believe that the fundamental right to keep and bear arms should not be infringed upon in a significant way by the United States government.

[M]y opinions about guns have not changed that much since my first paper, despite my continued effort to keep an open mind.

These end-of-semester reflections suggest something very important about our country's heated debate over guns: It may be informed, but will not be resolved, by empirical data about guns, self-defense, crime, violence, suicide, accidents, or anything else. Powerful cultural forces ensure this.

Law professors Dan Kahan and Donald Braman argue that fundamental cultural worldviews profoundly shape individuals' views of guns. These worldviews are not strongly influenced by empirical evidence; to the contrary, individuals interpret empirical evidence based on whether it agrees or disagrees with their pre-existing worldviews. Because of this, Kahan and Braman suggest that debates over guns should not set aside people's fundamental cultural beliefs and values to focus exclusively on "the evidence." Rather, in a culturally diverse society with a pluralistic political system, differences need to be brought to the fore. People on different sides of the gun debate often embrace competing visions of what a good life and a good society look like in the first place. As Kahan and Braman argue, "In order to civilize the gun debate, then, moderate citizens—the ones who are repulsed by cultural imperialism of all varieties—must ... talk through their competing visions of the good life without embarrassment. They must, in the spirit of genuine democratic deliberation, appeal to one another for understanding and seek policies that accommodate their respective worldviews."[34]

My students were skeptical when they read Kahan and Braman's value-based deliberative solution because in our acrimonious political culture—especially as it concerns guns—we do not have good models for engaging in civilized conversation. They have observed over and over how people on both sides view their opponents not only as different but as wrong, not only as wrong but as corrupt, not only as corrupt but as evil. I reminded them that over the course of the semester they modeled the kind of respectful discussion and disagreement that Kahan and Braman recommend. It may be possible to talk through our differences toward democratically agreed-upon practices and policies that would "reduce the problems of misuse while preserving the benefit of normal prudent use" of firearms, as Cook and Goss suggest.[35]

Even though the Sociology of Guns seminar did not change anyone's fundamental views about guns, having civil conversations did affect the students in important ways. This was again evident in their final class reflections:

> I think I have come to truly embrace a middle-ground approach that is less politically dogmatic, and I know for sure that I have a far more vested interest in the continued conversation of addressing the role that guns should and do play in our society.
>
> The significant ideological diversity of those in this seminar made it possible to hear a variety of viewpoints on guns, some of which I had never heard before, in an open, respectful setting. For that I am especially grateful because opportunities to debate contentious issues in such a way do not occur very often in today's partisan political environment.

My students—from a Christian pacifist to a card-carrying member of the NRA—did an amazing job of engaging in reasoned and respectful discussions with each other across their differences. They treated each other as fellow citizens. This has implications beyond the walls of our classroom. Ideological diversity is not just a fact of life in the U.S. today but, as social psychologist Jonathan Haidt has argued, can be a deliberative strength when "individuals feel some common bond or shared fate that allows them to interact civilly."[36]

To reclaim the benefits of civil conversations about guns, we need to get out of our echo chambers. I agree with pathbreaking gun studies scholar Jennifer Carlson that a robust democracy in America depends on the willingness of gun people and non-gun people across the political spectrum to approach each other with civic grace. Civic grace is "political compassion toward one's fellow citizens" and acceptance of their "sincerity of political expression and legitimacy of political standing." Ultimately, it allows us to embrace each other "as equal citizens and fellow humans" despite our differences.[37]

Because so many gun spaces are traditionally occupied by conservatives, becoming a gun owner got me out of my blue bubble. I was not "red-pilled," as some alt-right culture warriors might hope. When I became an armed American, I did not cease to be a liberal professor. I have, however, gotten to know many people who are demographically and culturally different from those I know best from my twenty-five years of full-time work as a sociologist. My journey inside American gun culture has allowed me to meet and befriend many people with whom I have little in common other than our citizenship and humanity. This is the most important lesson of all.

Chapter Notes

Preface

1. Kaufman, Scott Barry. "The Opposite of Toxic Positivity." *The Atlantic* (online), August 18, 2021. https://www.theatlantic.com/family/archive/2021/08/tragic-optimism-opposite-toxic-positivity/619786/; Yamane 2017, 2022.
2. Kidd and Hayden 2015.
3. Berger 1963, pp. 23–24.
4. Winkler 2011.

Introduction

1. Thanks to my friends John Correia of Active Self Protection and Robin Lindner of RLI Media, a video of this speech is available on my "Light Over Heat" YouTube channel (http://www.lightoverheat.com).
2. Karl Marx, "18th Brumaire of Louis Bonaparte" (1852), https://www.marxists.org/archive/marx/works/1852/18th-brumaire/ch01.htm.
3. After my father died in February 2023, I learned that he owned a revolver that he gave to my mom's brother before traveling overseas in the 1960s.
4. Hofstadter 1970.
5. Haag 2016.
6. In this sense, *Gun Curious* can be read as an updating and extension of Abigail A. Kohn's underappreciated book, *Shooters* (Kohn 2004).
7. 1999 and 2013 data from Pew Research Center, "Why Own a Gun? Protection Is Now Top Reason," 12 March 2013, http://www.people-press.org/2013/03/12/why-own-a-gun-protection-is-now-top-reason/; 2019 data from Siegel and Boine 2020.

In addition to this survey data, another way of picturing the change in the center of gravity of American gun culture is to look at the predominant themes in advertising over time. With my son, Paul, and another Wake Forest University undergraduate, I examined advertisements in the National Rifle Association's official magazine, *The American Rifleman*, from 1918 to 2017 and *Guns* magazine from 1955 to 2019. We found the prevalence of hunting and sport/recreational shooting themes declined in an almost mirror image to the increase in personal protection and concealed carry themes over these time periods, with the Gun Culture 1.0 and Gun Culture 2.0 themes crossing over in the early 2010s. See Yamane, Ivory, and Yamane 2019 and Yamane, Yamane, Ivory 2020.

8. The history of gun culture above is an abbreviated version of what can be found in my scholarly publications. See Yamane 2017, 2022.

Chapter 1

1. David Yamane, "Why Surveys Underestimate Gun Ownership Rates in the U.S.," *Gun Curious* (blog), 11 February 2019, https://guncurious.wordpress.com/2019/02/11/why-surveys-underestimate-gun-ownership-rates-in-the-u-s/. On gun ownership surveys, see also Bond, et al. 2023; LeCount 2022; Kellerman, et al. 1990. My calculation of 400 million guns owned is based on the Small Arms Survey's estimate of 393 million civilian firearms in the U.S. in 2018, adjusted upward for the subsequent two years. Given the great gun buying spree of 2020

and 2021, 400 million is likely an underestimate today. See Small Arms Survey,
"Global Firearms Holdings," https://www.
smallarmssurvey.org/database/global-
firearms-holdings.

2. Although I believe most surveys
underestimate the rate of gun ownership in the United States, the number of
gun owners used in these calculations is
30 percent (from the Pew Research Center) of 255.2 million adults in 2019, or
76.5 million. Because the denominator
is so large in these calculations, using a
higher estimate of personal gun ownership rates would only change these results
slightly in any event. Figures for homicide and suicide in 2019 are from UC
Davis Health, "Facts and Figures," https://
health.ucdavis.edu/what-you-can-do/
facts.html. Accidental death for 2019 is
from the Gun Violence Archive, https://
www.gunviolencearchive.org/reports.
Nonfatal firearms injury for 2017 is from
Everytown Research & Policy, "A More
Complete Picture: The Contours of Gun
Injury in the United States," 4 December 2020, https://everytownresearch.org/
report/nonfatals-in-the-us/.

3. Kurzman 2019.

4. Yamane 2017.

5. Wright and Marston 1975, p. 106;
O'Connor and Lizotte 1978, p. 428. James
Wright's 1995 essay, "Ten Essential Observations on Guns in America," has been
foundational to my thinking about guns.

6. Patrick Sauer, "Bullets Travel at 1,700
Miles Per Hour. These Stunning Images
Capture What Happens After Impact," *The
Trace*, 28 July 2017, https://www.thetrace.
org/2017/07/hail-garret-hansen-guns-
fine-arts/.

7. From Hansen's website, "HAIL Statement," https://www.garrettohansen.com/
hail/statement.

8. Legault, Hendrix, and Lizotte 2019,
p. 533.

9. Mitenbuler 2015.

10. Centers for Disease Control and Prevention, "Alcohol Use and Your Health,"
23 March 2023, https://www.cdc.gov/
alcohol/fact-sheets/alcohol-use.htm.

11. Ted Alcorn, "Blind Drunk," *New
Mexico In Depth*, 24 July 2022, https://
nmindepth.com/2022/blind-drunk/;
Consortium for Risk-Based Firearm Policy and Center for Gun Violence Solutions

at the Johns Hopkins Bloomberg School of
Public Health, "Alcohol Misuse and Gun
Violence: An Evidence-Based Approach
for State Policy," May 2023, https://
publichealth.jhu.edu/sites/default/files/
2023-05/2023-may-cgvs-alcohol-misuse-
and-gun-violence.pdf.

12. To quote a historic front-page *New
York Times* editorial following the terrorist attack at the Inland Regional Center in
San Bernardino, California in December
2015. "End the Gun Epidemic in America,"
5 December 2015, https://www.nytimes.
com/2015/12/05/opinion/end-the-gun-
epidemic-in-america.html.

13. Alcorn, "Blind Drunk."

14. Parker, et al. 2017.

15. Phillip B. Levine and Robin McK-
night, "Three Million More Guns: The
Spring 2020 Spike in Firearm Sales," *Brook-
ings* (blog), 13 July 2020, https://www.
brookings.edu/blog/up-front/2020/07/13/
three-million-more-guns-the-spring-
2020-spike-in-firearm-sales/. COVID-19
buying spree: Trent Steidley, "How Unprecedented Was the Gun Buying Spree of
March 2020," *Gun Curious* (blog), 19
April 2020, https://guncurious.wordpress.
com/2020/04/19/how-unprecedented-
was-the-gun-buying-spree-of-march-
2020-by-trent-steidley/. Obama gun sales:
Depetris-Chauvin 2015.

16. Trent Steidley, "Quick Compare:
2020 vs 2019 NICS Numbers" (personal
blog), 14 January 2021, https://socsteidley.
com/2021/01/14/quick-compare-2020-
vs-2019-nics-numbers/; National Shooting Sports Foundation, "Taking Stock
of a Record-Setting 2020 Firearm Year,"
7 January 2021, https://www.nssf.org/
taking-stock-of-record-setting-2020-
firearm-year/.

17. Sabrina Tavernise, "An Arms Race
in America: Gun Buying Spiked During
the Pandemic. It's Still Up," *New York
Times*, 29 May 2021, https://www.nytimes.
com/2021/05/29/us/gun-purchases-
ownership-pandemic.html; Miller, Zhang,
and Azrael 2022.

18. McPherson, Smith-Lovin, and Cook
2001.

19. Joslyn 2020.

20. Jonathan Metzl, "Social Science and the Future of Gun Research,"
Items: Insights from the Social Sciences
(blog), 2 October 2018, https://items.ssrc.

org/understanding-gun-violence/social-science-and-the-future-of-gun-research/. Also Metzl 2019a, 2019b, 2024.

21. "These Are the 10 Most Redneck Cities in North Carolina," *RoadSnacks,* 13 August 2015, https://www.roadsnacks.net/most-redneck-cities-in-north-carolina/.

Chapter 2

1. "Survivor: The Australian Outback," *Wikipedia,* https://en.wikipedia.org/wiki/Survivor:_The_Australian_Outback.
2. "The Liberal Gun Owners Mission," https://www.liberalgunowners.org/our-mission; "The Founding of the Liberal Gun Owners Online Discussion Community," https://www.liberalgunowners.org/our-story.
3. *The Human-Weapon Relationship* is the first of four papers ("pillars") Randy Miyan has planned. As the subtitle declares, they will collectively constitute *A Comprehensive, Contemporary Analysis of the Relationship between Humans and Firearms in Four Pillars.* The forthcoming Pillars 2 through 4 will address law, culture and society, and policy.
4. Miyan 2021, pp. 1, 2, 60; Shea 2009.
5. Shea 2009.
6. Human uniqueness problem: Marean 2015. Prosociality: Bingham 2000, 248. Punish cheaters: Bingham 1999, p. 135.
7. Bingham and Souza 2009, pp. 4–5.
8. Miyan 2021, p. 67.
9. Miyan 2021, p. 67.
10. David Kopel, "Firearms Technology and the Original Meaning of the Second Amendment," *Washington Post,* 3 April 2017, https://www.washingtonpost.com/news/volokh-conspiracy/wp/2017/04/03/firearms-technology-and-the-original-meaning-of-the-second-amendment/.
11. Miyan 2021, p. 73.
12. Miyan 2021, p. 47.
13. Miyan 2021, p. 129.
14. Brown 2016, p. 152, quoted in Miyan 2021, p. 59; Bingham and Souza 2009, p. 484, quoted in Miyan 2021, p. 46.
15. Carlson 2019. *District of Columbia vs. Heller,* 554 U.S. 570 (2008) available online at https://supreme.justia.com/cases/federal/us/554/570/; *McDonald v. City of Chicago,* 561 U.S. 742 (2010)

available online at https://supreme.justia.com/cases/federal/us/561/742/; and *New York State Rifle & Pistol Association, Inc. v. Bruen,* 597 U.S. ___ (2022) available online at https://supreme.justia.com/cases/federal/us/597/20-843/.
16. Lindgren and Heather 2002.

Chapter 3

1. Lois Beckett, "Meet America's gun super-owners—With An Average of 17 Firearms Each," *The Trace,* 20 September 2016, https://www.thetrace.org/2016/09/gun-super-owners-harvard-survey/; Lois Beckett, "Gun Inequality: U.S. Study Charts Rise of Hardcore Super Owners," *The Guardian,* 19 September 2016, https://www.theguardian.com/us-news/2016/sep/19/us-gun-ownership-survey; Bryan Schatz, "This Stat about Gun Ownership in America Is Nuts," *Mother Jones,* 19 September 2016, https://www.motherjones.com/politics/2016/09/gun-ownership-america-super-owners/. Published findings from 2015 National Firearms Survey: Azrael, et al. 2017. These "hardcore super owners" claimed personal arsenals ranging from 8 to 140 firearms. A replication of this National Firearms Survey in 2019 by the same research team again found that approximately three percent of the U.S. adult population owns half of all guns, though the largest collection reported in the survey increased to 302 guns. See Berrigan, Azrael, and Miller 2022.
2. Subsequently published as Yamane 2016.
3. Hepburn, et al. 2007.
4. Joslyn 2020, p. 117.
5. Berrigan, Azrael, and Miller 2022. I am using "arsenal" here in the colloquial sense of a collection of firearms rather than the technical sense of a place where arms are manufactured, stored, and/or repaired.
6. Chase 2008, p. 25.
7. North Carolina State Statutes, Article 52A: Sale of Weapons in Certain Counties, G.S. 14–402: Sale of certain weapons without permit forbidden, modified by SL 2023–8 (S41), https://www.ncleg.gov/Laws/GeneralStatuteSections/Chapter14.
8. Barrett 2012.
9. Azrael, et al. 2017, p. 44.

10. Beckett, "Meet America's gun super-owners."

11. Elizabeth MacBride, "The Second Amendment Is a Marketing Slogan, and Other Lessons from the Gun Business Beat," *Forbes*, 1 March 2019, https://www.forbes.com/sites/elizabethmacbride/2019/03/01/the-second-amendment-is-a-marketing-tool-and-other-lessons-from-the-gun-business-beat/.

Chapter 4

1. Following McWhirter and Elinson 2023, for simplicity's sake, I use "AR-15" to stand for all rifles descended from the light infantry weapon designed by Eugene Stoner and adopted by the U.S. military as the M16 rifle and M4 carbine.

2. McWhirter and Elinson 2023, pp. 292, 305.

3. Although this conversation is hypothetical, "built on the backs of the grade school children who continually forfeit their lives" is a quote from a review of my proposal for this book, and "Come on. You're too smart to buy what you are peddling here" is a quote from a college friend of mine who reviewed of an earlier version of this chapter.

4. For those wanting AR-15 red meat to chew on see pro-gun Halbrook 2022 and anti-gun Diaz 2013.

5. Taylor 2013.

6. I am indebted to Ashley Hlebinsky for input on this point. On competition and diversion: Cramer 2018.

7. As political philosopher Timothy Luke has written about the AR-15, "The condemnation of this particular gun as a weapon of war is perplexing" (2019, p. 79).

8. I am indebted to feedback I received on this point from my fellow sociologist and Academy Professor in the Army Cyber Institute Maj. Jessica Dawson, Ph.D.

9. McWhirter and Elinson 2023, p. 46. See also Bartocci 2004; Chivers 2010; Rose 2008; Stevens and Ezell 2004.

10. Rose 2008, pp. 359–61; McWhirter and Elinson 2023, pp. 37–41.

11. Rose 2008, p 362.

12. Quote is from McWhirter and Elison 2023, p. 65. I received additional input from Reed Knight, Stoner's friend and collaborator, via Ashley Hlebinsky.

13. McWhirter and Elinson 2023, p. 152.

14. McWhirter and Elinson 2023, pp. 153–54, 208, 239; also Busse 2021.

15. Todd C. Frankel, Shawn Boburg, Josh Dawsey, Ashley Parker, and Alex Horton, "The Gun That Divides a Nation," *Washington Post* 27 March 2023, https://www.washingtonpost.com/nation/interactive/2023/ar-15-america-gun-culture-politics/; Alex Horton, Monique Woo, and Tucker Harris, "Flannel, Muddy Girl Camo and Man Cards. See the Ads Used to Sell the AR-15," *Washington Post*, 11 April 2023, https://www.washingtonpost.com/business/interactive/2023/history-of-ar-15-marketing/.

On militarization as an old strategy for marketing guns: David Yamane, "Is Gun Culture Becoming Militarized?" *Gun Curious* (blog), 28 February 2020, https://guncurious.wordpress.com/2020/02/28/is-gun-culture-becoming-militarized/. For my thoughts on AR-15s and defensive gun training see: "Why Can't the U.S. Stop Mass Shootings?" *VICE News*, 15 December 2022, https://www.youtube.com/watch?v=z3yihywux_o.

16. Guskin, Emily, Aadit Tambe, and Jon Gerberg, "Why Do Americans Own AR-15s?" *Washington Post*, 27 March 2023, https://www.washingtonpost.com/nation/interactive/2023/american-ar-15-gun-owners/.

17. McWhirter and Elinson 2023, p. xii. Tom Gresham tweeting from his @Guntalk account, 24 November 2021.

18. Josh Altimari and Dave Kovner, "Courant Exclusive: More Than 1,000 Pages of Documents Reveal Sandy Hook Shooter Adam Lanza's Dark Descent into Depravity," *Hartford Courant*, 9 December 2018, https://www.courant.com/news/connecticut/hc-news-sandy-hook-lanza-new-documents-20181204-story.html.

19. Erik Spanberg, "Charlotte Gun Shop Breaks Sales Records after Newtown," *Charlotte Business Journal*, 20 December 2012, https://www.bizjournals.com/charlotte/blog/queen_city_agenda/2012/12/charlotte-gun-shop-breaks-sales.html.

20. "Sandy Hook Families' Lawsuit against Gunmaker Heads to Connecticut Supreme Court," *CBS This Morning*, 14 November 2017, https://www.cbsnews.

com/news/sandy-hook-families-lawsuit-remington-ar-15-connecticut-supreme-court/.

21. "Man card" campaign: McWhirter and Elinson 2023, pp. 251–53. Hegemonic masculinity and guns: Stroud 2016. More complex analyses of gender and guns: Browder 2006; McCaughey 1997; Yamane, Satterwhite, and Yamane 2021.

22. Though the Sig Sauer MCX rifle used in the Pulse Nightclub shooting bears a family resemblance to the AR-15, its internal functioning differs so many do not consider it a direct descendent of the AR-15. Thanks to Danny Michael for guidance on this distinction.

23. Kieran Healy, "Rituals of Childhood," *Kieran Healy* (blog), 3 August 2019, https://kieranhealy.org/blog/archives/2019/08/03/rituals-of-childhood/.

24. On twentieth-century mass murder: Duwe 2007. Violence Project data: "Key Findings," *The Violence Project* (webpage), https://www.theviolenceproject.org/key-findings/. On *Mother Jones* data: Chris Wilson, "41 Years of Mass Shootings in the U.S. in One Chart," *Time,* 16 April 2021, https://time.com/4965022/deadliest-mass-shooting-us-history/.

25. For the inverse of this argument, see Buttrick 2020.

26. Oliver Roeder, "The Phrase 'Mass Shooting' Belongs to the 21st Century," *FiveThirtyEight* (blog), 21 January 2016. https://fivethirtyeight.com/features/we-didnt-call-them-mass-shootings-until-the-21st-century/. Culture of fear: Glassner 2010; Gardner 2008.

27. Follman 2022; Schweit 2021; Van Dreal 2016; Peterson and Densley 2021.

28. My elaborated reply: "New York Times Editorial Morally Shames Gun Owners," *Gun Culture 2.0* (blog), 5 December 2015, https://gunculture2point0.wordpress.com/2015/12/05/new-york-times-editorial-morally-shames-gun-owners/.

29. Adam Gopnik, "In the Wake of the Las Vegas Shooting, There Can Be No Truce with the Second Amendment," *The New Yorker,* 12 October 2017, https://www.newyorker.com/news/daily-comment/after-the-las-vegas-shooting-there-can-be-no-truce-with-the-second-amendment.

30. Luke 2019, p. 85. Of course, "sporting purposes" is legal language that has been used to restrict guns, so the most fervent supporters of the Second Amendment right to own AR-15s rarely emphasize sport as a fundamental argument for ownership.

31. Jon Stokes, "The AR-15 Is More Than a Gun. It's a Gadget," *Wired,* 25 February 2013, https://www.wired.com/2013/02/ar-15/. Stokes extends this take to cover many additional reasons, including hunting and self-defense, in "Why Millions of Americans—Including Me—Own the AR-15," *Vox,* 20 June 2016, https://www.vox.com/2016/6/20/11975850/ar-15-owner-orlando. Also Baum 2013, ch. 1. On everyday craftspeople: Luke 2019, p. 84.

32. "Did Democrat Rep. Eric Swalwell 'Suggest Nuking' Gun Owners Who Resist Confiscation?" *Snopes* (website), 19 November 2018, https://www.snopes.com/fact-check/eric-swalwell-gun-owners-nukes/.

33. Hammes 2006.

34. Miyan 2021, pp. 102–104, 117–119.

35. Leonhard 2019.

36. Guskin, Tambe, and Gerberg, "Why Do Americans Own AR-15s?"; English 2022, p. 34.

37. Jennifer Brett, "'He had an AR-15, but so did I.' Sutherland Springs hero hailed by NRA," *Atlanta Journal-Constitution,* 6 May 2018, https://www.ajc.com/blog/buzz/had-but-did-sutherland-springs-hero-hailed-nra/QAO2FwB8GcBBNdrax24lGO/; Hannah Leone, "Gun instructor uses AR-15 to stop attacker in Oswego," *Chicago Tribune,* 1 March 2018, https://www.chicagotribune.com/suburbs/aurora-beacon-news/ct-abn-oswego-stabbing-charges-st-0227-20180227-story.html; David K. Li, "Pregnant Florida woman uses AR-15 to fatally shoot armed intruder," *NBC News,* 4 November 2019, https://www.nbcnews.com/news/us-news/home-invader-fatally-shot-florida-pregnant-woman-ar-15-n1076026.

38. "John Johnston: No One Needs a Gun Until They Do," *Gun Culture 2.0* (blog), 11 October 2020, https://gunculture2point0.wordpress.com/2020/10/11/john-johnston-no-one-needs-a-gun-until-they-do/.

Chapter 5

1. *District of Columbia vs. Heller,* 554 U.S. 570 (2008) available online at

https://supreme.justia.com/cases/federal/ us/554/570/; *McDonald v. City of Chicago*, 561 U.S. 742 (2010) available online at https://supreme.justia.com/cases/ federal/us/561/742/; and *New York State Rifle & Pistol Association, Inc. v. Bruen*, 597 U.S. ___ (2022) available online at https://supreme.justia.com/cases/federal/ us/597/20-843/.

2. This chapter focuses on the *concealed* carry of firearms in public. While concealed carry rights have fluctuated over time, *open* carry of firearms in public has often been legal even in states that restricted concealed carry. North Carolina has always allowed anyone eighteen years of age or older who can legally possess a firearm to carry it in public without a permit (with the exception of a Civil War-era Confederate law banning open carry from 1861 to 1865). Similarly, in Wyoming "peaceable open firearm carriage has almost always been allowed everywhere" in the 150 years since it was organized as a U.S. territory (Mocsary and Person 2021, p. 343).

3. On the extraordinarily dynamic consequences of the *Bruen* decision generally, two key works are Johnson, et al. 2021 and Charles 2023.

4. Limp-wristing, I came to learn, is a colloquial expression for not having a strong enough grip and a firm enough wrist to allow a semi-automatic pistol to cycle properly.

5. I discuss this history at more length in Yamane 2021b. In addition to this southern model of banning concealed carry, a northern model of regulating public gun carry developed during this time. This "Massachusetts Model" was formalized in 1836 and later adopted by states including Maine, Pennsylvania, Wisconsin, Michigan, Minnesota, Oregon, and even the Old Dominion state of Virginia. This model limited public weapon carry to those who had "a reasonable cause to fear an assault or other injury, or violence to his person, or to his family or property." If another person had "reasonable cause to fear an injury, or breach of the peace," the accused would have to prove their good cause for carrying a weapon. If a justice of the peace found a violation of the law, the defendant would have to provide "sureties for his keeping the Peace"—essentially

posting a bond that would be forfeited upon a further violation of the public carry law in a certain time period. If the bond could not be posted, as was often the case, the accused could be jailed, fined, or both (Ruben and Cornell 2015). In time, these Massachusetts Model surety laws were replaced by the kind of discretionary concealed carry permitting systems exemplified by New York's Sullivan Law and other may issue permitting regimes (Charles 2016).

6. On Sullivan Laws: Kennett and Anderson 1975, pp. 172–75. On discretionary permitting systems: Cramer and Kopel 1994, p. 681.

7. CA Penal Code Section 26150 (2022), https://law.justia.com/codes/ california/2022/code-pen/part-6/title-4/ division-5/chapter-4/section-26150/.

8. Tehama County Sheriff's Office, "Concealed Weapons," https://tehamaso. org/concealed-weapons. When Kain was elected Sheriff-Coroner in 2023, he kept the same language as his predecessor, Dave Hencratt, who served from 2011 to 2023. For an interactive map showing California Department of Justice data on concealed carry permits issued by county, see Ben Christopher, "A Boom for Concealed Carry Classes, but Long Waits for Permits," *CalMatters*, 21 March 2023, http://calmatters.org/politics/2023/03/ california-concealed-carry-permits/.

9. Christopher, "A Boom for Concealed Carry Classes."

10. Paul Gackle, "Naked man who allegedly terrorized BART riders arrested in S.F.," *San Francisco Examiner*, 18 June 2013, https://www.sfexaminer.com/news/ naked-man-who-allegedly-terrorized-bart-riders-arrested-in-s-f/.

11. See data from California Department of Justice's Bureau of Firearms for 2014 reported by Matt Drange, "Want to carry a concealed gun? Live in Sacramento, not San Francisco," *Reveal*, 12 June 2015, https://www.revealnews.org/article/ want-to-carry-a-concealed-gun-live-in-sacramento-not-san-francisco/. Recent data from Christopher, "A Boom for Concealed Carry Classes."

12. Connecticut's high permitting rate shows the difficulty of classifying it as clearly either may issue or shall issue. Delaware's permit application process is

particularly onerous. See Yamane 2021b, pp. 82–83n21 on Connecticut and pp. 27–28 on Delaware. Data on 2022 permitting rates are from Lott 2022.

13. On the Concealed Carry Improvement Act: Bernabei 2023. On the issue of "sensitive places": Charles, Blocher, and Miller 2023.

14. Cramer and Kopel 1994, p. 687. Washington's early shall issue law also occasioned the first empirical study of concealed weapon permits, Northwood, Westgard, and Barb, Jr. 1978.

15. Cramer and Kopel, 1994, p. 687; Grossman and Lee 2008; Steidley 2019.

16. Yamane 2021b, Table 1, pp. 38–39.

17. Language in the Supreme Court's *Heller* decision highlights the constitutionality of these restrictions on where citizens can carry concealed weapons: "[N]othing in our opinion should be taken to cast doubt on longstanding prohibitions on ... laws forbidding the carrying of firearms in sensitive places such as schools and government buildings" (*District of Columbia vs. Heller*, 554 U.S. 570, 629 [2008]). Limits on sensitive places are allowable according to the concurring opinion in the *Bruen* case written by Justices Kavanaugh and Roberts. In the post-*Bruen* era now unfolding, states like New York, New Jersey, California, and Maryland are attempting to define expansively the Constitutionally allowable "sensitive places" where gun carrying can be forbidden. See Darrell A.H. Miller, "The Next Front in the Fight Over Guns," *Washington Post*, 6 July 2022, https://www.washingtonpost.com/outlook/2022/07/01/bruen-guns-rights-carry-sensitive-places/. On "sensitive places doctrine" more generally: Charles, Blocher, and Miller 2023.

18. The permit arrived in the mail a month later. Mike Stuckey, "22 Minutes for a Concealed-Weapon Permit," *NBC News,* 25 March 2010, https://www.nbcnews.com/id/wbna35839541.

19. Jennifer Mascia, "26 States Will Let You Carry a Concealed Gun Without Making Sure You Know How to Shoot One," *The Trace*, 2 February 2016, http://www.thetrace.org/2016/02/live-fire-training-not-mandatory-concealed-carry-permits/.

20. Needing a 70 percent hit rate to pass, Johnston scored 78 percent (195/250) and Baker scored 76 percent (191/250). From Chris Baker, "Shooting a Carry Permit Test Blindfolded," *Lucky Gunner Lounge* (blog), 23 April 2019, https://www.luckygunner.com/lounge/shooting-a-carry-permit-test-blindfolded/.

21. Rehn and Daub 2019, p. 5.

22. Thanks to Karl Rehn for providing this important historical observation.

Chapter 6

1. Pinker 2011, p. xxi. See sociologist Andrew Papachristos's work on the network structure of gun injury and death: Papachristos, Braga, Hureau 2012; Papachristos and Wildeman 2014; Papachristos, Wildeman, and Roberto 2015.

2. I presented this as yet unpublished paper, "The Standard Model of Explaining the Irrationality of Defensive Gun Ownership," at a workshop on "The Ethics, Law, and Social Science of Firearms and Self Defense" at Saint Anselm College in November 2022.

3. Cultural theory of gun-risk perceptions: Kahan and Braman 2003. Guns not needed: Stroebe, Leander, and Kruglanski 2017, p. 1079.

4. Buttrick 2020, p. 835; Hemenway and Solnick 2015.

5. Low confidence in government: Yamane 2016. RAND Corporation, "The Challenges of Defining and Measuring Defensive Gun Use," March 2, 2018, https://www.rand.org/research/gun-policy/analysis/essays/defensive-gun-use.html.

6. Parker, et al. 2017, p. 43.

7. Cherin C. Poovey, "Lins, Strong," *Wake Forest Magazine*, 1 February 2018, https://magazine.wfu.edu/2018/02/01/lins-strong/; John Hinton, "WFU Student Recovers from Gunshot Injury," *Winston-Salem Journal*, 11 July 2016, https://journalnow.com/news/crime/wfu-student-recovers-from-gunshot-injury/article_106f9a83-96cc-5c76-bd1f-1a8bf2491a9d.html.

8. Barry Saunders, "After Being Shot and Left for Dead, College Student Is 'Good to Go,'" *The Sacramento Bee*, 4 July 2016), https://www.sacbee.com/opinion/article87608922.html.

9. Cherin C. Poovey, "Lins, Strong."

10. Ayoob 1980.

11. David Yamane, "Kyle Rittenhouse Does Not Represent American Gun Owners

Today," *The Hill*, 23 November 2021, https://thehill.com/opinion/criminal-justice/582758-kyle-rittenhouse-does-not-represent-american-gun-owners-today/.

12. James Towle, "Bad Idea," *Stop the Threat* (Sportsman Channel), 2 September 2013, http://stopthethreat.tv/stop-the-threat-bad-idea-season-3-episode-10/.

13. Becker 1998.

14. Gila Hayes, "Balancing Dangers: An Interview with John Farnam," *Armed Citizens' Legal Defense Network*, February 2012, https://armedcitizensnetwork.org/archives/253-february-2012.

15. Metzl 2019a, p. 50.

16. Will Petty quoted by John Johnston on "Full House" (Episode 211), *Ballistic Radio*, 6 June 2017, https://ballisticradio.com/2017/06/07/full-house-podcast-season-5-ballistic-radio-episode-211-june-4th-2017/. I owe the safer sex analogy to my Sociology of Guns student Bevin Burns. See her course reflection paper, "Education Really Does Have the Power to Change Lives," *Gun Curious* (blog), 23 December 2020, https://guncurious.wordpress.com/2020/12/23/sociology-of-guns-seminar-student-final-reflection-5-education-really-does-have-the-power-to-change-lives/.

17. A.C. Haskins, "Guns and (Relative) Risk Management," *Gun Culture 2.0* (blog), 22 October 2017, https://gunculture2point0.wordpress.com/2017/10/22/guns-and-relative-risk-management-by-a-c-haskins/.

18. Massad Ayoob, "The Semi-Auto Advantage," *Gun Digest,* Spring 2015, p. 17; Patrick 2009, p. 72.

Chapter 7

1. Kellermann, et al. 1992; Kellermann, et al. 1993. On the Dickey Amendment: Carlson and James 2022.

2. Kellermann, et al. 1993, p. 1090; Kellermann 1997, p. 912.

3. Dowd, et al. 2012.

4. Guns as "tools": Shapira and Simon 2018. Feature not bug: Open Source Defense, "OSD 120: Guns Are Dangerous. That's a Feature, Not a Bug," *Open Source Defense* (Substack), 7 June 2021. https://opensourcedefense.substack.com/p/osd-120-guns-are-dangerous-thats.

5. These headlines were harvested from the website of the British newspaper *The Independent* using the topic tag "accidental shooting." See https://www.independent.co.uk/topic/accidental-shooting.

6. Manseau 2016, pp. xi, 28, 30, vxiii.

7. Jennifer Mascia, "How Often Are Guns Involved in Accidental Deaths?" *The Trace*, 9 December 2022, https://www.thetrace.org/2022/12/accidental-shootings-cdc-data-children/. On paradox: Carlson and Cobb 2017.

8. The move away from the term accident reflects a broader 20th-century shift among public health scholars. Since the 1980s, accidental firearms injuries and deaths have been increasingly framed "as a social problem for which we bear both individual and collective responsibility" (Carlson and Cobb 2017, p. 398).

9. Available through *The Tactical Professor* website at https://thetacticalprofessor.net/serious-mistakes-gunowners-make/.

10. Claude Werner, "The Tactical Professor's SHOT Show Odyssey (Part II)—Site Visit to the Duel at the Dumbster," *The Tactical Professor* (blog), 28 January 2019, https://thetacticalprofessor.net/2019/01/28/the-tactical-professors-shot-show-odyssey-part-ii-site-visit-to-the-duel-at-the-dumbster/.

11. Dan Keating, "Guns Killed More Young People Than Cars Did for the First Time in 2020," *Washington Post*, 26 May 2022, https://www.washingtonpost.com/health/2022/05/25/guns-kill-more-kids-than-cars/; Lee, Douglas, and Hemenway 2022; Goldstick, Cunningham, and Carter 2022.

12. "FACT CHECK: Many More Children Die from Road Violence Than Gun Violence," *Streetsblog New York City*, 28 December 2022, https://nyc.streetsblog.org/2022/12/28/fact-check-many-more-children-die-from-road-violence-than-gun-violence/.

13. Data on accidental death were extracted from the IHME GBD study data visualizer, available at https://vizhub.healthdata.org/gbd-results/. The analyses summarized here can be found in my blog post, "From Relative Risk to Absolute Risk of Negative Outcomes with Firearms—and Back." *Gun Curious* (blog), 17 April 2023, https://guncurious.wordpress.com/2023/04/17/from-relative-risk-to-

absolute-risk-of-negative-outcomes-with-firearms-and-back/.

14. Katherine Schaeffer, "Key Facts about Americans and Guns," *Pew Research Center* (blog), 13 September 2021, https://www.pewresearch.org/fact-tank/2021/09/13/key-facts-about-americans-and-guns/. CDC data from "FastStats: Homicide," https://www.cdc.gov/nchs/fastats/homicide.htm and "FastStats: Suicide and Self-Harm Injury," https://www.cdc.gov/nchs/fastats/suicide.htm. Lifetime risk of death: Sehgal 2020.

15. Homicide data were extracted from the IHME GBD study data visualizer at https://vizhub.healthdata.org/gbd-results/. OECD member nations is from https://www.oecd.org/about/members-and-partners/. The analyses summarized here can be found in my blog post, "Exploring America's Violent Exceptionalism via the Global Burden of Disease Collaborative Network (Homicide)." *Gun Curious* (blog), 15 April 2023, https://guncurious.wordpress.com/2023/04/15/exploring-americas-violent-exceptionalism-via-the-global-burden-of-disease-collaborative-network-homicide/.

16. To wit: The death rate from drowning in Hawaii (3.09 per 100,00) is four times as high as Pennsylvania (0.68). See CDC, "Drowning Data," https://www.cdc.gov/drowning/data/index.html. The lifetime risk of death by motor vehicle accident in the U.S. is 0.93 percent, but in New York State it is only 0.42 percent and in the District of Columbia 0.46 percent (Sehgal 2020).

17. Ray 2018, p. 32.

18. Anscombe 1973.

19. Johns Hopkins Center for Gun Violence Solutions, *A Year in Review: 2020 Gun Deaths in the U.S.,* 28 April 2022, https://publichealth.jhu.edu/sites/default/files/2022-05/2020-gun-deaths-in-the-us-4-28-2022-b.pdf. Lifetime risk: Sehgal 2020.

20. Daniel Kay Hertz, "The Debate Over Crime Rates Is Ignoring the Metric That Matters Most: 'Murder Inequality,'" *The Trace,* 25 July 2016, https://www.thetrace.org/2016/07/murder-inequality-urban-violence-statistics/. State rates: Johns Hopkins Center for Gun Violence Solutions, *A Year in Review.* County rates: Reeping, et al. 2023.

21. Author's analysis of 2019 data from the IHME GBD study data visualizer at https://vizhub.healthdata.org/gbd-results/.

22. "15 Census Tracts, 97 Fatal Shootings, and the Two Different Sides to American Gun Violence," *The Trace,* 22 March 2017, https://www.thetrace.org/2017/03/gun-violence-deadliest-census-tracts/. United Nations Office on Drugs and Crime, *Global Study on Homicide,* 2019 edition, https://www.unodc.org/unodc/en/data-and-analysis/global-study-on-homicide.html.

23. Chalfin, Kaplan, and Cuellar 2021.

24. Fowler, et al. 2015; Papachristos, Braga, and Hureau 2012; Papachristos and Wildeman 2014.

25. On trauma: Madison Armstrong and Jennifer Carlson, "We've Spent Over a Decade Researching Guns in America. This Is What We Learned," *New York Times,* 26 March 2021, https://www.nytimes.com/2021/03/26/opinion/politics/gun-reform-us.html. On injury: Lee 2012. On indirect effects: Sharkey 2018.

26. Open Source Defense, "OSD 241: Violence Is like Getting into Harvard." *Open Source Defense* (Substack), 2 October 2023, https://opensourcedefense.substack.com/p/osd-241-violence-is-like-getting.

27. Heath Druzin, "The Majority of U.S. Gun Deaths Are Suicides, But a New Poll Suggests Few Americans Know It," *Guns & America,* 1 October 2019, https://gunsandamerica.org/story/19/10/01/the-majority-of-u-s-gun-deaths-are-suicides-but-a-new-poll-suggests-few-americans-know-it/; National Center for Health Statistics, "Suicide Mortality in the United States, 2001–2021," NCHS Data Brief No. 464, April 2023, https://www.cdc.gov/nchs/products/databriefs/db464.htm.

28. Martínez-Alés, et al. 2022.

29. The analyses summarized here can be found in my blog post, "Further Exploring American Exceptionalism via the Global Burden of Disease Study (Suicide)," *Gun Curious* (blog), 16 April 2023, https://guncurious.wordpress.com/2023/04/16/further-exploring-american-exceptionalism-via-the-global-burden-of-disease-study-suicide/.

30. Christopher W. Drapeau and John

L. McIntosh, "U.S.A. Suicide: 2021," *Suicide Awareness Voices of Education (SAVE)*, 12 January 2023, https://save.org/about-suicide/suicide-statistics.

31. National Center for Health Statistics, "Suicide Mortality in the United States, 2001–2021."

32. Thanks to B.J. Campbell for guidance on this point. See Siegel and Rothman 2016. One estimate of case fatality ratios for different methods of intentional self-harm finds firearms range from 83–91%, drowning ranges from 66–84%, and suffocation/hanging ranges from 61–83% (Azrael and Miller 2016).

33. Jones and Podolsky 2015.

34. Studdert, et al. 2020.

35. Lagerfeld 2000.

36. Nars 1999.

37. "National Healthcare Provider Directory," *Walk the Talk America* (website), https://walkthetalkamerica.org/provider-directory/.

38. Hemenway, et al. 2017.

39. Betz, et al. 2021.

40. Tamara Keel, "Boomsticks: CCW Safety, or 'Stop Touching That!'" *View from the Porch* (blog), 19 September 2006, https://booksbikesboomsticks.blogspot.com/2006/09/boomsticks-ccw-safety-or-stop-touching.html; Mike Weisser, "What Should Physicians Do About Guns? Tell the Truth," *Mike the Gun Guy* (blog), 18 December 2014, https://mikethegunguy.social/2014/12/18/what-should-physicians-do-about-guns-tell-the-truth/.

41. Claude Werner, "Standards (Part VIII—Trainer Standards)," *Tactical Professor* (blog), 21 May 2017, https://thetacticalprofessor.net/2017/05/21/standards-part-viii-trainer-standards/. On gun owners as liabilities, see my blog post "Distinguishing Responsibly Armed Citizens from Mere Gun Owners," *Gun Culture 2.0* (blog), 26 September 2018, https://gunculture2point0.wordpress.com/2018/09/26/distinguishing-responsibly-armed-citizens-from-mere-gun-owners/.

Chapter 8

1. Possibly coined by Jeff Cooper 2006, p. 43.

2. Michael Austin, "Virtue and Guns." *Psychology Today* (blog), 9 January 2019, https://www.psychologytoday.com/blog/ethics-everyone/201901/virtue-and-guns. See my response: David Yamane, "A Counterargument to 'Virtue and Guns.'" *Psychology Today* (blog), 24 May 2019, https://www.psychologytoday.com/us/blog/ethics-everyone/201905/counterargument-virtue-and-guns.

3. Harel Shapira, "Firearms Classes Taught Me, and America, a Very Dangerous Lesson." *The New York Times*, 16 May 2023, https://www.nytimes.com/2023/05/16/opinion/firearms-guns-america-safety.html.

4. This is what I call the Master Narrative of Democracy Destroying Right-Wing Gun Politics. Pieces of it can be found in several recently published books on guns in America, including Busse 2021; Lacombe 2021; McKevitt 2023; and Spitzer 2022.

5. Quotes in the list of conditions to be met are from *Concealed Carry Handgun Training* (Salemburg, NC: North Carolina Justice Academy, 2020), pp. 8–9. The labels in the list are adopted from Branca 2016. "Good plea bargain" is from Andrew Branca's June 2014 "Law of Self Defense" seminar I attended in Charlotte, North Carolina. Branca also made clear, "Nothing you learn today will enable you to manipulate the law of self-defense in order to commit bad acts and escape punishment."

6. "Shoot First Laws, Also Known as Stand Your Ground Laws, Are Dangerous. How Do They Encourage Violence?" *Everytown for Gun Safety* (website), 22 February 2022, https://www.everytown.org/shoot-first-stand-your-ground-laws-are-dangerous/.

7. *Concealed Carry Handgun Training,* pp. 11–13.

8. Howe 2011, p. xii.

9. Steinbeck 2008, p. 193.

10. Gibson 1994, p. 174. *New Yorker* staff writer Rachel Monroe recently characterized Cooper as "an imperious and erudite racist" in "The Last Gun I Shot," *The New Yorker*, 23 September 2023, https://www.newyorker.com/news/the-weekend-essay/the-last-gun-i-shot. My friend Jurjen Smies pointed me to the Wikipedia entry for Cooper that includes the following: "In 1991, Cooper wrote in *Guns & Ammo* magazine that 'no more

than five to ten people in a hundred who die by gunfire in Los Angeles are any loss to society. These people fight small wars amongst themselves. It would seem a valid social service to keep them well-supplied with ammunition.' In 1994, Cooper said 'Los Angeles and Ho Chi Minh City have declared themselves sister cities. It makes sense: they are both Third World metropolises formerly occupied by Americans.'" See "Jeff Cooper," *Wikipedia*, https://en.wikipedia.org/w/index.php?title=Jeff_Cooper&oldid=1176852598.

11. Morrison and Cooper 1991.

12. In her foundational study of public gun carry, Jennifer Carlson argues that "the everyday practice of gun carry sustains a model of citizenship—the citizen-protector—that celebrates the protection of self *and others* as an everyday civic duty" (emphasis added). It is common for those who advocate armed citizenship to highlight "the defense of self and others," and the Nebraska state constitution even includes language about "the right to keep and bear arms for security or defense of self, family, home, and others." But most times these "others" are within the person's immediate circle of concern. Carlson, by contrast, highlights a broadened duty to protect that for some citizen-protectors includes strangers. See Carlson 2015, pp. 19–20, 105–110.

13. Sherman A. House, "Becoming the Civilian Defender," *Civilian Defender* (blog), 14 April 2016, https://civiliandefender.com/2016/04/14/becoming-the-civilian-defender/.

14. Tam Keel, "Can't Lose a Fight You're Not In," *View From The Porch* (blog), 13 October 2018, https://booksbikesboomsticks.blogspot.com/2018/10/cant-lose-fight-youre-not-in.html.

15. Chuck Haggard, "How to Pepper Spray," *RECOIL Concealment,* 8 July 2018, https://www.recoilweb.com/how-to-pepper-spray-139086.html.

16. Claude Werner, "Another Serious Mistake," *Tactical Professor* (blog), 12 January 2016, https://thetacticalprofessor.net/2016/01/12/another-serious-mistake/.

17. David Yamane, "Stand Your Ground Laws Do Not Allow You to 'Shoot First and Ask Questions Later,'" *The Hill*, 12 April 2023, https://thehill.com/opinion/civil-rights/3962701-stand-your-ground-laws-do-not-allow-you-to-shoot-first-and-ask-questions-later/.

18. Anderson 2021; Dunbar-Ortiz 2018; Light 2017.

Conclusion

1. Bruce-Briggs 1976. "The meaning of guns" is an adaptation of the philosopher Ludwig Wittgenstein's famous contention that "For a *large* class of cases—though not for all—in which we employ the word 'meaning' it can be defined thus: the meaning of a word is its use in the language" (Wittgenstein 2009, Sect. 43).

2. David Yamane, "Taking Students to the Range to Learn About Gun Culture Firsthand," *The Conversation*, 26 June 2023, http://theconversation.com/taking-students-to-the-range-to-learn-about-gun-culture-firsthand-205553.

3. Crowder, Forrester, and Morgan 2016, p. 267.

4. Anthropologist Abigail Kohn uses the phrase "gun enthusiasm" to characterize the orientation of the sport shooters she studied. "At its most basic, gun enthusiasm is an enjoyment of and enthusiasm for firearms" (Kohn 2004, p. 9).

5. This is the subject of my next book on guns and is explained in Yamane 2017, 2022.

6. Luke 2019, p. 75. Concern about defensive gun ownership: Buttrick 2020; Donohue 2022.

7. Buttrick 2020; Donohue 2022.

8. Cobb 2015, p. 7.

9. King quoted in Cobb 2015, pp. 8–9; Blackstone 1979. See also Hessbruegge 2017.

10. Miyan 2021, p. 111.

11. Stroud 2012, p. 216; Fiske and Rai 2014, p. 30.

12. Luke 2019, p. 75; Fiske and Rai 2015, p. 36.

13. Pinker 2011, p. xxi. At least as concerns interpersonal physical violence, not structural violence, and only if we consider the 12,000 years since the agricultural revolution around 10,000 BCE, according to peace studies scholar Douglas P. Fry's review of Pinker ("Peace in Our Time," *Bookforum*, January 2012). Larkin 2017, pp. 5, 134.

14. Larkin 2017, p. 3.
15. Firmin DeBrabander, "The Gun-Rights Movement Fed America's Insurrectionist Fever Dreams," *The Atlantic*, 11 January 2021, https://www.theatlantic.com/ideas/archive/2021/01/nra-americas-insurrectionist-fever-dreams/617627/.
16. Yamane 2021a, p. 177.
17. Turner 1967, ch. 4.
18. POTUS-45 AR-15 lower receiver: David Yamane, "I May Never Be Fully at Home in Gun Culture." *Gun Culture 2.0* (blog), 18 January 2018, https://gunculture2point0.wordpress.com/2018/01/18/i-may-never-be-fully-at-home-in-gun-culture/.
19. See also Annette S. L. Evans, "As an Asian American Woman, I've Realized No One Is Coming to Save Me," *Philadelphia Inquirer*, 15 April 2021, https://www.inquirer.com/opinion/commentary/asian-americans-attacks-safety-self-defense-gender-violence-20210415.html.
20. In addition to David Frum in this chapter, another recent example is Project Unloaded (projectunloaded.org) and their "SNUG campaign" targeting teens on social media with the message: Safer Not Using Guns. See also founder and Executive Director Nina Vinik's opinion, "I Sat Next to a Gun 'Fanatic' on a Plane. When I Told Him What My Job Is, Things Got Interesting," *HuffPost* (website), 17 October 2023, https://www.huffpost.com/entry/second-amendment-fanatic-gun-violence_n_6505e5a7e4b045a142a4c2a0.
21. On master narrative: Dunbar-Ortiz 2018; Anderson 2021; Light 2017. On alternative narratives: Johnson 2014; McCaughey 1997; Combs 2022.
22. Miller, Zhang, and Azrael 2022.
23. On the NRA's creation of a politically conservative gun owner identity over the years: Lacombe 2021. Tragic

optimism: Kaufman, "The Opposite of Toxic Positivity."
24. David Frum, "Responsible Gun Ownership Is a Lie," *The Atlantic*, October 2021, https://www.theatlantic.com/magazine/archive/2021/10/responsible-gun-ownership-is-a-lie/619811/.
25. Gössling, Kees, and Litman 2022; Andor, et al. 2020.
26. Rob Pincus, "Gun Rights and Responsibility Manifesto," *Second Amendment Organization* (blog), 29 September 2018, https://www.2ao.org/gun-rights-and-responsibility-manifesto/.
27. David Frum, "Responsible Gun Ownership Is a Lie."
28. Responsible storage and staging: Rob Pincus's perspective is clearly reflected in the article quoted here, Betz, et al. 2021. On storage of firearms in homes with children: Miller and Azrael 2022. The Kids S.A.F.E. (Safe Around Firearms Education) Foundation website is https://kidssafefoundation.org/.
29. On vehicle storage: Tucker, et al. 2023.
30. On firearm training data: Rowhani-Rahbar, et al. 2018.
31. David Yamane, "What We Talk About When We Talk About 'Gun Safety,'" *BulletPoints Project* (blog), 18 October 2022, https://www.bulletpointsproject.org/blog/what-we-talk-about-when-we-talk-about-gun-safety/.
32. Wicked problem: Taken from conversations with Randy Miyan, who attributes the concept to Rittel and Webber 1973. On conversation and empathy: Turkle 2015.
33. Cook and Goss 2014, p. 220.
34. Kahan and Braman 2003, pp. 1321–22.
35. Cook and Goss 2014, p. 220.
36. Haidt 2013, p. 105.
37. Carlson 2023, pp. 174, 181.

Bibliography

I list here books, scholarly articles, and other major sources referenced in the Chapter Notes. Full citations to online sources, blogs, news stories, and the like are provided in the notes.

Anderson, Carol. 2021. *The Second: Race and Guns in a Fatally Unequal America*. New York: Bloomsbury.

Andor, Mark A., Andreas Gerster, Kenneth T. Gillingham, and Marco Horvath. 2020. "Running a Car Costs Much More Than People Think—Stalling the Uptake of Green Travel." *Nature* 580 (7804): 453–55.

Anscombe, F.J. 1973. "Graphs in Statistical Analysis." *The American Statistician* 27 (1): 17–21.

Ayoob, Massad F. 1980. *In the Gravest Extreme: The Role of the Firearm in Personal Protection*. Concord, NH: Police Bookshelf.

Azrael, Deborah, and Matthew J. Miller. 2016. "Reducing Suicide Without Affecting Underlying Mental Health." In *The International Handbook of Suicide Prevention*, 637–62. New York: Wiley.

Azrael, Deborah, Lisa Hepburn, David Hemenway, and Matthew Miller. 2017. "The Stock and Flow of U.S. Firearms: Results from the 2015 National Firearms Survey." *RSF: The Russell Sage Foundation Journal of the Social Sciences* 3 (5): 38–57.

Barrett, Paul M. 2012. *Glock: The Rise of America's Gun*. New York: Broadway Books.

Bartocci, Christopher R. 2004. *Black Rifle II: The M16 Into the 21st Century*. Cobourg, Ontario: Collector Grade Publications.

Baum, Dan. 2013. *Gun Guys: A Road Trip*. New York: Knopf.

Becker, Gavin de. 1998. *The Gift of Fear: And Other Survival Signals That Protect Us from Violence*. New York: Dell.

Berger, Peter L. 1963. *Invitation to Sociology: A Humanistic Perspective*. New York: Anchor.

Bernabei, Leo. 2023. "Taking Aim at New York's Concealed Carry Improvement Act." *Fordham Law Review* 91 (1): 103–42.

Berrigan, John, Deborah Azrael, and Matthew Miller. 2022. "The Number and Type of Private Firearms in the United States." *The ANNALS of the American Academy of Political and Social Science* 704 (1): 70–90.

Betz, Marian E., Jill Harkavy-Friedman, Fatimah Loren Dreier, Rob Pincus, and Megan L. Ranney. 2021. "Talking About 'Firearm Injury' and 'Gun Violence': Words Matter." *American Journal of Public Health* 111 (12): 2105–10.

Bingham, Paul M. 1999. "Human Uniqueness: A General Theory." *The Quarterly Review of Biology* 74 (2): 133–69.

———. 2000. "Human Evolution and Human History: A Complete Theory." *Evolutionary Anthropology: Issues, News, and Reviews* 9 (6): 248–57.

Bingham, Paul M., and Joanne Souza. 2009. *Death from a Distance and the Birth of a Humane Universe: Human Evolution, Behavior, History, and Your Future*. Charleston, SC: BookSurge Publishing.

Blackstone, William. 1979. *Commentaries on the Laws of England: A Facsimile of the First Edition of 1765-1769, Vol. 1.* Chicago: University of Chicago Press.

Bond, Allison E., Aleksandr T. Karnick, Daniel W. Capron, and Michael D. Anestis. 2023. "Predicting Potential Underreporting of Firearm Ownership in a Nationally Representative Sample." *Social Psychiatry and Psychiatric Epidemiology*, June.

Branca, Andrew F. 2016. *The Law of Self Defense: The Indispensable Guide to the Armed Citizen.* 3rd edition. West Bend, WI: Delta Defense.

Browder, Laura. 2006. *Her Best Shot: Women and Guns in America.* Chapel Hill: University of North Carolina Press.

Brown, William F. 2016. *Perspectives: The Evolution of the Cosmos, Life, Humans, Culture and Religion and a Look Into the Future.* Victoria, BC: FriesenPress.

Bruce-Briggs, B. 1976. "The Great American Gun War." *The Public Interest,* no. 45 (Fall): 37–62.

Busse, Ryan. 2021. *Gunfight: My Battle Against the Industry That Radicalized America.* New York: PublicAffairs.

Buttrick, Nicholas. 2020. "Protective Gun Ownership as a Coping Mechanism." *Perspectives on Psychological Science* 15 (4): 835–55.

Carlson, Jennifer. 2015. *Citizen-Protectors: The Everyday Politics of Guns in an Age of Decline.* New York: Oxford University Press.

———. 2019. "Revisiting the Weberian Presumption: Gun Militarism, Gun Populism, and the Racial Politics of Legitimate Violence in Policing." *American Journal of Sociology* 125 (3): 633–82.

———. 2023. *Merchants of the Right: Gun Sellers and the Crisis of American Democracy.* Princeton: Princeton University Press.

Carlson, Jennifer, and Jessica Cobb. 2017. "From Play to Peril: A Historical Examination of Media Coverage of Accidental Shootings Involving Children." *Social Science Quarterly* 98 (2): 397–412.

Carlson, Jennifer, and Rina James. 2022. "Conspicuously Concealed: Federal Funding, Knowledge Production, and the Criminalization of Gun Research." *Sociological Perspectives* 65 (1): 196–215.

Chalfin, Aaron, Jacob Kaplan, and Maria Cuellar. 2021. "Measuring Marginal Crime Concentration: A New Solution to an Old Problem." *Journal of Research in Crime and Delinquency* 58 (4): 467–504.

Charles, Jacob D. 2023. "The Dead Hand of a Silent Past: Bruen, Gun Rights, and the Shackles of History." *Duke Law Journal* 73 (1): 67–155.

Charles, Jacob D., Joseph Blocher, and Darrell A.H. Miller. 2023. "'A Map Is Not the Territory': The Theory and Future of Sensitive Places Doctrine." SSRN Scholarly Paper. Rochester, NY. https://papers.ssrn.com/abstract=4325454.

Charles, Patrick. 2016. "The Faces of the Second Amendment Outside the Home, Take Two: How We Got Here and Why It Matters." *Cleveland State Law Review* 64 (3): 373–481.

Chase, Kenneth. 2008. *Firearms: A Global History to 1700.* Cambridge: Cambridge University Press.

Chivers, C.J. 2010. *The Gun.* New York: Simon & Schuster.

Cobb, Charles E. Jr. 2015. *This Nonviolent Stuff'll Get You Killed: How Guns Made the Civil Rights Movement Possible.* Durham: Duke University Press.

Combs, Thatcher Phoenix. 2022. "Queers with Guns? Against the LGBT Grain." *Sociological Perspectives* 65 (1): 58–76.

Cook, Philip J., and Kristin A. Goss. 2014. *The Gun Debate: What Everyone Needs to Know.* New York: Oxford University Press.

Cooper, Jeff. 2006. *Principles Of Personal Defense.* Revised. Boulder, CO: Paladin Press.

Cramer, Clayton E. 2018. *Lock, Stock, and Barrel: The Origins of American Gun Culture.* Santa Barbara: Praeger.

Cramer, Clayton E., and David B. Kopel. 1994. "Shall Issue: The New Wave of Concealed Handgun Permit Laws." *Tenn. L. Rev.* 62: 679–757.

Crowder, Trae, Corey Ryan Forrester, and Drew Morgan. 2016. *The Liberal Redneck Manifesto: Draggin' Dixie Outta the Dark.* New York: Atria Books.

Depetris-Chauvin, Emilio. 2015. "Fear of Obama: An Empirical Study of the Demand for Guns and the U.S. 2008 Presidential Election." *Journal of Public Economics* 130 (October): 66–79.

Diaz, Tom. 2013. *The Last Gun: How Changes in the Gun Industry Are Killing Americans and What It Will Take to Stop It*. New York: The New Press.

Donohue, John J. 2022. "The Effect of Permissive Gun Laws on Crime." *The ANNALS of the American Academy of Political and Social Science* 704 (1): 92–117.

Dowd, M. Denise, Robert D. Sege, H. Garry Gardner, Kyran P. Quinlan, Michele Burns Ewald, Beth E. Ebel, Richard Lichenstein, et al. 2012. "Firearm-Related Injuries Affecting the Pediatric Population." *Pediatrics* 130 (5): e1416–23.

Dunbar-Ortiz, Roxanne. 2018. *Loaded: A Disarming History of the Second Amendment*. San Francisco: City Lights Publishers.

Duwe, Grant. 2007. *Mass Murder in the United States: A History*. Jefferson, NC: McFarland.

English, William. 2022. "2021 National Firearms Survey: Updated Analysis Including Types of Firearms Owned." SSRN Scholarly Paper. Rochester, NY.

Fiske, Alan Page, and Tage Shakti Rai. 2014. "Violence for Goodness' Sake." *New Scientist* 224 (2997): 30–31.

———. 2015. *Virtuous Violence: Hurting and Killing to Create, Sustain, End, and Honor Social Relationships*. Cambridge: Cambridge University Press.

Follman, Mark. 2022. *Trigger Points: Inside the Mission to Stop Mass Shootings in America*. New York: Dey Street Books.

Fowler, Katherine A., Linda L. Dahlberg, Tadesse Haileyesus, and Joseph L. Annest. 2015. "Firearm Injuries in the United States." *Preventive Medicine* 79 (October): 5–14.

Gardner, Daniel. 2018. *The Science of Fear: Why We Fear the Things We Shouldn't—and Put Ourselves in Greater Danger*. New York: Dutton.

Gibson, James William. 1994. *Warrior Dreams: Violence and Manhood in Post-Vietnam America*. New York: Hill & Wang.

Glassner, Barry. 2010. *The Culture of Fear: Why Americans Are Afraid of the Wrong Things: Crime, Drugs, Minorities, Teen Moms, Killer Kids, Mutant Microbes, Plane Crashes, Road Rage, & So Much More*. Anniversary edition. New York: Basic Books.

Goldstick, Jason E., Rebecca M. Cunningham, and Patrick M. Carter. 2022. "Current Causes of Death in Children and Adolescents in the United States." *New England Journal of Medicine* 386 (20): 1955–56.

Gössling, Stefan, Jessica Kees, and Todd Litman. 2022. "The Lifetime Cost of Driving a Car." *Ecological Economics* 194 (April): 107335.

Grossman, Richard S., and Stephen A. Lee. 2008. "May Issue Versus Shall Issue: Explaining the Pattern of Concealed-Carry Handgun Laws, 1960–2001." *Contemporary Economic Policy* 26 (2): 198–206.

Haag, Pamela. 2016. *The Gunning of America: Business and the Making of American Gun Culture*. New York: Basic Books.

Haidt, Jonathan. 2013. *The Righteous Mind: Why Good People Are Divided by Politics and Religion*. New York: Vintage.

Halbrook, Stephen P. 2022. *America's Rifle: The Case for the AR-15*. New York: Bombardier Books.

Hammes, Thomas X. 2006. *The Sling and the Stone: On War in the 21st Century*. St. Paul, MN: Zenith Press.

Hemenway, David, and Sara J. Solnick. 2015. "The Epidemiology of Self-Defense Gun Use: Evidence from the National Crime Victimization Surveys 2007–2011." *Preventive Medicine* 79 (October): 22–27.

Hemenway, David, Steven Rausher, Pina Violano, Toby A. Raybould, and Catherine W. Barber. 2019. "Firearms Training: What Is Actually Taught?" *Injury Prevention* 25 (2): 123–28.

Hepburn, Lisa, Matthew Miller, Deborah Azrael, and David Hemenway. 2007. "The US Gun Stock: Results from the 2004 National Firearms Survey." *Injury Prevention* 13 (1): 15–19.

Hessbruegge, Jan Arno. 2017. *Human Rights and Personal Self-Defense in International Law*. New York: Oxford University Press.

Hofstadter, Richard. 1970. "America as a Gun Culture." *American Heritage,* October 1970.

Howe, Paul R. 2011. *Leadership and Training for the Fight: Using Special Operations Principles to Succeed in Law Enforcement, Business, and War.* New York: Skyhorse.

Johnson, Nicholas. 2014. *Negroes and the Gun: The Black Tradition of Arms.* Amherst, NY: Prometheus Books.

Johnson, Nicholas J., David B. Kopel, George A. Mocsary, E. Gregory Wallace, and Donald E. Kilmer. 2021. *Firearms Law and the Second Amendment: Regulation, Rights, and Policy.* 3rd edition. New York: Aspen Publishing.

Jones, David S., and Scott H. Podolsky. 2015. "The History and Fate of the Gold Standard." *The Lancet* 385 (9977): 1502–3.

Jooyoung Lee. 2012. "Wounded: Life After the Shooting." *The ANNALS of the American Academy of Political and Social Science* 642 (1): 244–57.

Joslyn, Mark R. 2020. *The Gun Gap: The Influence of Gun Ownership on Political Behavior and Attitudes.* New York: Oxford University Press.

Kahan, Dan M., and Donald Braman. 2003. "More Statistics, Less Persuasion: A Cultural Theory of Gun-Risk Perceptions." *University of Pennsylvania Law Review* 151 (4): 1291–1327.

Kellermann, Arthur L. 1997. "Comment: Gunsmoke—Changing Public Attitudes toward Smoking and Firearms." *American Journal of Public Health* 87 (6): 910–13.

Kellermann, Arthur L., Frederick P. Rivara, Grant Somes, Donald T. Reay, Jerry Francisco, Joyce Gillentine Banton, Janice Prodzinski, Corinne Fligner, and Bela B. Hackman. 1992. "Suicide in the Home in Relation to Gun Ownership." *New England Journal of Medicine* 327 (7): 467–72.

Kellermann, Arthur L., Frederick P. Rivara, Joyce G. Banton, Donald T. Reay, and Corinne Fligner. 1990. "Validating Survey Responses to Questions about Gun Ownership among Owners of Registered Handguns." *American Journal of Epidemiology* 131 (6): 1080–84.

Kellermann, Arthur L., Frederick P. Rivara, Norman B. Rushforth, Joyce G. Banton, Donald T. Reay, Jerry T. Francisco, Ana B. Locci, Janice Prodzinski, Bela B. Hackman, and Grant Somes. 1993. "Gun Ownership as a Risk Factor for Homicide in the Home." *New England Journal of Medicine* 329 (15): 1084–91.

Kennett, Lee, and James LaVerne Anderson. 1975. *The Gun in America: The Origins of a National Dilemma.* Westport, CT: Praeger.

Kidd, Celeste, and Benjamin Y. Hayden. 2015. "The Psychology and Neuroscience of Curiosity." *Neuron* 88 (3): 449–60.

Kohn, Abigail A. 2004. *Shooters: Myths and Realities of America's Gun Cultures.* New York: Oxford University Press.

Kurzman, Charles. 2019. *The Missing Martyrs: Why Are There So Few Muslim Terrorists?* 2nd edition. New York: Oxford University Press.

Lacombe, Matthew J. 2021. *Firepower: How the NRA Turned Gun Owners into a Political Force.* Princeton: Princeton University Press.

Lagerfeld, Karl. 2000. *Karl Lagerfeld: Escape from Circumstances.* Göttingen: Steidl.

Larkin, Tim. 2017. *When Violence Is the Answer: Learning How to Do What It Takes When Your Life Is at Stake.* New York: Little, Brown.

LeCount, Ryan Jerome. 2022. "Who Wants to Know? White Racial Attitudes and Survey Item Refusal on Gun Ownership Questions." *Sociological Inquiry* 92 (1): 153–99.

Lee, Lois K., Katherine Douglas, and David Hemenway. 2022. "Crossing Lines—A Change in the Leading Cause of Death among U.S. Children." *New England Journal of Medicine* 386 (16): 1485–87.

Legault, Richard L., Nicole Hendrix, and Alan J. Lizotte. 2019. "Caught in a Crossfire: Legal and Illegal Gun Ownership in America." In *Handbook on Crime and Deviance,* edited by Marvin D. Krohn, Nicole Hendrix, Gina Penly Hall, and Alan J. Lizotte, 533–54. Handbooks of Sociology and Social Research. New York: Springer.

Leonhard, Robert R. 2019. "Case Studies in Insurgency and Revolutionary Warfare: The Patriot Insurgency (1763–1789)." Fort Bragg, NC: US Army Special Operations Command.

Light, Caroline. 2017. *Stand Your Ground: A History of America's Love Affair with Lethal Self-Defense.* Boston: Beacon Press.

Lindgren, James, and Justin Heather. 2002. "Counting Guns in Early America." *William & Mary Law Review* 43 (5): 1777–1842.

Lott, John R. 2022. "Concealed Carry Permit Holders Across the United States: 2022." SSRN Scholarly Paper. Rochester, NY.

Luke, Timothy W. 2019. "Counting Up AR-15s: The Subject of Assault Rifles and the Assault Rifle as Subject." In *The Lives of Guns,* edited by Jonathan Obert, Andrew Poe, and Austin Sarat, 70–92. New York: Oxford University Press.

Manseau, Peter. 2016. *Melancholy Accidents: Three Centuries of Stray Bullets and Bad Luck.* Brooklyn: Melville House.

Marean, Curtis W. 2015. "An Evolutionary Anthropological Perspective on Modern Human Origins." *Annual Review of Anthropology* 44 (1): 533–56.

Martínez-Alés, Gonzalo, Tammy Jiang, Katherine M. Keyes, and Jaimie L. Gradus. 2022. "The Recent Rise of Suicide Mortality in the United States." *Annual Review of Public Health* 43 (1): 99–116.

McCaughey, Martha. 1997. *Real Knockouts: The Physical Feminism of Women's Self-Defense.* New York: NYU Press.

McKevitt, Andrew C. 2023. *Gun Country: Gun Capitalism, Culture, and Control in Cold War America.* Chapel Hill: University of North Carolina Press.

McPherson, Miller, Lynn Smith-Lovin, and James M Cook. 2001. "Birds of a Feather: Homophily in Social Networks." *Annual Review of Sociology* 27 (1): 415–44.

McWhirter, Cameron, and Zusha Elinson. 2023. *American Gun: The True Story of the AR-15.* New York: Farrar, Straus and Giroux.

Metzl, Jonathan M. 2019a. *Dying of Whiteness: How the Politics of Racial Resentment Is Killing America's Heartland.* New York: Basic Books.

———. 2019b. "What Guns Mean: The Symbolic Lives of Firearms." *Palgrave Communications* 5 (1): 1–5.

———. 2024. *What We've Become: Living and Dying in a Country of Arms.* New York: W.W. Norton.

Miller, Matthew, and Deborah Azrael. 2022. "Firearm Storage in US Households With Children: Findings From the 2021 National Firearm Survey." *JAMA Network Open* 5 (2): e2148823.

Miller, Matthew, Wilson Zhang, and Deborah Azrael. 2022. "Firearm Purchasing During the COVID-19 Pandemic: Results From the 2021 National Firearms Survey." *Annals of Internal Medicine* 175 (2): 219–25.

Mitenbuler, Reid. 2015. *Bourbon Empire: The Past and Future of America's Whiskey.* New York: Viking.

Miyan, Randy. 2021. "The Liberal Gun Owner Lens, Pillar 1: The Human-Weapon Relationship—Evolution, Anthropology, and Human Innateness." https://lgolens.com/anthropillar/.

Mocsary, George, and Debora Person. 2021. "A Brief History of Public Carry in Wyoming." *Wyoming Law Review* 21 (2): 341–68.

Morrison, Gregory B., and Jeff Cooper. 1991. *The Modern Technique of the Pistol.* Paulden, AZ: Gunsite Press.

Nars, Francois. 1999. *X-Ray.* New York: powerHouse Books.

Northwood, Lawrence K., Richard Westgard, and Charles E. Barb. 1978. "Law-Abiding One-Man Armies." *Society* 16 (1): 69–74.

O'Connor, James F., and Alan Lizotte. 1978. "The 'Southern Subculture of Violence' Thesis and Patterns of Gun Ownership." *Social Problems* 25 (4): 420–29.

Papachristos, Andrew V., and Christopher Wildeman. 2014. "Network Exposure and Homicide Victimization in an African American Community." *American Journal of Public Health* 104 (1): 143–50.

Papachristos, Andrew V., Anthony A. Braga, and David M. Hureau. 2012. "Social Networks and the Risk of Gunshot Injury." *Journal of Urban Health* 89 (6): 992–1003.

Papachristos, Andrew V., Christopher Wildeman, and Elizabeth Roberto. 2015. "Tragic, but Not Random: The Social Contagion of Nonfatal Gunshot Injuries." *Social Science & Medicine* 125 (January): 139–50.

Parker, Kim, Juliana Horowitz, Ruth Igielnik, Baxter Oliphant, and Anna Brown. 2017. "America's Complex Relationship with Guns." Washington, D.C.: Pew Research Center. https://www.pewresearch.org/social-trends/2017/06/22/americas-complex-relationship-with-guns/.

Patrick, Brian Anse. 2009. *Rise of the Anti-Media: In-Forming America's Concealed Weapon Carry Movement.* Lanham, MD: Lexington Books.

Peterson, Jillian, and James Densley. 2021. *The Violence Project: How to Stop a Mass Shooting Epidemic.* New York: Harry N. Abrams.

Pinker, Steven. 2011. *The Better Angels of Our Nature: Why Violence Has Declined.* New York: Viking.

Ray, Larry. 2018. *Violence and Society.* Second edition. Los Angeles: Sage.

Reeping, Paul M., Allison Mak, Charles C. Branas, Ariana N. Gobaud, and Michael L. Nance. 2023. "Firearm Death Rates in Rural vs Urban US Counties." *JAMA Surgery* 158 (7): 771–72.

Rehn, Karl, and John Daub. 2019. *Strategies and Standards for Defensive Handgun Training.* Lincoln, TX: KR Training.

Rittel, Horst W. J., and Melvin M. Webber. 1973. "Dilemmas in a General Theory of Planning." *Policy Sciences* 4 (2): 155–69.

Rose, Alexander. 2008. *American Rifle: A Biography.* New York: Delacorte Press.

Rowhani-Rahbar, Ali, Vivian H. Lyons, Joseph A. Simonetti, Deborah Azrael, and Matthew Miller. 2018. "Formal Firearm Training among Adults in the USA: Results of a National Survey." *Injury Prevention* 24 (2): 161–65.

Ruben, Eric M., and Saul Cornell. 2015. "Firearm Regionalism and Public Carry: Placing Southern Antebellum Case Law in Context." *Yale Law Journal Forum* 125: 121–35.

Schweit, Katherine. 2021. *Stop the Killing: How to End the Mass Shooting Crisis.* Lanham, MD: Rowman & Littlefield.

Sehgal, Ashwini R. 2020. "Lifetime Risk of Death From Firearm Injuries, Drug Overdoses, and Motor Vehicle Accidents in the United States." *The American Journal of Medicine* 133 (10): 1162–1167.e1.

Shapira, Harel, and Samantha J. Simon. 2018. "Learning to Need a Gun." *Qualitative Sociology* 41 (1): 1–20.

Sharkey, Patrick. 2018. *Uneasy Peace: The Great Crime Decline, the Renewal of City Life, and the Next War on Violence.* New York: W.W. Norton.

Shea, John J. 2009. "A Spark or an Ember?" *The Human Spark* (blog). December 10, 2009. https://www.pbs.org/wnet/humanspark/blog/expert-blogger-a-spark-or-an-ember-by-john-shea/315/.

Siegel, Michael, and Emily F. Rothman. 2016. "Firearm Ownership and Suicide Rates Among US Men and Women, 1981–2013." *American Journal of Public Health* 106 (7): 1316–22.

Siegel, Michael B., and Claire C. Boine. 2020. "The Meaning of Guns to Gun Owners in the U.S.: The 2019 National Lawful Use of Guns Survey." *American Journal of Preventive Medicine* 59 (5): 678–85.

Spitzer, Robert J. 2022. *The Gun Dilemma: How History Is Against Expanded Gun Rights.* New York: Oxford University Press.

Steidley, Trent. 2019. "Sharing the Monopoly on Violence? Shall-Issue Concealed Handgun License Laws and Responsibilization." *Sociological Perspectives* 62 (6): 929–47.

Steinbeck, John. 2008. *The Acts of King Arthur and His Noble Knights.* New York: Penguin.

Stevens, R. Blake, and Edward C. Ezell. 2004. *The Black Rifle: M16 Retrospective.* 2nd edition. Cobourg, Ontario: Collector Grade Publications.

Stroebe, Wolfgang, N. Pontus Leander, and Arie W. Kruglanski. 2017. "Is It a Dangerous World Out There? The Motivational Bases of American Gun Ownership." *Personality and Social Psychology Bulletin* 43 (8): 1071–85.

Stroud, Angela. 2012. "Good Guys With Guns Hegemonic Masculinity and Concealed Handguns." *Gender & Society* 26 (2): 216–38.

———. 2016. *Good Guys with Guns: The Appeal and Consequences of Concealed Carry.* Chapel Hill: University of North Carolina Press.

Studdert, David M., Yifan Zhang, Sonja A. Swanson, Lea Prince, Jonathan A. Rodden, Erin E. Holsinger, Matthew J. Spittal, Garen J. Wintemute, and Matthew Miller. 2020. "Handgun Ownership and Suicide in California." *New England Journal of Medicine* 382 (23): 2220–29.

Taylor, Jimmy D. 2013. *American Gun Culture: Collectors, Shows, and the Story of the Gun.* 2nd edition. El Paso, TX: LFB Scholarly Publishing.

Tucker, Raymond P., Jeff Powers, Sarah Pardue-Bourgeois, Nicolas Oakey-Frost, Emma H. Moscardini, Shawn P. Gilroy, Daniel W. Capron, Craig J. Bryan, and Michael D. Anestis. 2023. "Vehicle Firearm Storage: Prevalence and Correlates in a Sample of Male Firearm Owners." *Archives of Suicide Research* 27 (2): 479–93.

Turkle, Sherry. 2015. *Reclaiming Conversation: The Power of Talk in a Digital Age.* New York: Penguin.

Turner, Victor. 1967. *The Forest of Symbols: Aspects of Ndembu Ritual.* Ithaca, NY: Cornell University Press.

Van Dreal, John. 2016. *Assessing Student Threats: Implementing the Salem-Keizer System.* 2nd edition. Lanham, MD: Rowman & Littlefield.

Winkler, Adam. 2011. *Gunfight: The Battle Over the Right to Bear Arms in America.* New York: W.W. Norton.

Wittgenstein, Ludwig. 2009. *Philosophical Investigations.* Malden, MA: Blackwell Publishing.

Wright, James D. 1995. "Ten Essential Observations on Guns in America." *Society* 32 (3): 63–68.

Wright, James D., and Linda L. Marston. 1975. "The Ownership of the Means of Destruction: Weapons in the United States." *Social Problems* 23 (1): 93–107.

Yamane, David. 2016. "Awash in a Sea of Faith and Firearms: Rediscovering the Connection Between Religion and Gun Ownership in America." *Journal for the Scientific Study of Religion* 55 (3): 622–36.

———. 2017. "The Sociology of U.S. Gun Culture." *Sociology Compass* 11 (7): e12497.

———. 2021a. "Understanding and Misunderstanding America's Gun Culture." In *Understanding America's Gun Culture,* edited by Lisa Fischer and Craig Hovey, Second Edition, 175–92. Lanham, MD: Lexington Books.

———. 2021b. *Concealed Carry Revolution: Liberalizing the Right to Bear Arms in America.* Updated Edition. Hiawassee, GA: Shades Creek Press.

———. 2022. "Gun Culture 2.0: The Evolution and Contours of Defensive Gun Ownership in America." *The ANNALS of the American Academy of Political and Social Science* 704 (1): 20–43.

Yamane, David, Paul Yamane, and Sebastian L. Ivory. 2020. "Targeted Advertising: Documenting the Emergence of Gun Culture 2.0 in Guns Magazine, 1955–2019." *Palgrave Communications* 6 (1): 1–9.

Yamane, David, Riley Satterwhite, and Paul Yamane. 2021. "A Woman's Place in Gun Advertisements: The American Rifleman, 1920–2019." In *Understanding America's Gun Culture,* edited by Lisa Fisher and Craig Hovey, Second Edition, 91–111. Lanham, MD: Lexington Books.

Yamane, David, Sebastian L. Ivory, and Paul Yamane. 2019. "The Rise of Self-Defense in Gun Advertising: The American Rifleman, 1918–2017." In *Gun Studies: Interdisciplinary Approaches to Politics, Policy, and Practice,* edited by Jennifer Carlson, Kristen Goss, and Harel Shapira, 9–27. New York: Routledge.

Index